W9-BKX-896

The Rape of the Text

Frontispiece from Pierre Charron's *Of Wisdom*.
(Courtesy of The Folger Shakespeare Library, Washington, D.C.)

The Rape of the Text

Reading and Misreading Pope's *Essay on Man*

Harry M. Solomon

The University of Alabama Press
Tuscaloosa & London

Tuscaloosa, Alabama 35487–0380

Manufactured in the United States of America

designed by zig zeigler

∞

The paper on which this book is printed meets the minimum requirements of American National Standard for Information Science-Permanence of Paper for Printed Library Materials, ANSI Z39.48–1984.

Library of Congress Cataloging-in-Publication Data

Solomon, Harry M.
The rape of the text : reading and misreading Pope's Essay on man / Harry M. Solomon.
p. cm.
Includes bibliographical references and index.
ISBN 0-8173-0696-X (alk. paper)
1. Pope, Alexander, 1688–1744. Essay on man. 2. Pope, Alexander, 1688–1744—Criticism and interpretation—History. 3. Philosophy, English—18th century. 4. Philosophy in literature. 5. Man in literature. I. Title.
PR3627.S64 1993
821'.5—dc20 92-38675

British Library Cataloging-in-Publication Data available

To Alexander Pope,
in respect for his "strong Antipathy
of Good to Bad";
and to my colleagues who share his vehemence,
especially Ben Fitzpatrick, Dennis Rygiel,
and Martha Solomon

CONTENTS

Acknowledgments ix
Introduction: "A Poetic Disaster" 1
1. Trivializing *An Essay on Man* 6
2. Disseminating Theodicy 32
3. The Self as Aporia 57
4. Optimism and Pessimism 89
5. Academic Discourse 114
6. Paradox Against the Orthodox 146
Conclusion: Naturalizing Philosophical Poetry 183
Notes 191
Bibliography 219
Index 237

ACKNOWLEDGMENTS

To the many librarians who helped me.

To the many libraries whose repositories made my research possible, especially the libraries of Auburn University, the University of Maryland at College Park, the University of North Carolina at Chapel Hill, the University of Wisconsin, the University of Minnesota, and the New York Public Library, the British Library, and the Folger Library.

To the professional and generous staff of The University of Alabama Press, especially Nicole Mitchell.

There is a long-standing quarrel
between poetry and philosophy.

—*Plato*

INTRODUCTION

"A Poetic Disaster"

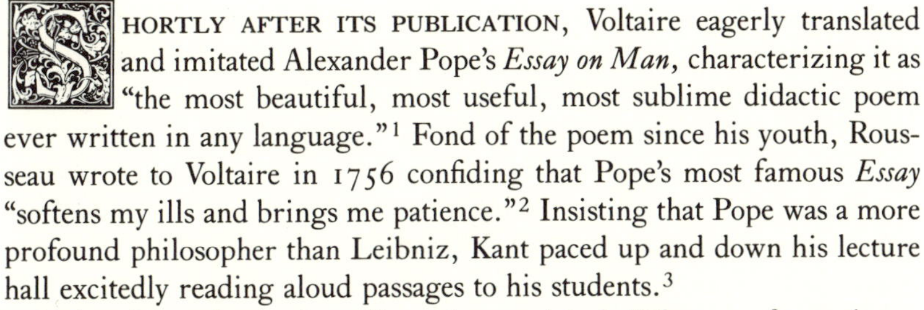

SHORTLY AFTER ITS PUBLICATION, Voltaire eagerly translated and imitated Alexander Pope's *Essay on Man*, characterizing it as "the most beautiful, most useful, most sublime didactic poem ever written in any language."[1] Fond of the poem since his youth, Rousseau wrote to Voltaire in 1756 confiding that Pope's most famous *Essay* "softens my ills and brings me patience."[2] Insisting that Pope was a more profound philosopher than Leibniz, Kant paced up and down his lecture hall excitedly reading aloud passages to his students.[3]

Today this enthusiastic audience has vanished. What was formerly regarded as the Mount Everest of eighteenth-century poetry now languishes unread and enjoys, at best, "a currency wholly honorific."[4] When the *Essay* is read at all, it is as a quaint period piece, as a repository of dead and outdated ideas, as a curious relic irrelevant to our current sensibilities. "Pope piquing himself on philosophical or theological profundity and acumen is intolerable," F. R. Leavis asserts. "No one, I imagine, willingly reads through the *Essay on Man*."[5] And why should anyone? Harold Bloom recently reaffirms. Pope's *Essay* is, as we all know, a "poetic disaster."[6] Thank goodness, Robert M. Adams concludes, the *Essay*'s "sense of hierarchy, its commitment to order, and its rather withering optimism . . . are all ancient history by now."[7]

Reviewing Miriam Leranbaum's 1977 study of *An Essay on Man*, G. S. Rousseau reluctantly concludes that she joins a lengthy file of previous scholars who have failed to convince readers that Pope's "system" still deserves our study: "not even [Maynard] Mack could turn the tide of two centuries."[8] The most recent book-length commentary on the *Essay* does not even attempt to praise Pope's poem but elects instead to bury it. Finding Kant's admiration of the *Essay* incomprehensible and noting that the twentieth century has had little interest in the *Essay,* A. D. Nuttall treats Pope's poem as a moribund remainder of a "half-alien culture." We are forced to read the poem, Nuttall argues, not because it is a notable philosophical poem, for its "philosophy is not systematically consistent," but as "THE philosophical poem of the age in that it assembles, in a sort of brilliant disarray, the fractured systems of the age."[9] In his *Times Literary Supplement* review of this latest disparagement of Pope's poem, David Nokes speaks for most eighteenth-century scholars when he empathizes with Nuttall's difficulty in interpreting a work that is "not only demanding but also deeply unsatisfactory both as poetry and philosophy."[10]

Clearly, as Maynard Mack concluded in 1985, "Poems in the genre of the *Essay* are not, as the saying goes, our thing."[11] Over a hundred years ago an earlier Pope biographer posed the problem one way: "The modern reader of the *Essay on Man* finds a difficulty in understanding the manner in which it impressed contemporary imagination. He is astonished that such a farrago of fallacies should ever have been accepted as a work of philosophy."[12] I would state the problem differently: Why can we no longer read what Voltaire and so many of Pope's contemporaries regarded as "the most beautiful, most useful, most sublime didactic poem ever written in any language"?

This book is an explanation of, as recent Heideggerians grandly phrase it, our alienation from the Being of Pope's text. Even the best-intentioned readers of *An Essay on Man* inevitably perceive a historical artifact with no authentic relationship to current concerns. For quite clear reasons Pope's *Essay* has been systematically misread, trivialized, and—consequently—relegated to the trash heap of mere literary history. The six chapters characterize these strategies of misreading; simultaneously, they suggest more productive approaches to *An Essay on Man* in particular and the genre of philosophical poetry generally.

My project is doubly presumptuous. Emboldened by the deconstructive enthusiasms of Jacques Derrida, William Spanos, and G. Douglas Atkins, I presume to "destroy" the reified *Essay* embalmed in histories of literature or philosophy; and then, deconstructing to reconstruct, I presume to substitute my own allegedly superior reading. My justification is a desire to make Pope's poem readable again. Not a single modern critic,

G. S. Rousseau observes, has succeeded in showing us why the *Essay* is "so important as philosophy that we today should change our minds about it."[13] I agree that most commentary on *An Essay on Man* is in a deadening critical rut; but I also think that the work of scholars like Thomas R. Edwards, Dustin Griffin, Maynard Mack, and David Morris is subtle and interesting and sympathetic. Yet, too often even the best contemporary criticism is imprisoned in a mode of discourse that necessitates blindness to the poem's greatest strengths. As Lawrence Lipking notes, even the most laudatory treatments of the *Essay* are "weary and defensive" like rear-guard actions in a lost war.[14]

The vast majority of criticism of *An Essay on Man*, however, is about as subtle as surgery with sledgehammers. In chapter one I contend that most readers of philosophical poetry are unconscious prisoners of one of two mutually antagonist modes of discourse: the Logocentric and the Aesthetic. Recent textual criticism designates this dichotomy variously as logical and literary, as philosophical and poetic, as cognitive and emotive, as real and rhetorical, or as intelligible and sensuous. "Logocentric," literally "word-centered," characterizes the ideal of most Western philosophy to speak the rational word that perfectly correlates with the world. In contrast, "Aesthetic," deriving from the Greek word for "things perceptible by the senses," has come to signify an arational and amoral concern with the beautiful.[15] Each discourse mode assumes interpretive authority for speaking the truth about Pope's text; and if *An Essay on Man* proves recalcitrant to the unquestioned canons of that discourse mode, it is dismissed as bad philosophy or bad poetry or both.

As has been eloquently and adequately demonstrated, most philosophers distrust literariness in propositional discourse. They are trained to "separate the chaff of persuasive tone and manner from the logical kernel," as John Richetti says in his rhetorical analysis of Locke, Berkeley, and Hume.[16] Most literary critics, in contrast, abominate argument in verse.[17] Beginning with an interpretive bias against the union of philosophy and poetry, both discourse camps misread and distort; and both have done so from the initial publication of the *Essay*. Thus, I believe—as Paul de Man says of commentary on Rousseau—that the tradition of interpretation of *An Essay on Man* "stands in dire need of deconstruction."[18]

Over a hundred years ago, Mark Pattison argued that his age "could no longer read the *Essay on Man*"; but he argued that the deficiency was not his misreading but Pope's writing. "We find its arguments confused, and its dry rationalism unedifying," he concludes. "The subject has not lost its interest, but the questions which are involved are all advanced into a further stage."[19] The related concepts of intellectual progress and literary periodization unite to empower critics to dismiss the *Essay* as a period piece, as a text interesting only to intellectual archaeologists attempting either to reconstruct the antiquated mind of an earlier age or to pigeonhole Pope ever more precisely in the "history of ideas." Given this state of affairs the challenge is to destroy the historicity of the *Essay* so we can read it afresh. Michael Ayers rightly condemns the "intellectually disreputable" approach of Locke scholars who rest satisfied with a superficial description of the philosopher's textual and cultural context.[20] Analogously, both Richetti and de Man argue that Locke is unreadable until we "disregard the commonplaces about his philosophy that circulate as reliable currency in the intellectual histories of the Enlightenment."[21] As long as we substitute Rousseau's interpreters for Rousseau's text, de Man insists, we are blind.[22]

In chapter one I demonstrate that Pope's *Essay* is an extreme example of a text that attracts the kind of critical incrustation that blinds readers. "Interpretation drives to control, insists on order, demonstrates authority," Vincent Leitch argues.[23] Believing that most readings of the *Essay* have been the "acts of willed mastery" that deconstructionists decry and, as such, systematic and largely unconscious extensions of critics' ideologies, I characterize and attempt to account for the predominant patternings in these prior interpretive orderings. Chapter two characterizes and rebuts the traditional debunkings of Pope as either an indiscriminate eclectic or a servile imitator. Chapter three deconstructs the usual caricature of Pope as a smug rational optimist somewhat along the lines of a lesser Leibniz. Chapters four and five argue against logocentric attempts to devalue the *Essay* by demonstrating its logical incoherence and suggest instead reading the *Essay* within an alternative world of discourse shared by Pope and his contemporaries. Chapter six uses that alternative world of discourse to argue against criticisms that Pope's use of paradox and metaphor "contaminates" his philosophic text. The conclusion generalizes from interpretation of *An Essay on Man* to philosophical poetry generally and urges the "naturalization" of the genre.

Although each chapter begins as a destruction of patterns of prior interpretation, the substance of each chapter is a reconstruction of the discourse context in which the *Essay* was written and consequent recommendations for new reading strategies. As Martin Heidegger suggests in *Being and Time,* his call for a *destruktion* of the history of ontology has nothing to do with "a pernicious relativizing of ontological standpoints" but is instead essential to recognizing the positive possibilities to which tradition has blinded us.[24] We deconstruct to reconstruct on better foundations, as even Jacques Derrida has been quoted as saying.[25] In attempting Pope's revaluation I borrow shamelessly from recent criticism; yet beneath the veneer of that postmodern terminology, many readers will recognize something familiar. Fashionable phraseology forces us to read differently partly by acknowledging what we always already knew. Thus my appropriations and distortions of recent theory are means and not ends. They are strategies for placing us, as readers of *An Essay on Man*, where Voltaire, Hume, Rousseau, and Kant already are.

How his editors and biographers have hated Pope!

—F. W. Bateson (1961)

ONE

Trivializing *An Essay on Man*

F THE QUESTION were asked, What ought to have been the best of Pope's poems?" Thomas De Quincey wrote, "most people would answer, the *Essay on Man*. If the question were asked, What is the worst? all people of judgement would say, the *Essay on Man*."[1] Ours must be an age of judgment, for the current consensus is indisputable: *An Essay on Man* is fundamentally flawed. The textbook of eighteenth-century British literature most frequently used in American universities concludes: "To write sustainedly on Man in prose . . . calls for powers that few poets possess, and from the start Pope had to face his deficiencies as an exact philosopher. *An Essay on Man*, then, could never be more than a partial success."[2] Although the poem contains isolated passages of great power, Leopold Damrosch, Jr., writes in 1987, it "never quite becomes a great poem."[3] These and a plenitude of similar pronouncements are the most recent reinscriptions of a consensus developed two centuries earlier.

The development of this consensus has never been described in any detail; and it is interesting literary history involving as it does the triumph of Samuel Johnson over Alexander Pope, a triumph reinscribed in A. D. Nuttall's concluding of his recent book-length study of the *Essay* with an otherwise inexplicable chapter praising Johnson's intellect as "manifestly greater" than Pope's. More important than the intrinsic interest of the trivialization of the *Essay*, however, is the possibility that once the historical development of this consensus is understood we may be able to write about *An Essay on Man* without being compelled to reinscribe the interpretative status quo and, perhaps, to answer De Quincey's question differently.

"THE SAGE'S WISDOM, AND THE POET'S FIRE"

The warfare that is a wit's life on earth was raging at full tide in the early 1730s following the publication of Pope's *Dunciad Variorum*. Knowing that his enemies would pounce upon and ravage any poem bearing his name, Pope took elaborate precautions to disguise his authorship as the separate epistles of the *Essay* were published. In the year from January 1733 to January 1734 when the four epistles of the *Essay* were being published anonymously by a bookseller not earlier associated with him, Pope was simultaneously publishing new works bearing his name and the imprint of his usual booksellers.[4] In one of these, *The First Satire of the Second Book of Horace*, Pope celebrates his Twickenham retirement where "*St. John* mingles with my friendly Bowl, / The Feast of Reason and the Flow of Soul."[5] The epistles of the *Essay* were in subsequent editions to be addressed to Pope's friend and neighbor Henry St. John, Viscount Bolingbroke. But knowing that inclusion of Bolingbroke's name in the poem would encourage speculation that Pope was the author, the first epistle was issued in February 1733 addressed to "LAELIUS" rather than "ST. JOHN":

> AWAKE, my LAELIUS! leave all meaner things
> To low ambition, and the pride of Kings.
> Let us (since Life can little more supply
> Than just to look about us and to die)
> Expatiate free o'er all this scene of Man;
> A mighty maze! of walks without a plan.[6]

Pope's deception worked. Even recently abused dunces like Leonard Welsted and Bezaleel Morrice croaked forth unqualified praise of this new wonder of philosophical poetry. *An Essay on Man* is "above all commendation," Welsted wrote, as Pope reminded him in subsequent editions of the *Dunciad*.[7] Recurrent in initial responses to the anonymous poem is praise for its simultaneous success as poetry and as philosophy. Representatively, the *London Evening Post* praised the first epistle of the *Essay* for its inspired blending of the charms of verse with the ratiocinative rigor of prose: "Go on, Great Genius, with thy bold Design, / And

Prose's Strength with Verse's Softness join." Most reviews, following the *Weekly Miscellany*'s judgment upon the publication of the third epistle, found it "difficult to know which Part to prefer, when all is equally beautiful and noble." A correspondent from Bath lauds the *Essay* as an "inimitable" poem "calculated on the noblest Basis of Philosophy and Divinity." In the same issue a commendatory poem "To the Unknown AUTHOR of the Essay on Man" begins:

> To praise thy judgment or commend thy strain,
> In this were all superfluous or vain.
> Hail, then, instructing bard (whoe'er thou art)
> That opens thus our eyes and clears our heart![8]

Similarly, a correspondent from the north of England writes the *Gentleman's Magazine* praising the *Essay* as uniting "the most Nervous Reasoning in the Advancement of profound natural Truths" with "the sublimest . . . Poetry in its Kind." When read "with deliberate Attention," the writer concludes, the *Essay* "at once enlarges the Understanding, convinces the Judgment, and touches the Heart."[9] The aspiring footman Robert Dodsley encapsulated contemporary response when he celebrated Pope's incarnation of the Philosophic Poet: "GREAT Bard! in whom united we admire / The Sage's Wisdom, and the Poet's Fire."[10]

However, as Pope anticipated, once Bolingbroke was acknowledged as the "guide, philosopher, and friend" addressed in the epistles, Pope's authorship was suspected; and both their enemies attacked with greater vehemence for having been gulled into immoderate praise. On New Year's Day 1734 Pope wrote his friend John Caryll mentioning both that a "poetical war" against him had been initiated by Lord Hervey and that Pope thought that the forthcoming fourth epistle of the *Essay on Man* would allay Caryll's apprehension that the author was not distinctively Christian.[11] Clearly by early February Hervey's friend and collaborator in the war against Pope, Lady Mary Wortley Montagu, knew who had written the much-lauded *Essay*. In *The Dean's Provocation For Writing the Lady's Dressing-Room*, she compares Swift's sexual impotence to Pope's philosophical ineptitude:

> Poor Pope Philosophy displays on
> With so much Rhime and little reason,
> And tho he argues ne'er so long
> That, all is right, his Head is wrong.[12]

Lady Mary continued the attack with an abusive epistle from "Pope to Bolingbroke"; and in addition to personal enemies, their Opposition politics brought out Robert Walpole's literary minions.

In March of 1734 the author of *The False Patriot* criticizes Pope for using "immortal lines" to praise the Jacobite Bolingbroke: "Recall your Muse, lur'd into Factions Cause / And sing, great Bard, of Heav'ns and Natures Laws."[13] As late as October, according to a criticism in *The Present State of the Republic of Letters*, "no one [had] expressly own'd" the poem. However, allusions to Pope's satiric epistles leave no question that he is the "peevish *Satyrist*" and "proud *Dictator*" whose plagiarism of Shaftesbury provides the apparent "Sublimity of the Thoughts" in *An Essay on Man*. Consequently, the writer undertakes to disabuse the rhetorically ravished by laying "before you in plain and genuine Colours" the content of the first epistle "undisguised by any *Arts*, unassisted by the *Magick* of his *Numbers*" so that "some may thereby be cur'd of their implicit Submission to his *Dictates*, and it may weaken his Power of enchanting the Multitude *when he pleases* into *Error*."[14] Alluding directly to Pope's "Libel" on Lord Hervey as Sporus in *An Epistle to Dr. Arbuthnot*, an outraged reader of *The Prompter* fulminates against the impiety of an *Essay* which, "I vow to God" goes "a Bar's Length beyond Lucretius."[15] Thomas Bentley, smarting from Pope's ridicule of his famous uncle, explicitly linked Bolingbroke's alleged atheism with the ideology of Pope's poem. His *Letter to Mr. Pope* regrets that the impious Bolingbroke should be celebrated in Pope's "immortal verse," and asks, "Are you then really content to go down to Posterity with that Gentleman . . . ? Can you think the Christian religion true . . . and not fear being damned with him?"[16]

When neither Pope's nor Bolingbroke's name was associated with the *Essay*, the poem's piety seems not to have been a salient consideration. With various degrees of difficulty the *Essay* was assimilated to the preexisting theology of its admirers, some even attributing its authorship to a Christian divine. "The design of concealing myself was good," Pope confided to Swift, "and has had its full effect; I was thought a divine, a philosopher and what not? and my doctrine had a sanction I could not have given to it."[17] With Bolingbroke now ensconced as Pope's addressee strictly orthodox readings became more problematic. What was there, after all, specifically Christian in *An Essay on Man*? "We ought to be *respectful* to Parts and Ingenuity," an essayist in the *Weekly Miscellany* concludes of the still anonymous author of the *Essay*, "but the *Bible is*

Sacred." Good poets are seldom "*close Logicians*," the writer argues; and "tho' the *Art* of *Poetry* be *Divine*, we have had but very few *Divine Poets*." The powers of poetry "all conspire to captivate the Affections"; but because "the *Poetical* and the *Reasoning Faculties* seldom unite in the same Person," poets like the author of *An Essay on Man* are "as dangerous as they are delightful."[18]

"I am far from charging Mr. POPE with any Design against Christianity," one Mr. Bridges wrote in the preface to his imitative *Divine Wisdom and Providence;* "but if he builds upon such Principles as appear to others entirely destructive of the Foundation of the Christian System," he must expect criticism. Bridges excuses Pope's implicit heterodoxy by suggesting that the poet fails to perceive the implications of his arguments. Pope's immortal style only unintentionally perpetuates immoral content; but in so doing the *Essay* exists as a pretext for Bridges's own work, which he humbly acknowledges cannot aspire "to give the same Poetical Entertainment" but does claim the virtue of consistent piety.[19] Only a few years later Edward Young makes the same claim for his *Night Thoughts* as a pious though aesthetically inferior supplement to Pope's *Essay.* "Night the First" concludes with an explicit contrast between Pope's natural "darkness" and Young's supernatural "day":

> *Man* too [Pope] sung: *Immortal* man I sing;
> Oft bursts my Song beyond the bounds of Life;
> What, *now,* but Immortality, can please?
> O had *He* press'd his Theme, pursu'd the track,
> Which opens out of Darkness into Day!
> O had he mounted on his wing of Fire,
> Soar'd where I sink, and sung *Immortal* man!
> How had it blest mankind? and rescued me?[20]

As in England the first European responses to the *Essay* stressed Pope's inspired union of the mental faculties of reason and imagination: "C'est un philosophe profound & un poete vraiment sublime," one distinguished French cleric pronounced.[21] Also as in England, when Pope inserted Bolingbroke's name the text became suddenly suspicious. Isolated phrases and even general tendencies of argument were now seen as susceptible to pantheistic or fatalistic interpretation. In the preface to his 1736 prose translation of the *Essay,* Etienne de Silhouette felt obliged to defend Pope's orthodoxy against mounting criticisms of "Spinosisme." Similarly, when on the heels of four quick editions of the prose translation Jean-François

Du Resnel published his verse translation of the *Essay,* he prefaced his bloated version with a defense of Pope against those who found in the poem "a lurking Poison, and charge it with the Absurdities of *Spinoza's* System." French readers were confused, Du Resnel asserted, because of their discomfort with a subtle British poetic that demanded a great deal of readers. Convinced that the "Order of its Parts is not very easily discovered by those accustomed to the exact Regularity of our Treatises in Prose," he added, deleted, and rearranged passages from the *Essay* to render its "System" accessible to French readers. Correctly conceived, Du Resnel concluded, Pope's poem is not only entirely orthodox but the only modern example of a true philosophical poem: it is "an Honour reserved in the later Ages for Mr. *Pope*" to unite "the Extasies and Flights of the Poet, and the Nicety and cool Argumentation of the abstracted Reasoner."[22]

The Roman Catholic Church was now having none of it; and there were whispers that young Voltaire had encouraged the verse translation of the *Essay.* In June 1736 the Jesuit journal *Mémoires de Trévoux* had praised Pope's pious work; the following year the same periodical reversed its assessment and condemned the doctrine and moral tendency of Pope's poem. Nor were Roman Catholics the only ones unconvinced by the apologies put forward by Pope's translators. Also in 1737, Jean Paul de Crousaz, a Protestant professor at Lausanne, a logician and theologian who understood no English, wrote an extended denunciation of the *Essay*'s "Spinozist" and "Leibnizian" tendencies in *Examen de l'Essai de M. Pope sur l'Homme.* Told that the prose translation upon which he based his criticisms in the *Examen* was faulty, Crousaz used Du Resnel's much-altered version as the basis for a laboriously pedantic *Commentaire sur la traduction en vers . . . de l'Essai . . . sur l'Homme.*

As Maynard Mack correctly observes, "a less happy confrontation of minds and methods could scarcely have been imagined" than Pope and Crousaz.[23] Yet by November of 1738 the London booksellers realized that because of their target Crousaz's blunderbusses were certain to sell. Pope's old enemy the "abominable" Edmund Curll published an abridged translation of the *Commentaire* by Charles Forman, advertising it as a "critical Satire" on the *Essay* which Pope was obliged to answer. The same week the bookseller Anne Dodd published Elizabeth Carter's translation of the *Examen.* Her friend Samuel Johnson helped with the advertisements that promised "an Enquiry what View Mr. Pope might have in touching upon the Leibnitzian Philosophy." Also, and most significantly,

Dodd also had Johnson's own translation of the *Commentaire* with notes ready for sale. Thus, in a one-week period, three translations of Crousaz's critiques were being hawked on the streets of London.

In December an aspiring British cleric, William Warburton, came to Pope's defense and in the first of a series of letters in the *History of the Works of the Learned* began the response Curll said Pope was obliged to give to Crousaz. Each month thereafter through April another installment of Warburton's tendentious rebuttal lumbered out; and all were collected and augmented for publication as *A Vindication of Mr. Pope's Essay on Man* on 15 November 1739.[24] With the publication of Johnson's translation of Crousaz's *Commentaire* in November 1738 and Warburton's "Vindications" in the December, January, February, March, and April issues of the *Works of the Learned* the die was cast for most subsequent interpretations of the poem to the present day. As A. D. Nuttall admits, "Criticism of the *Essay on Man* has tended ever since to be either Crousazian or Warburtonian."[25]

Inasmuch as the terms of Warburton's defense were set by Crousaz's attack, the truth is that the basis for all subsequent discussion of *An Essay on Man* in English was established by a man judged by all subsequent scholars from Warburton and Joseph Warton to Maynard Mack and A. D. Nuttall to be an unsympathetic, unsubtle pedant whose sole motive was to discredit Pope's work as dangerously heterodox. "Crousaz seems to be unequipped mentally for dealing with any sentence," Nuttall says, "in which there is some shadow of irony, or play of metaphor and paradox."[26] Nonetheless, Crousaz established the salient points of subsequent discussion—the concept of plenitude or the importance of "Whatever IS, is RIGHT," for example—without having read a word of Pope's poem. He only knew the prose and verse deformations produced for a French taste, as Resnel flatly admits, "accustomed to . . . exact Regularity."

"DISCORDANT SENSE"

In his *Life of Pope* Samuel Johnson powerfully reinscribed the objections he had translated over forty years earlier; but the fountainhead is clearly Crousaz. The professor used three interrelated tactics to discredit Pope's *Essay.* He asserted that as theology the poem was heretical, that as philosophy it was illogical, and that as poetry it was ravishingly beautiful. The first tactic is obvious and is aptly encapsulated in Crousaz's rhetorical question in the *Commentaire:* "Has Mr. *Pope* ever read the Scripture?"

Discussion of the third tactic will be reserved for the following section. The logician's second tactic most interests a modern reader because it was in denigrating the reasoning in Pope's poem that Crousaz did his most enduring damage.

Crousaz uses every yardstick logic can supply to demonstrate Pope's perpetual inconsistency. At times, using a single word or image, he will situate Pope compromisingly in the history of ideas. After finding the sources of the *Essay* in heterodox philosophers like Leibniz and Spinoza, Crousaz then proves Pope's inconsistency by showing that other parts of the *Essay* contradict the metaphysical systems of his putative "sources." In response, William Warburton goes to grotesque lengths to find analogues for Pope's arguments in reputable places. The principle of plenitude may figure in the metaphysics of Leibniz and Spinoza, Warburton counters, but it likewise enjoys an august pedigree in "the most celebrated and orthodox *Fathers* and *Divines* of the ancient and modern Church." However, Warburton capitulates unintentionally to Crousaz's indictment of Pope's intellectual competence when he concurs with the logician in questioning the truth of the "Notion" of plenitude.

Warburton feels he has accomplished his rhetorical purpose when he has demonstrated Pope's piety; and despite the special pietistic pleading of his *Vindication*, Warburton seems to have had no high opinion of Pope's reasoning powers.[27] Bolingbroke subsequently wrote a pamphlet against Warburton as the "Most Impudent Man Living"; and Warburton spent some energy trying to write Bolingbroke out of Pope's *Essay*. To dissociate Pope from Bolingbroke's deism (and thereby to vindicate his own *Vindication*), Warburton quotes Bolingbroke as saying disparagingly that Pope "understood nothing of his own principles nor saw to what they naturally tended." This position allows Warburton, in his *View of Lord Bolingbroke's Philosophy*, to contrast Pope's "real vindication of Providence against Libertines and Atheists" in the *Essay* with Bolingbroke's attempts "to discredit the *Being of a God*."[28]

After Pope's death Warburton quarreled bitterly with both Bolingbroke and Robert Dodsley, the young footman-poet who praised *An Essay on Man* and whom Pope subsequently made his bookseller. Eventually, an ally of Dodsley—Joseph Warton—took Warburton to task for his distorting interpretation of the *Essay;* but the damage was already done. Warburton's Christian reading of the poem together with his denunciation of the impious Bolingbroke made Pope look philosophically naive in acknowledging St. John as his "guide"; and although Warton finds Warburton's dogged piety absurdly strained, he nonetheless agrees that Pope never really understood Bolingbroke's philosophy. Two questions are central to Warton's interpretation of the *Essay:* Is the poem orthodox? and Is Pope aware of the implications of his arguments? Whereas Warburton had answered yes to both questions while stressing Pope's deliberate deviations from Bolingbroke's atheism, Warton says no to both, characterizing Pope as a naive "disciple" of his noble friend.[29]

Warton's "deistic" reading of the *Essay* and his characterization of Pope's philosophical naiveté occur both in the second volume of *An Essay on the Genius and Writings of Pope* (1782) and in his edition of Pope's *Works* (1797). A generation later in his own edition of Pope's *Works* (1824), William Roscoe sought to reclaim Pope's poem for the pious by relying heavily on Warburton's annotations to attack Warton's "erroneous" interpretation.[30] Roscoe's approach was, by then, atavistic; more indicative of the prevailing assessment of Pope as philosopher was De Quincey's denigration in his review of Roscoe's edition. In turn, Whitwell Elwin quotes De Quincey's indictment of both the poem and the poet who would be a philosopher in the voluminous commentary to his "definitive" edition of the *Essay* (1871). The theologian Elwin, convinced that Pope had "renounced Christianity," agrees with Warton that the poem is deistic but also agrees with De Quincey that Warton evinces "reckless neutrality" in the face of Pope's impiety rather than an appropriate Christian zeal. All blunderbuss and thunder, Elwin fulminates against an ignorant Pope misled by Bolingbroke's more powerful satanic intellect. A "puerile" *Essay on Man* is laboriously belittled as "a tissue of inconsistency and incoherence" unworthy of serious interpretation.[31]

Elwin's edition of the *Essay* remained standard for eighty years and set the tone for subsequent commentary including that of Mark Pattison and Leslie Stephen, both men whose denigration of Pope's poem could not be dismissed as wounded piety. In a review of Elwin's edition, Pattison adopted wholesale the image of Pope's confused incompetence. Similarly, in his *Men of Letters* volume on Pope, Leslie Stephen diminishes Pope's *Essay* as merely a confused versification of Bolingbroke's *Essays*. Thus, rather than attack *An Essay on Man* directly, Stephen rails against Bolingbroke's "superficial and arrogant" philosophical essays. The "half-read" poet and his incoherent "mosaic" are treated as marginal adjuncts to the history of Bolingbroke's half-baked ideas.[32]

The mosaic metaphor, which Stephen admits he is borrowing from Pattison, vivifies the objection to Pope's indiscriminate borrowing and resultant inconsistency inherited from Crousaz. "If I could flatter myself that this Essay has any merit," Pope asserts in the "Design" prefixed to all editions from 1734 on, "it is in steering betwixt the extremes of doctrines seemingly opposite" (p. 7). Almost immediately, the enemy he attached as "Sporus" in his *Epistle to Arbuthnot* alleged that Pope's eclecticism was, in fact, the central flaw of the *Essay*. "Resolving to turn Philosopher," Lord Hervey snidely says, "he has, in order to fit himself for Execution of that Task, read every speculative Book upon the Subject he treats; and whenever a Passage happen'd to strike him in any of these different Authors, writing upon different Principles . . . and consequently maintaining different Opinions, and exhibiting different Sentiments, he has put them into most *harmonious Verse*, I confess, but such *discordant Sense* . . . that his whole Work is nothing but a Heap of poetical Contradictions, and a jarring Series of Doctrines, Principles, Opinions and Sentiments, diametrically opposite to each other; making an *Olio, Hodge-Podge Mess of Philosophy.*"[33]

In an ambitious work like the *Essay*, De Quincey argues, "eclecticism ceases to be possible. . . . The parts lose their support, their coherence, their very meaning."[34] The coexistence of pious (Warburton, Roscoe) and impious (Crousaz, Warton) interpretations of the *Essay* reinforced this Argument from Inconsistency that increasingly pervaded discussions of Pope's poem. *An Essay on Man* "is indeed the realization of anarchy," De Quincey asserts, "and one amusing test of this may be found in the fact that different commentators have deduced from it the very opposite doctrines." This is the recurrent motif in Elwin, Pattison, and Stephen. Pope's "weak attempt to use language which would fit both infidelity and belief led," Elwin objects, "to sorry conclusions" and makes the *Essay* a shoddy assemblage of "clashing theories" best fitted to document Pope's astonishing "ignorance of philosophy."[35] Readers should not approach Pope's poetry looking for "the higher range of religious and philosophical ideas," Pattison wrote in a review of Elwin's edition for the *British Quarterly Review*. "When he attempted them, as in the *Essay on Man*, he found himself out of his depth."[36]

Within a decade three sage Victorians appropriated Crousaz's denigration and chiseled in granite the condescending estimate of Pope's *Essay* which has been reinscribed ever since. To his 1869 edition of the *Essay* for the Clarendon School series, Mark Pattison provided a lengthy and very hostile preface. Within a decade it went through six editions and continued to serve as a standard school text well into the next century. Elwin's edition and voluminous commentary, destined to become the definitive edition for scholars until 1950, appeared in 1871. In his review the following year, Pattison secularized Reverend Elwin's zeal; and in 1880 Leslie Stephen provided the capstone. Discussing *An Essay on Man* in his *Alexander Pope*, Stephen concludes that "anything like sustained reasoning was beyond Pope's reach." Stephen's ridicule of the *Essay* shows his familiarity with Johnson's adaptation of Crousaz in his own *Life of Pope*. "When [Pope's] wonder-working sounds sink into sense," the pious Johnson had judged, the reader recognizes nothing more profound than the jejune "talk of his mother and his nurse." Stephen concludes with Johnsonian definitiveness, "The reasonings in the essay are confused, contradictory, and often childish." Stephen also wrote the entries for both Pope and Bolingbroke for the *Dictionary of National Biography*, cross-referencing his denunciation of Bolingbroke's *Essays* with his denigration of Pope's *Essay*. Thus, at the close of the nineteenth century the most authoritative sources, Pope's editors and biographers, concurred in dismissing the *Essay* as a worthless "realization of anarchy": "puerile," "ignorant," and "childish."[37]

Almost all subsequent commentary presumes this Victorian assessment of the *Essay*'s incoherence. "Pope's very inconsistent poem," one critic writes, "is known to be a hodge-podge of incompatible philosophies."[38] Another finds "no real logical order" in the poem;[39] and another criticizes its "illogicality."[40] "The eclecticism of the *Essay*," still another writes, is "a major source of the poem's failure to achieve . . . coherent thought."[41] Entirely worthless as philosophy, another contends, Pope's poem is "no more than rhetoric."[42] Even the most subtle and astute recent critics conclude that "Readers who approach *An Essay on Man* in search of philosophical richness" will be disappointed because Pope was incapable of the "sustained conceptual thinking" we expect of a Locke or a Leibniz.[43] The judgment of recent critics that Pope's unfortunate "eclecticism" led to his "hodge-podge" poem literally reinscribes Lord Hervey's 1742 attack. Through the authoritative alchemy of literary scholarship what was initially an expression of tendentious, personal hostility has been transmuted into the sagest of received wisdom, exactly the kind of received idea that blinds us to author and work alike.[44]

"HARMONIOUS VERSE"

Crousaz's second tactic was to discredit Pope as philosopher; his third tactic was to celebrate Pope as poet. Crousaz inherited a philosopher's allegiance in the antique antagonism of Plato to Homer and, like Hobbes and Locke, distrusted poetry. At best, they agreed, poetry and philosophy were different discourse modes whose marriage inevitably resulted in obscurity and inconsistency. Both the poetical philosopher and the philosophic poet were unnatural couplings. The point made by his translator Resnel in praising Pope's dual success as "Poet" and "abstracted Reasoner" is to highlight his unique ability "in this latter Age" to unite "Poetry and Metaphysics [which] are generally considered as two Kinds of Writing inconsistent with each other." Johnson included this laudatory assessment in his translation of Crousaz, correctly seeing the Swiss theologian's attack as a deconstruction of its assertion that Pope, unique among the moderns, had bridged the generic gap and written a successful philosophical poem.[45]

Contemporary consensus was on Crousaz's side in dissociating the genres. In 1721 John Clarke representatively criticized Cicero's *Nature of the Gods* along with "the later arguments of the *Academicks,* as rather oratorical and poetical Descriptions, than Arguments," as rhetorical tricks "calculated more to excite the Passions and captivate the Imaginations of the vulgar, than to convince the Reason and satisfy the Judgment."[46] Following Plato's dichotomy in the *Republic,* Clarke's contemporaries reserved the empyrean realm of real Knowledge for rational philosophical discourse and relegated poetical effusions to the ash heap of passionate Opinion. During the composition of *An Essay on Man* even Bolingbroke affirmed the dichotomy in a letter to Pope: "The business of the philosopher is to dilate," he wrote, "to press, to prove, to convince; and that of the poet to hint, to touch his subject with short and spirited strokes, to warm the affections, and to speak to the heart."[47]

In the division of human spoils, the head goes to the philosopher, the heart to the poet. The "long process of reasoning," which distinguishes the philosopher, Bolingbroke tells Pope, sinks the poet. Similarly, when David Hume argues that the poet, unlike the philosopher, does not hitch his reputation to a syllogism so that "Addison, perhaps, will be read with pleasure when Locke shall be entirely forgotten,"[48] he is presupposing the same dichotomy between the bewitching rhetorician and the empiricist-logician which Locke advocates in *An Essay Concerning Human Understanding*. "If we would speak of things as they are," Locke soberly advises, "we must allow that all the art of rhetoric . . . all the artificial and figurative application of words eloquence hath invented, are for nothing else but to insinuate wrong *ideas,* move the passions, and thereby mislead the judgment."[49] This statement accords perfectly with the resolution of Locke's fellows in the Royal Society of London for the Improving of

Natural Knowledge to banish "this beautiful deceipt," "this vicious abundance of *Phrase*," "this trick of *Metaphor*" and replace it with a "manner of Discourse . . . as near the Mathematical plainness" as possible.[50]

Thus the generic stage was set for Crousaz's indictment of Pope's aspirations to be simultaneously singer and sage. A philosopher is committed to truth and must adopt a rigorously rational methodology, Crousaz asserts, "whereas, a Poet is the Master of the Subject, and . . . disposes it as he thinks proper. The Philosopher takes a Pride in giving Instructions, in resolving Difficulties, and dissipating Doubts and Obscurities. But the Poet, without any Intention to deceive, aims to surprise, to agitate, and wholly to engage his Reader." Many of Pope's images and ideas "are magnificent," Crousaz admits, "but not all are equally clear; they are expressed in Terms proper to give Verse an Air of Sublimity, and which occur of themselves to a Poet. He is pleased with them, and makes use of them. A Philosopher does not admit them so easily." Rather than prove, Pope proclaims, offering sound where sense was promised. Irritated by the string of antinomies that closes Pope's attack on "Reasoning Pride" in the first epistle, Crousaz demands: "Does the Right of Poets extend so far as boldly to publish the greatest Paradoxes, provided they be deliver'd in pompous Expressions?"[51]

Crousaz's objection to Pope's mixing of discourse modes—to Pope's "beautiful deceipt"—was immediately Anglicized. In 1739, shortly after Johnson's translation of Crousaz's *Commentary* appeared, William Ayre prefaced his epistle on *Truth* (self-promoted as a "Counterpart" to Pope's poem) with the admonition that such philosophical matters as Pope's *Essay* expatiated upon "must be consider'd without any regard to Poetry."[52] This criticism of *An Essay on Man* enters the biographical tradition that Johnson inherited when, a year after Pope's death, the same William Ayre argues in his *Memoirs* of Pope that the glorious poetry of the *Essay* suspends all exercise of the reader's rational faculties.[53] Johnson's authoritative dismissal of the *Essay* in his *Life of Pope* reinscribes some of the phrases by Crousaz he translated earlier. "Mr. *Pope* seems," Johnson translates, "to express a great deal in a few Words, but upon Reflection, we learn nothing from him." "The reader feels his mind full," Johnson writes forty years later, "though he learns nothing." Like Crousaz and Ayre, Johnson attributes the illusion of profundity to rhetorical bewitchment. *An Essay on Man* "affords an egregious instance," he complains, "of the predominance of genius, the dazzling splendour of imagery, and the seductive powers of eloquence. Never were penury of knowledge and vulgarity of sentiment so happily disguised."[54]

While bookseller Curll was promoting sales of Crousaz's "Satire" of Pope's *Essay,* Joseph Warton was defining his own vocation as a poet in contradistinction to Pope's practice. In both the preface to his *Odes* and in the preface to his *Essay on the Genius and Writings of Pope* an adamantine barrier separates the prose and the poetic worlds of discourse; and he agrees with Crousaz that to mix the modes is inevitably self-contradictory. However, unlike Crousaz, Ayre, and Johnson, Warton is troubled neither by Pope's impiety nor by his lapses in logic. In fact, Warton admits that Pope's *Essay* "is as close a piece of argument . . . as perhaps can be found in verse." What Warton denies is that such "verse" can ever be poetry. Retaining the binary opposition, Warton privileges the Poet over the Philosopher.

Appropriately, Warton's *Essay on Pope* is dedicated to Edward Young whose supplementary *Night Thoughts* offered the "transcendently sublime" strain which Pope as "Le Poete de la Raison" lacked. Warton records that Young pressed Pope "to write something on the side of Revelation, in order to take off the impression of those doctrines which the Essay on Man were supposed to convey."[55] Pope's earthbound art, as Samuel Richardson wrote to Young, "was not the genius *to lift our souls to Heaven,* had it soared ever so freely, since it soared not in the Christian beam." In contrast to Pope's naturalism, Richardson praises Young for soaring like an eagle to "apotheosis."[56] "What is there transcendently sublime . . . in Pope?" Warton pointedly asks, arguing that bards degrade themselves by descending to the ratiocinative.[57] De Quincey's fundamental objection is identical. "To address the *insulated* understanding is to lay aside Prospero's robe of poetry," he insists. Consequently, *An Essay on Man,* like all didactic verse, is destroyed by its own "self-contradiction."[58] Elwin invokes De Quincey's authority before concluding that "the false scheme of embodying scientific philosophy in verse determined in advance the failure of the *Essay.*"[59] This "Romantic" objection is reincarnated frequently, most recently in Harold Bloom's pronouncement that Pope's *Essay* attempts an "aesthetic impossibility." Because Pope's project was "not suited to the Muse," it could only result in a "poetic disaster."[60] As Johnson wrote two hundred years earlier, Pope's "subject is perhaps not very proper for poetry."[61]

Harold Bloom is beating the dead; but in Johnson's day opponents of Pope's *Essay* were faced with the astonishing popularity of the poem. The enemy was not only alive but esteemed. Therefore, antagonists were compelled to explain why, if the poem was so very bad, it seemed so good. The answer was readily extrapolated from the dichotomy of rational philosopher and passionate poet. Like Eve with Adam, Pope pandered to readers' lower faculties and by overheating their bodies befuddled their minds. Pope's enemies were willing to acknowledge his artistry if they could simultaneously deny his adequacy as a systematic thinker. "Your Essays on Man . . . are much read and commended," Thomas Bentley wrote in March 1735. "Yet I have met with very knowing People, that think you are not equal to the Undertaking. . . . There are Starts and Flights of Poetry very fine, but you *prove* nothing."[62] To account for passages of apparent sense in the *Essay,* Pope's admitted eclecticism was invoked. When, to his chagrin, Bezaleel Morrice learned that the poem he had extravagantly praised in his own *Essay on the Universe* in 1733 was by his nemesis Pope, he alleges plagiarism to account for any intellectual substance in the *Essay:*

> If thy *Essay on Man* some value shows,
> 'Tis what the bounteous *Shaft'sbury* bestows;
> His only, all that's solid and sublime;
> Thine are the measure, and melodious chime.[63]

Insidiously, this depiction of Pope as the mindless rhymester of other men's ideas grew. When Boswell told Johnson that Lord Bathurst had affirmed that Bolingbroke wrote a prose draft of *An Essay on Man* and that Pope "did no more than put it into verse," Johnson offers a caveat but essentially concurs: "Sir, this is too strongly stated. Pope may have had from Bolingbroke the philosophic stamina of his *Essay* . . . but the poetical imagery, which makes a great part of the poem, is his."[64] Joseph Spence reported that Pope acknowledged how obliged he was to Bolingbroke "for the thoughts and reasonings in his moral work,"[65] and Spence was friends with Joseph Warton who lamented that Bolingbroke drew Pope away from "poetry" into the wasteland of ethical epistles (1782). A hundred years later Leslie Stephen concurred (1880); and another hundred years later (1984) Brean Hammond reinscribed the judgment of Pope's lines as "an attempt to render [Bolingbroke's view] into dramatically compelling verse."[66] By the alchemy of academic contempt what began as praise was transmuted to blame. In 1737 *Common Sense: Or, The Englishman's Journal* lauded Pope's *Essay* and urged "Minor Poets" not to attempt philosophical poetry since "their Motions must be round their own Axis, and within their own Sphere." Their feeble imitations are to Pope's poem "what the *Satellites* of *Jupiter* are to that Planet: Humble

Attendants made to roll round him at a Distance."[67] By 1880 Leslie Stephen could confidently reverse the metaphor by characterizing Pope's subordination to Bolingbroke as akin "to one of the inferior bodies of the solar system, whose orbit is dependent upon that of some more massive planet."[68]

Even Warburton ungraciously contributed to Pope's intellectual denigration. "'Tis perhaps singularly remarkable in Mr. Pope," Warburton told Spence with specific reference to *An Essay on Man*, that "his imagination [was] stronger than his judgment when he grew old."[69] Warburton took great satisfaction in having rescued Pope's *Essay* from his enemy Bolingbroke by interpretative fiat; and he listened smugly as flatterers said of his *Vindication*, "If you did not find Pope a philosopher, you have made him one." In acid prose Johnson etched a shallow, immature Pope inebriate on a little learning: "the poet was not sufficiently master of his subject; metaphysical morality was to him a new study, he was proud of his acquisitions, and, supposing himself master of great secrets, was in haste to teach what he had not learned. . . . The positions which he transmitted from Bolingbroke he seems not to have understood."[70] At exhausting length Elwin, Pattison, and Stephen repeat Johnson's judgment. "It is much to be lamented," Pattison writes, "that Pope attempted philosophy. He was very ignorant; ignorant of everything except the art of versification. Of philosophy he knew nothing beyond the name."[71] Johnson's judgment still dominates discussion of *An Essay on Man*. John Sparrow concludes that Pope erred in "attempting to expound in verse a philosophy he did not understand."[72] "However splendid his cosmic panorama, however beguiling his vision of ultimate harmony," George Fraser writes, "Pope lacks the muscle of a really strong thinker."[73]

Although Pope is a philosophical weakling, Fraser argues, he is nonetheless "a true poet"; and, in fact, both assertions were central to the trivialization of the *Essay* from the first. "I do not remember," Crousaz writes in Johnson's translation, "that ever I experienced the Power of Poetry so strongly as in Mr. Pope's *Essay*." Yet it was pathos without logos: rhyme without reason. "The Reader, carried away by the Beauty of the Poetry, reads with Eagerness, and supposes, often contrary to Truth, that the Facts are as the Poet represents them." The *Essay*, Crousaz insists, is simultaneously "grand and magnificent" and "confused" because "Mr. *Pope's* Physics smell of the Poet."[74] Although he detests the philosophy of the *Essay*, William Ayre says, Pope has written "a strain of Poetry so wonderfully sublime" that he is bewitched: "I love the music, but condemn the song." In his *Life of Pope,* Ayre ends his summary of the *Essay* with cold words for the content but with adulation for the style: "Such was Mr. Pope's Philosophy, and such his fine Poetry; which, as it never had, perhaps never will have any Equal in our Language."[75]

A contemporary pamphlet alleges that Pope "has attended to nothing but the Sound of his Words, when he was writing" but that the power of his poetry has blinded readers to the fact that "every thing this celebrated Author says, has not only a tendency to debauch and corrupt the Manners of Mankind, but, throughout the whole Performance, Contradictions and Inconsistencies reign triumphant over all Understanding and good Sense."[76] Predictably, Samuel Johnson said it most memorably. Although when Pope's "wonder-working sounds sink into sense" the reader should be able to see Pope's "penury of knowledge," Johnson fears the dangerous prevalence of Pope's power over the imagination: "The vigorous contraction of some thoughts, the luxuriant amplification of others, the incidental illustrations, and sometimes the dignity, sometimes the softness of the verses, enchain philosophy, suspend criticism, and oppress judgment by overpowering pleasure."[77]

Johnson's formulation of the disjunction of Pope's "harmonious Verse" and "discordant Sense" was accepted eventually by scholars as authoritative; but initially it had no effect on enthusiasm for *An Essay on Man.* "Why is the *Essay on Man* still read," Pattison is still obliged to answer a hundred years after Johnson's dictum, "when many a volume of the same age, of the same shallow metaphysics, is forgotten?" Since he is so obviously inadequate as a philosopher, Stephen asks, "How, then, could Pope obtain even an appearance of success?" Both Pattison and Stephen are somewhat surprised that Elwin devotes so many pages to demonstrating the *Essay*'s incompetence. That Pope's poem is but "a tissue of incoherence and inconsistence," Pattison affirms, "is a charge which no one can attempt to deny." Why, then, is it still being reprinted, read, and written about even by enemies like Elwin, Pattison, and Stephen?[78]

Johnson's image of poetry binding philosophy in chains provides the answer; and nineteenth-century rationalizations of the *Essay*'s popularity are attenuations of Johnson's phrases. "When we turn from the matter of the *Essay* to the execution," Pattison admits, "dissatisfaction gives way to admiration. We then see the secret of the eminence which Pope attained, and which he must always retain as long as the English language continues to be read." In *An Essay on Man* "the elegance of the phrase hides the absence of an idea. . . . [Pope] has masked an unmanageable matter by his inimitable art of expression. Such is the importance of style."[79] In his *Life of Alexander Pope,* Elwin's co-editor wrote: "To the question, How the 'Essay on Man' could ever have been accepted as embodying a philosophical system; the answer is, that . . . its poetical qualities blinded men's judgments to its philosophical defects." Courthope admits that many of the most able eighteenth-century logicians, including Voltaire, Marmontel, and Kant, paid the poem extravagant praise; but "that such praise should have been extorted from eminent doctors of philosophy" need not trouble us, he argues, if we realize that Pope's rhetorical power left them no freedom to reflect on "the weakness or inconsistency of the argument."[80] Popular histories and literary handbooks merely reflected this scholarly consensus. H. A. Taine's popular summary is representative: although Pope's "ideas are mediocre, the art of expressing them is truly marvelous: marvelous is the word."[81] "Read the poem for its poetical merits," a popular guide to *The Age of Pope* advised in 1894, "and you will forget its defects."[82]

An Essay on Man exists on the margins of two discourse worlds: the Logocentric (rational, logical, philosophical) and the Aesthetic (passionate, imaginative, poetic). When the *Essay* was published those worlds were mutually hostile: each mode suspicious of the other. It is no accident that Pope's poetic power is recurrently characterized as a dangerous enchantress, as a female playing upon men's passions to seduce them from the rational, as a poetic Circe turning whole herds of otherwise upright philosophers into swine. Crousaz was literally a professor of logic; but even he admitted that he had been tempted by the most powerful rhetoric he had ever read. The equally logocentric Warburton exuded no ink in defending Pope as poet precisely because that was never in question in Crousaz's attacks. Instead, Warburton's entire tendentious tome is a *Philosophical Commentary* on the poem as "a System of Philosophy."[83]

In 1755 the Prussian Royal Academy proposed an examination of Pope's "System" as the subject for their yearly philosophical prize. Kant made some notes toward a submission that would have argued Pope's philosophical superiority to Leibniz.[84] Gotthold Lessing and Moses Mendelssohn responded to the logocentric bias of the Academy with an ironic analysis of Pope's "system" in *Pope ein Metaphysiker!* the same year. Assuming that poets and philosophers inhabit different worlds of discourse, they ridiculed the practice of looking for philosophical "systems" in poems. The poet may borrow promiscuously from incompatible philosophies since poetry's concern is with sensuous, sprightly emotional stimulation whereas philosophy is obliged to order consistently precisely defined words divorced from all emotional connotations. An art for art's sake aestheticism is implied in their argument that Pope is performing a primarily nonrational function distinct from that of the philosopher and should be evaluated differently.[85] Aesthetically, Warton and De Quincey agree; but they fault Pope for attempting to bridge the discourse worlds. To Crousaz's objection that Pope's "Physics smell of the Poet," Warton and De Quincey retort that Pope's "Poetry stinks of the Philosopher." Significantly, sympathetic modern commentary on the *Essay* inevitably stresses the criteria appropriate to an aesthetic discourse isolated from logocentric considerations. Martin Kallich, for example, finds it praiseworthy in the *Essay* that "the poet appears to be in complete control over the philosopher."[86]

Thus, from the first, whether hostile or sympathetic, critics have made separate studies of the philosophy and poetry of the *Essay*. Elwin, Pattison, and Stephen first discuss the logic of the poem and only when that is debunked do they consider its aesthetics. "We may take the thought as a given material," Pattison says, "and make a separate study of the setting and workmanship." Although the *Essay* is entirely worthless as philosophy, "the young scholar [of rhetoric] cannot propose to himself a more instructive model to dwell upon and to analyze."[87] Maynard Mack's splendid Twickenham edition continues this dichotomy. Separate sections of his introduction deal with "The *Essay* and 'Philosophy'" and "The *Essay* as a Poem." The quotation marks around "Philosophy" suggest Mack's aesthetic and sympathetic bias. He believes that a study of "the materials philosophy supplied" and the resultant "ideas, postulates, conclusions (and right and wrong) of the poem's logical meaning and organization" are less important than the poem's "implicit organization, its attitudes, images, emotions, and its developing theme."[88] Despite his informed affection for the *Essay*, Mack unavoidably perpetuates the inherited separation of the poetic from the philosophic ("the thought as a given material" in Pattison; "the materials philosophy supplied" in Mack). Two subsequent book-length studies of the *Essay* make the dichotomy absolute. Believing that "no careful examination of the whole work as poem . . . has yet been made," Martin Kallich studies Pope's rhetoric exclusively.[89] In contrast, Douglas White is concerned exclusively with the "Manipulation of Ideas" in *An Essay on Man*, with situating Pope's arguments in the history of philosophy.[90]

JOHNSON'S "MORE MASSIVE INTELLECT"

The only other full-length study of *An Essay on Man* since Mack's Twickenham edition is that by A. D. Nuttall, which surprisingly ends with a chapter praising "Johnson's intellect as manifestly more powerful than Pope's." As it stands Nuttall's final chapter seems a quirky conclusion to a volume on the *Essay;* it seems less so when we realize how pervasive and determining Johnson's response to *An Essay on Man* has been to subsequent interpretation. Presently only literary scholars write about Pope's poem; and they invariably reinscribe Johnson's Crousazian dichotomy of "wonder-working sound" and "penury of knowledge." Nuttall's pedigree is archetypal: broadly dividing the history of interpretation into Crousazian and Warburtonian camps, he says that "Johnson is Crousazian" and that his own "book is Crousazian."[91]

Although virtually every Pope scholar quotes Johnson's denigration of the *Essay,* none has sought to explain Johnson's hostility. Perhaps after the definitive dismissals of Pattison, Elwin, and Stephen in the late nineteenth century, the question of personal animus seems irrelevant. There is no question of ideological bias in Johnson's assessment because he was just speaking a truth which, in Pattison's phrase, "no one can attempt to deny." There is, however, more to it than that. Interpretations are not neutral descriptions but admissions and assertions of self; Johnson's judgment of Pope's poem tells us about Johnson. His praise of Pope's "seductive powers of eloquence" in the *Essay* is sincere; and it was that powerful and "egregious" bewitchment that had to be silenced for the sake of Johnson's soul.

As Nicholas Hudson correctly notes, Johnson's hostility to theodicy was shared widely by other orthodox moralists and theologians,[92] but the persistence of that hostility from his early career (his translation of Crousaz) through his middle years (his review of Soame Jenyns's *Free Inquiry*) to the writing of the life of Pope late in his career is suggestive. His translation and annotation of Crousaz probably inclined Johnson to categorize Pope's *Essay* as a theodicy; it certainly established the association in Johnson's mind between the ideology of his *bête noire,* Bolingbroke, and Pope.[93] However, the truth is more complex because it was not—according to the received dichotomy repeated to him by Boswell—Bolingbroke's arguments that troubled him but Pope's poetry. As Martin Maner observes, Johnson's critique of the poem gives it "an evil, almost satanic overtone, as though the *Essay on Man* were a forbidden fruit on the tree of knowledge."[94]

Johnson's diaries and prayers are a record of a private struggle over decades against "tumultuous imaginations," a continuing effort not to be "depraved with vain imaginations." "My thoughts," Johnson confided to his God, "have been clouded with sensuality" and "my appetites have predominated over my reason." Recurrently, he vowed "to study the Scriptures" (1761), "to read the Scriptures" (1764), "to read the whole Bible" (1777), "*Biblia legenda*" (1777). Increasingly, the vain imaginings took the form of religious skepticism. "*Scruplis obsistendum,*" he pledged in April 1777: "resist religious doubts." He resolved "to gather the arguments for Christianity" (1777) and "to study Divinity, particularly the Evidences of Christianity" (1778). Despite extensive readings in the Bible and in church fathers like Aquinas and Chrysostom, he was beset by "terrour and anxiety." He implored God to deliver him "from needless scruples and oppressive terrours" (1777): "Ease, if it shall please thee the doubts of my mind" (1779); "let me be . . . no longer doubtful" (1780); "remove from me all such scruples and perplexities as encumber and obstruct my mind" (1784); "strengthen my mind against useless perplexities" (1784). In his continual "endeavour to conquer scruples," as his death drew near Johnson compiled a list of eleven causes of the "Skepticism" that tormented him.[95]

It was at the height of these fears that he worked on the prefaces to a new edition of the English poets. "Last week I published the lives of the poets," he confided in April of 1779, "written I hope in such a manner, as may tend to the promotion of Piety." They were not all written until 1781, at which time he was still struggling "Against Inquisitive and Perplexing Thoughts," which plagued him until his death.[96] Johnson does not specify how he thought his lives might promote piety; but it seems certain that he saw his inclusion of Sir Richard Blackmore's *Creation* in this light. Although John Dennis had celebrated Blackmore's philosophical poem as the work of a Christian Lucretius when it was published in 1712, Pope's destruction of Blackmore in *Peri Bathos* had ended *Creation*'s astonishing popularity; and Johnson's booksellers had no intention of including anything by Blackmore in their collection, much less a physico-theological poem of epic length. Johnson insisted that *Creation* be included.[97]

Johnson agrees with the Popian consensus that damns Blackmore's other poems; but he lavishly praises *Creation,* affirming that had Blackmore written nothing else it alone "would have transmitted him to posterity among the first favorites of the English Muse." Johnson praises *Creation*'s inspired union of "philosophical judgment and poetical spirit": "it wants neither harmony of numbers, accuracy of thought, nor elegance of diction."[98] It is, in essence, what a philosophical poem ought to be: elegant as poetry and accurate as philosophy. It was also—as a deliberate attack on the latter-day disciples of Epicurus including Descartes, Spinoza, and Hobbes—unremittingly pious.[99]

Moreover, *Creation* was to Johnson the opposite of Pope's "egregious" *Essay on Man*. After resigning Blackmore to the oblivion of duncedom, Pope supplanted *Creation* with his own philosophical poem that whether deist or Spinozist or Leibnizian or Shaftesburian or Bolingbrokian was certainly not distinctively Christian. Pope was, he flatly asserted, "Slave to no Sect." Knowing the immense popularity of the *Essay* with the public, Johnson could not exclude the *Essay* from the collection; but what he could do, he did. Through ridicule of his weaknesses and appropriations of his strength, Pope had deposed Blackmore as poet and philosopher. As will be shown in a subsequent chapter, from the sluggish Christian ore of *Creation*'s lines Pope coined golden couplets. Johnson's pious aim was to reestablish Blackmore's priority and to obliterate Pope's disturbing influence. His attempt to rewrite literary history by reinscribing Blackmore's *Creation* failed; but his trivialization of the *Essay* succeeded as well as he could have wished.

Whether it worked for Johnson himself is doubtful. "O Lord," he wrote in 1784, "while it shall please thee to continue me in this world where much is to be done and little to be known, teach me by thy Holy Spirit to withdraw my Mind from unprofitable and dangerous enquiries, from difficulties vainly curious, and doubts impossible to be solved." "Enable me," he prayed to God in that final year of his life, "to drive from me all such unquiet and perplexing thoughts as may mislead or hinder me in the practice of those duties which thou hast required." Delirious and dying, Johnson stared at the vacuity at the end of his bed and demanded, "Will that man never have done talking poetry at me?"[100]

The full story of Johnson's need to exorcise Pope belongs elsewhere; but perhaps what has been said is sufficient to interpret his trivialization of the *Essay* as "written . . . to the promotion of Piety." The interpretive tools were ready-to-hand. The age had its discourse lines drawn to separate poetry and philosophy. "A Description in *Homer*," Joseph Addison announced, "has charmed more Readers than a Chapter in *Aristotle*." While it is true that the "Pleasures of the Imagination" are not "so refined as those of the Understanding," Addison admits, the enchantments of the imagination are more salubrious. "The Pleasures of the Fancy are more conducive to Health, than those of the Understanding, which are worked out by Dint of Thinking, and attended with too violent a Labour of the Brain."[101] When Pope presumed to marry wit and judgment, Crousaz was quick to ridicule a Homer trying to write like an Aristotle.

Johnson's adoption of this dichotomy allowed him to trivialize the *Essay* into a glittering rhetorical bauble of no intrinsic worth. By admitting the poem's power and artistry, Johnson appears even-handed at the same time that he rationalizes the popularity of the *Essay* as an "enchantment" or "bewitchment" or "enchaining" of the intellect by literary language, a "seduction" into "vain imaginings." Once written, Johnson's judgment was repeated by subsequent editors. Elwin is typical: "The Essay was altogether a mistake. . . . His thoughts are often gems rendered lustrous by the skill of the cutter, but . . . when examined are found worthless."[102] Even the *Essay*'s greatest admirers now presuppose Johnson's assessment. Although a reader must be "dubious . . . over the logic," Geoffrey Tillotson exclaims, Pope's poetry "towers in a splendor that is massive."[103] There is now scarcely a writer on the *Essay* who fails to quote Johnson's charge that Pope's verses "enchain philosophy." Representatively, in *The Imaginative World of Alexander Pope* (1987), Leopold Damrosch quotes Johnson repeatedly in dismissing Maynard Mack's defense of the *Essay* as a "formed *Weltanschauung*" which works "not through theorem but through symbol."[104] No amount of the kind of Renaissance parallels Mack offers, Damrosch insists, "can conceal the dissonance between rhetorical procedure and metaphysical claims. . . . A strong intelligence can easily take the poem apart."[105]

Johnson authorized what Pope's editors subsequently did to the *Essay*. For eighty years the student or scholar turning to Elwin's definitive edition found a massive critical apparatus, much longer than the *Essay* itself, which even the hostile Pattison described as a "furious" denunciation of the poem it pretended to perpetuate. Nuttall inaccurately characterizes Maynard Mack's Twickenham edition, which replaced Elwin's, as "Warburtonian." Mack is sympathetic to the poem, but unlike Warburton he does not attempt a pious interpretation. Believing "ratiocinative rigour . . . impossible in poetry and probably undesirable," Mack is really allied with aesthetic interpreters like Warton, De Quincey, and Bloom who find "philosophical poetry" an oxymoron.[106] True poets do not circumscribe the sublime with syllogisms.

Ironically, even those aesthetic critics who would praise Pope help to damn him. As Richard Rorty stresses, most philosophers are hostile to poetry. "To claim that its statements are structured by logic, reason, truth, and not by the rhetoric in which they are 'expressed,' philosophical discourse defines itself against writing." Philosophers trivialize poetry as a "nonserious margin" dangerous to serious conceptual discourse.[107] Crousaz's complaint that "Mr. Pope's Natural Philosophy seems somewhat infected by his Poetry" astutely encapsulates the logocentric objection that poetry is potential "infection," a kind of venereal disease of discourse. One is puzzled to see the mingling of recriminations in Johnson's prayers until one recognizes the latent connection between "sensual images," "vain imaginations," and religious doubts. The lower faculties are infecting the higher, to his soul's peril. As a recent critic affirms, Pope's ideas "might have doomed [the] *Essay* to oblivion" had not his poetry made its "appeal to our reason through our senses."[108] Johnson felt the appeal: Pope's eloquence is "seductive" and must be "disrobed" and seen "naked" if it is not to "oppress [our] judgment by overpowering pleasure." Stripped of her rhetorical robes, the whore is seen as unsound; but in expiation for his attraction, Johnson resurrected Blackmore and buried Pope.

Here too Johnson is paradigmatic. Indications are that he felt a powerful pull toward Pope's vortex of vain imaginings. Like Crousaz, he acknowledges Pope's "egregious . . . genius." Something of the same thing must be true of scholars like Elwin and Pattison who spent so much energy and ingenuity trying to destroy the poem they pretended to interpret. One wonders why, A. D. Nuttall writes, "if Elwin despised Pope so much, he was willing to expend so much labor on him?" The same must be asked of Nuttall himself for his recent book qualifies him as the latest in that line of scholars who come to bury the *Essay* rather than to praise it. Pope "was not . . . a clear-sighted philosopher"; he "was an unsystematic thinker," and, consequently, "the thought of *An Essay on Man*, philosophical or not, is notably unsystematic." Nuttall finds Pope to be a writer who only "obscurely senses" philosophical distinctions and has only a "dim" awareness of his own intentions, most of his energies going into "the production of a smooth and acceptable set of couplets." Pope's "rhetoric and logic," Nuttall argues, "are not working in perfect union." In fact, "the energy of Pope's genius perhaps works against the bias of his intellect"; but, whatever the cause, Pope's "slick yet intellectually inept" performance is "the sort of thing that gets poets a bad name with philosophers." Nearing his conclusion, Nuttall acknowledges his hostile tone: "there have probably been many occasions earlier in this book when I have seemed more contemptuous of Pope than I really am." In fact, if Nuttall has any intellectual respect for *An Essay on Man,* it does not come through his text. Random quotation cannot communicate the pervasiveness of his contempt and consequent condescension.[109]

So long as one considers Nuttall's book an "interpretation" of *An Essay on Man* it seems very strange. Once one realizes that it is not an interpretation of the *Essay* but is instead a destruction of Pope's philosophical poem and a vindication of Johnson's judgment of it, then Nuttall's work is no longer odd and his final chapter is explained. Nuttall's twenty-five-page "Coda" entitled "The End of Theodicy" lauds *Rasselas* as the philosophical alternative to *An Essay on Man.* Aware that "the evil of the world is not explained, it is only endured," Johnson—"most classical of authors"—replaces Pope's "stasis of optimistic theology" with "a stasis which is close to despair. But, in its very surrender," Nuttall concludes, "Johnson's intellect is manifestly more powerful than Pope's." Nuttall's demolition is complete. Whereas Johnson admitted his powerful attraction to Pope's dangerous style, Nuttall finds Johnson's style in *Rasselas* "deeply refreshing" after Pope's "usual flurry of humorous or evasive rhetorical defenses." Johnson's "style is utterly unlike that of Pope" in that it "simply says what it wishes to say." In his "Arnoldian moments," Nuttall admits, "it is suddenly blindingly clear that Pope is not a poet as Virgil, Dante, Shakespeare, Milton, and Keats are poets."[110]

What should be blindingly clear is that A. D. Nuttall cannot read *An Essay on Man.* He is frustrated on virtually every page that Pope will not "simply say" what he wishes to say. He is also blind to "the egregious . . . predominance of genius, the dazzling splendour of imagery, and the seductive powers of eloquence," which Johnson perceived. There is, Lord Byron asserted, "ten times more poetry in the *Essay on Man,* than in [Wordsworth's] *Excursion.*" Johnson could concur; Nuttall is having none of it. Nor are the rest of us.

William Spanos's extension of Heidegger's "de-struction of the Western onto-theo-logical tradition" to literary criticism helps explain Nuttall's disability and our own. The "onto-theo-logical" critics, the critics I have called "Logocentric" (Crousaz) and "Aesthetic" (Warton), cannot enter into a careful, dialogic encounter with the text because texts are "dangerous," potentially destructive "of reified formations and present beliefs."[111] Johnson's spiritual doubts make clear the grounds of his discomfort with *An Essay on Man.* Nuttall's grounds are equally clear. He is self-characterized as simultaneously "Arnoldian" and "Crousazian"; and, in fact, he is the epitome of both the Logocentric and the Aesthetic critic. As Logocentric critic he fulminates on almost every page against Pope's "superficial intelligence" and his inadequacy as a philosopher; as Aesthetic critic he finds it "blindingly clear" that Pope is not a real poet. Finally, Nuttall concludes, "the underlying trouble with Pope and his kind is not rationalism or futile metaphysics but the fact that they do not want enough." Pope and his kind lack "moral imagination."[112]

It may be objected that Nuttall is not a preeminent Pope scholar and that, consequently, his hostility is unrepresentative. However, Maynard Mack, the preeminent scholar of *An Essay on Man*, characterizes Nuttall's book as "brilliant"; and J. Douglas Canfield's review in *Eighteenth-Century Studies* applauds Nuttall's dogged denigration of Pope: "Indeed, we track through the poem line by line, shooting every one of Pope's philosophical follies that Nuttall's hounding mind can flush."[113] This benign response to Nuttall's Crousazianism by our scholarly community suggests the extent to which his "reified formations and present beliefs" are our own.[114]

Modern readers are capable of divorcing form from content and judging that the Essay *is a great poem, however negligible or even repulsive its philosophy may be.*
—*Brean S. Hammond (1984)*

TWO

Disseminating Theodicy

THE RATIONALE for the condemnatory rut imprisoning interpretation of Pope's *Essay* is evident in the discussion of "Philosophy and Poetry" in the *Princeton Encyclopedia of Poetry and Poetics*. A poem may be "philosophical" in either of two senses, Philip Wheelwright asserts. A poem "may serve as a vehicle of some philosophical teaching which is essentially independent of the poem itself and could therefore be paraphrased in a set of logically developed statements without loss or distortion of meaning." Lucretius' *De Rerum Natura* and Pope's *Essay* are cited as archetypes of this kind of philosophical poem. However, "a more deeply characteristic procedure," Wheelwright argues, is for a poem to "employ its full linguistic, rhythmic, and associational relationships to open up new insights into values, relationships, and significant possibilities, such as could not be adequately restated, except with gross distortion, outside the particular poem that has succeeded in expressing them." Wheelwright cites *King Lear*, Keats's "Ode on a Grecian Urn," and Eliot's *Four Quartets* as illustrations of this "more deeply characteristic" philosophical poem.[1] Perpetuating Joseph Warton's aestheticism, Wheelwright exiles the *Essay* to the poetic hinterland of paraphrasable propositions. Interpreters wielding the keen and delicate instruments of contemporary criticism are not challenged to tease out the poem's textual subtleties since it has none.

Inured as we are to the disjunction of philosophical and poetic discourse, Wheelwright's characterization of *De Rerum Natura* and *An Essay on Man* may seem not only accurate but inevitable. Yet to interpret a text, as Jonathan Culler usefully reminds us, is "to bring it within the modes of order which culture makes available, and this is usually done by talking about it in a mode of discourse which a culture takes as natural."[2] Our cultural episteme mandates the separation of poetic and philosophical discourse, authorizing the philosopher to be judge of one and the literary critic to be judge of the other. In effect, we have deconstructed and, thereby, discredited the genre of philosophical poetry. To be able to read philosophical poetry again we must, in the parlance of structuralism, "naturalize" poems like *An Essay on Man* rather than insist on translating them into another discourse mode. Tzvetan Todorov's discussion of the fantastic as a literary genre illustrates by analogy what has happened to philosophical poetry. For the genre of the fantastic to exist, Todorov insists, the reader must hesitate between a natural and a supernatural explanation of events. The fantastic exists between the neighboring genres of the strange and the supernatural; consequently, the reader who insists on either a wholly natural or a wholly supernatural interpretation deconstructs and destroys the genre.[3] The chapters that follow argue that Pope's *Essay* occupies an analogous "space of uncertainty" between the contiguous but distinguishable genres of philosophical prose and purely emotive poetry.

"PUTTING POPE IN HIS PLACE"

In interpreting Rousseau, Jacques Derrida speaks of the necessity to free his reading from inherited categories of judgment, "not only from the categories of the history of ideas and the history of literature but also, and perhaps above all, from the categories of the history of philosophy."[4] The same is true if there is to be any genuine reinterpretation and revaluation of *An Essay on Man*. The proof that this judgment is just and that the inherited tradition of interpretation characterized in the previous chapter is, in fact, a history of systematic misreading must take the form of a demonstration of a more adequate way of reading Pope's philosophical poem.

Robert M. Adams's review of Mack's biography of Pope is significantly entitled "Putting Pope in His Place." From the first, interpreters sought to locate Pope's poem in its appropriate ideological camp, to situate it accurately in the history of ideas, to say once and for all what it means. Yet from the first both Crousazians and Warburtonians acknowledged recalcitrant elements in the poem that made it equally difficult to dismiss as atheistic fatalism or to vindicate as providential theism. Roughly speaking, Crousazians acknowledged orthodox elements in a predominantly heterodox work and invoked Pope's alleged uncomprehending eclecticism to discredit the whole. Warburtonians, in contrast, made the poem orthodox by supplementing the poem with doctrines—such as the fall of man, the divinity of Jesus, or the existence of an afterlife—which they could not find unequivocally affirmed in Pope's text.

One way of dealing with aspects of a text that are recalcitrant to interpretation's desire to put things in order is to place the text in a context that supplements, and thereby clarifies, its meaning. Thus Crousaz argues that Pope's diction and imagery are only coherently explicable in the context of the "atheism" of Spinoza or Leibniz. Consequently, Crousaz invokes both men as Pope's dangerous precursors, as the "sources" for the ideology of *An Essay on Man.* Warburton acts identically using pious sources. In this way an identification of "sources" becomes the primary key to interpretive ordering. This placement may be done with subtlety as in Maynard Mack's delineation of Pope's "Renaissance *Weltanschauung*" or in Douglas White's recreation of Pope's "Context of Controversy"; or, far more usual, it may be done crudely by identifying a single author or genre or historical idea that becomes the philosophic planet around which Pope, the poetic satellite, revolves. Once identified, the pretext or "source" becomes the interpretative border that limits and makes manageable the meaning of Pope's perplexing text.[5]

The history of interpretation of *An Essay on Man* is a narrative of proposed precursors. Warburton writes as an intellectual terrorist exploding his adversaries' allegations of Pope's debts to Lucretius, Spinoza, Leibniz, Shaftesbury, and Bolingbroke and installing his own genealogy of Christian worthies. Archbishop William King's popular theodicy, *De Origine Mali,* was immediately seen as a key. In fact, in 250 years of commentary there have been no new nominees for Pope's precursor. Mark Pattison finds the *Essay* "a very narrow and incomplete rendering of Leibniz's *Theodicee.*"[6] John Herman Randall, Jr., reads Pope's poem as a "summary" of Shaftesbury, as does William Alderman.[7] Although he thinks that Bolingbroke is Pope's "philosophical mentor," Bernhard Fabian interprets the *Essay* as "a confident imitation of Lucretius."[8] Brean Hammond rebuts Fabian and reestablishes Bolingbroke's priority.[9] David Morris reasserts that "Pope's primary model . . . was undoubtedly Lucretius."[10] Nuttall concurs that Lucretius' *De Rerum Natura* is the "model" for the *Essay* while simultaneously insisting that Bolingbroke is "Pope's philosophical mentor," although he admits that the poem "is slightly more Leibnizian than it is Bolingbrokian."[11] Most recently, Damrosch redamns Pope by concluding that he "got his philosophical ideas very much secondhand, principally from Bolingbroke."[12]

Damrosch's allegation that Pope got his ideas secondhand certainly applies to most of Pope's interpreters; and the preceding enumeration of suggested "origins" while partial is indicative of the many articles proving: Pope's deism or Catholicism; his indebtedness to the grand received ideas of a great chain of being and Neoplatonic plenitude; his generic debt to theodicy; his servility to the greater minds of Lucretius, Locke, Leibniz, or their like. All such origin studies are placements erecting interpretative parameters, as the static metaphors suggest. Basil Willey places Pope against his eighteenth-century "background" of "Cosmic Toryism" and Douglas White puts Pope in his proper "Context of Controversy."[13] Characteristically, the explanatory key is an extra-textual template for judging Pope's poem. Thus A. O. Lovejoy assesses the *Essay* as a minor literary manifestation in the history of a bad idea (plenitude)[14] and Nuttall judges it as the last gasp of a no longer tenable genre (theodicy).[15] The chronological situating of Pope's poem in philosophical surveys like those of Lovejoy, Willey, Randall, and Nuttall also reinforces the assumption that Pope's poem is an outmoded period piece with no claim on our current sensibilities.[16] Moreover, the "paraphrases" of the *Essay* in Lovejoy and Willey exert disproportionate interpretative influence as obligatory readings for literary students seeking a "background" in eighteenth-century philosophy.[17]

However, as Vincent Leitch observes, "The careful and conscious constructions of scholarship and history rest upon a wild profusion whipped into order."[18] In Willey and Lovejoy *An Essay on Man* is whipped into order by interpretive paraphrases that render Pope indistinguishable from Soame Jenyns. The assumption that the identification of a single or a predominant "source" can provide the interpretive key to the *Essay* is mistaken. First, Pope—most allusive of poets—is too various. Moreover, in *An Essay on Man* he explicitly adopts a methodology of "steer[ing] betwixt" doctrines, which is fundamentally at odds with any approach that limits meaning by constructing rigid contextual boarders. Yet it is easy to understand the critics' longing for borders because those hermeneutical boundaries allow critics to demonstrate their mastery of the text, in some cases even their superiority.

The motive of most source studies from those of Crousaz and Lord Hervey to the present has not been to enrich or extend our understanding of Pope's text but to erect interpretive borders limiting intertextual play so that the critic may pronounce the last word on *An Essay on Man*. Only against a static frame of reference is the hostile critic able to say definitively when Pope is out of bounds as in Hervey's invocation of Pope's "uniform" and "Original" sources as the damning contrast to Pope's own incoherence and lack of originality. Perhaps this intrinsically coercive use of precursors explains why intertextual studies of the *Essay* continue to be unambitious reexaminations of the same set of suspects. To acknowledge Pope's intertextual genius for imitation and allusion, to acknowledge that *An Essay on Man* is a rich set of relations with many other texts, would frustrate critical closure and make absurd the interpretive aim of pronouncing a univocal final judgment.

IN MILTON'S SHADOW

Literary language resists final words: "literariness" implies resistance to paraphrase. As Shoshana Felman argues, good interpretation—like good psychoanalysis—does not seek coercively to banish every ambiguity and contradiction because as human beings, as Whitman says, we are large and contain multitudes.[19] Great poems, poems dense with human experience, require patience; but many of Pope's readers were and are impatient. *An Essay on Man*, Robert Dodsley wrote in 1734, confused many with its difficulty until rereading carefully they acknowledged its profundity and Pope's unique union of "the Sage's Wisdom, and the Poet's Fire":

> So when at first I view'd thy wond'rous Plan,
> Leading thro' all the winding Maze of Man;
> Bewilder'd, weak, unable to pursue,
> My Pride would fain have laid the Fault on You.
> This false, That ill-expresst, this Thought not good,
> And all was wrong which I misunderstood.[20]

Exactly 250 years later, coercive criticism having triumphed over the text, David Nokes commiserated with any critic having to interpret Pope's "demanding but also deeply unsatisfactory" *Essay*.[21]

Perhaps the best way to initiate careful rereading of Pope's text is to break down those contextual borders erected by critics to control dissemination. Most critics use Pope's "source" as the interpretative border;

they identify his Ur-text—almost invariably a work of philosophical prose—and treat any deviation from that "source" as error. Such simplistic reductionism runs directly counter not only to Pope's "poetry of allusion" but also to intertextuality's insistence that most texts, and especially literary texts, are constructs importantly dependent on, but complexly related to, prior texts. Anthropologists distinguish between thick and thin descriptions of a culture on analogy to the literary distinction between round and flat characters in fiction. From this perspective most work on Pope's *Essay* has been thin intertextual description, usually amounting to no more than a rehash of earlier editorial apparatus. Consequently, a thicker intertextual description that acknowledges the play of differences in and between texts can become a technique "for battling the tyranny of correct or controlled meaning."[22] By stressing the dissemination of meanings, intertextuality resists reducing texts to their pretexts as interpreters of *An Essay on Man* are doing perpetually.

Ironically, so thin and repetitive has commentary been that Pope has succeeded in one of his primary aims in the *Essay*: to obliterate an immediate and major "source" from literary history. Thicker description of Pope's rich intertextuality not only breaks down the borders of interpretive closure but also shows how critics' self-imposed blindness has abetted Pope in establishing priority over a major precursor. This complex textual struggle begins at the beginning with the first verse paragraph of the poem:

AWAKE, my ST. JOHN! leave all meaner things
To low ambition, and the pride of Kings.
Let us (since Life can little more supply
Than just to look about us and to die)
Expatiate free o'er all this scene of Man;
A mighty maze! but not without a plan;
A Wild, where weeds and flow'rs promiscuous shoot,
Or Garden, tempting with forbidden fruit.
Together let us beat this ample field,
Try what the open, what the covert yield;
The latent tracts, the giddy heights explore
Of all who blindly creep, or sightless soar;
Eye Nature's walks, shoot Folly as it flies,
And catch the manners living as they rise;
Laugh where we must, be candid where we can;
But vindicate the ways of God to Man.

(I:1–16)

On a manuscript of Epistle I, now at the Houghton Library at Harvard University, Pope wrote that line sixteen "sums up ye Moral and main Drift of ye whole, Justification of ye Ways of Provi."[23] What "whole" the note refers to and at what stage of composition it was written are ambiguous. In "THE DESIGN" prefixed to all editions of the *Essay,* Pope is unambiguous in characterizing his poem as a "system of Ethics" that deals with other matters only insofar as they are essential "to prove any moral duty, to enforce any moral precept" (p. 7). However, on the second page of his vindication of the *Essay,* Warburton asserts that line sixteen "tells us with what design" Pope wrote. Warburton's rhetorical purpose is to demolish Crousaz's allegation that Pope's real design is to discredit "the very being of a God,"[24] and that probably explains Warburton's emphasis. Subsequent criticism, however, has accepted Warburton's interpretation of the *Essay* as a theodicy and ignored Pope's explicit characterization of it as an "Ethics."

In concluding the first verse paragraph of *Paradise Lost,* Milton implores his "Heav'nly Muse":

> What in me is dark
> Illumine, what is low raise and support;
> That to the height of this great Argument
> I may assert Eternal Providence,
> And justify the ways of God to men.[25]

In the process of redefining Pope's ethics as a metaphysics, every interpreter cites the Miltonic allusion in line sixteen. Joseph Warton (1782), for example, opines that Pope "seems to have hinted, by his allusion to the Paradise Lost, that he intended his poem for a defence of providence, as well as Milton." According to Warton, Pope "proposes to prove, that of all possible systems, infinite wisdom has formed the best" and in so doing is "deeply indebted to the Theodicee of Leibnitz, to Archbishop King's Origin of Evil, and to the Moralists of Lord Shaftesbury."[26] Two hundred and two years later A. D. Nuttall (1984) mentions the same influences and instructs the reader innocent of philosophy that "the technical term for the justification of God is 'theodicy.'" The allusion to Milton, Nuttall says, is an "act of truly calculated presumption" with "an element of sheer 'cheek' but, at the same time, a firm assumption of the center of the literary stage." Warton notes that Pope's method of justification is "very different" from Milton's; Nuttall calls the *Essay* a "counter-Miltonic justification."[27]

Leibniz's neologistic "theodicee" marries the Greek roots for *god* and *justice* as an appropriate designation for an attempt to resolve the apparent logical contradiction between God's attributes of omniscience, omnipotence, and perfect goodness and the empirical evidences of a world abounding in suffering and injustice. In *Paradise Lost* Milton exonerates God not by logical argument but by reinscribing a story from Genesis: Adam's disobedience "Brought death into the world, and all our woe." Abandoning scriptural authority and the doctrine of the fall, Leibniz shifted from narrative to a rigorously logical mode modeled on mathematics. Succinctly stated, Leibniz's argument was that since even God cannot will a contradiction or square a circle there are limits on just how perfect, from a human perspective, a world can be; and although there are real problems with our world, it is perhaps the best possible and, consequently, consistent with the existence of a benevolent deity.

When Crousaz, Warton, and Nuttall characterize Pope's intention as identical with Leibniz's *Theodicy* as a "counter-Miltonic justification" they adopt canons of evaluation perhaps appropriate to Leibnizian mathematical logic but grotesquely distorting when applied to philosophical poetry. Pope's "objective," the *Oxford Companion to English Literature* assumes, "is to vindicate the ways of God to man; to prove that the scheme of the universe is the best of all possible schemes," attempts that "recall the efforts of Pangloss."[28] Professor Pangloss is Voltaire's lampoon of Leibniz; and just such a generic substitution of theodicy for philosophical poetry and of Pope for Pangloss-Leibniz permeates discussions of *An Essay on Man.* Nuttall examines virtually every verse paragraph of the *Essay* for evidences of Leibnizian "abstract rationalization"; and where he cannot find it he "senses that Pope's theodicy is beginning to break up through neglect," further evidence that Pope is "intellectually inept." For Nuttall, therefore, Pope's allusive line sixteen emphasizes the gulf separating the inspired poet from the versifying ephebe: "The difference between Milton and Pope is overwhelming."[29] And, of course, two centuries earlier Warton concluded his *Essay on the Genius and Writings of Pope* with a placement of Pope: "Not, assuredly, in the same rank with *Spenser, Shakespeare,* and *Milton.*"[30] The Miltonic pretext casts a condemnatory shadow over Pope's accomplishment.

The allusion to Milton in line sixteen is unmistakable, and critics are correct to see it as significant. The interpretative error is to see Pope's purpose as identical to Milton's or to Leibniz's and thereby to reduce the *Essay* to a metaphysical theodicy. With a vengeance critics do to the small world of Pope's text what they accuse Pope of doing to that great text, the world; while they indict him for simplifying the mysterious richness of the world into a few axioms of optimistic theology, they reduce his text to those very axioms themselves. In contrast, no critic has opened Pope's text to the play of deliberate dissemination by suggesting that "vindication" within line sixteen is an allusion within an allusion; but a fuller look at Pope's rhetorical context may encourage greater appreciation of the "shifting crevices at work" in Pope's poem and may illustrate how the reduction of Pope's text to a single dominant pretext is "a venture in foolhardy soothsaying."[31]

On the Houghton manuscript Pope glosses line sixteen as summing up the "main Drift of ye Whole, Justification of ye Ways of Provi." Another note at the bottom of the sheet reads: "16. Verse, To ye Subject wch runs thro ye Whole Design, Justification of ye Methods of Providence." At least three phrases are simultaneously present in Pope's mind:

> And justify the ways of God to men.
> (Milton, *Paradise Lost*)
>
> But vindicate the ways of God to Man.
> (Pope, *An Essay on Man*)
>
> Justification of ye Methods of Providence.
> (Pope, manuscript note on line sixteen)

I believe a primary connective in Pope's mind is Bishop William Sherlock's enormously popular *Discourse Concerning the Divine Providence* (1694), which anticipates Pope's methodology by advising readers to steer between "dangerous extremes on both sides" when considering theological questions. Sherlock brings the words "vindicate," "justify," and "providence" together when he describes what is necessary "for a fuller Vindication of the Justice of Providence."[32]

Sherlock rails against philosophers who "are impatient to think, that God should do any thing which they cannot understand," citing the verse from Job that "Vain man would be wise, tho man be born like a wild asses colt." He argues that "this is a matter of such vast consequence, to silence the Sceptical Humour of the Age, and to shame those trifling and ridiculous Pretenses to Wit and Philosophy, in Censuring the Wisdom and Justice of Providence, that it deserves a more particular Discourse." Pope's manuscript notes to line sixteen make it clear that he characterized the initial epistle as just such a discourse. Sherlock especially recommends stressing the limits of human reason: "There is not one thing in Nature, which they do understand: And if we cannot understand the Mysteries of Nature, why should we expect to understand all the unsearchable Depths and Mysteries of Providence?"[33] This tradition of apologetics inherited from the Hebrew scriptures and recently reinscribed in Matthew Prior's *Solomon* reaches its eighteenth-century acme shortly after publication of Pope's *Essay* in Joseph Butler's *Analogy of Nature* (1736). Immediately above his gloss to line sixteen on the Houghton manuscript, Pope notes the "Limits of Reason" as one theme of the "second book"; and near the beginning of Epistle II, Pope uses Isaac Newton as an example of the metaphysical blindness of even those who have seen most deeply into the mysteries of nature:

> Superior beings, when of late they saw
> A mortal Man unfold all Nature's law,
> Admir'd such wisdom in an earthly shape,
> And shew'd a NEWTON as we show an Ape.
> Could he, whose rules the rapid Comet bind,
> Describe or fix one movement of his Mind?

Revelatory of his debt, on the manuscript of Epistle II immediately beneath these lines on Newton, Pope has interlineated the identical verse cited by Sherlock: "Job. Man is as a wild ass."[34]

A case for Pope's hitherto unnoticed allusions to Sherlock could easily be elaborated by a systematic comparison of relevant passages. Establishing new "sources," however, is subsidiary to opening up the intertextual context by noting further relevant disseminations of "vindicate." In 1730, as Pope was settling down to serious work on the *Essay,* Arthur Ashley Sykes, friend and argumentative protégé of Samuel Clarke, published *The True Foundations of Natural and Reveal'd Religion Asserted,* an attempt at "a clear and consistent, and rational Scheme of defending Christianity . . . in debate with the Deists." Sykes laments the contentiousness within the orthodox camp: "I cannot but with the utmost concern lament the fate of our common Christianity . . . to see the man to whom the province of *vindicating the Scripture* is assigned, not treating his Adversary with Reason and Argument, but with *Contempt* and Haughtiness." The emphasis for *vindicating* is Sykes's own.[35] Similarly deploring those disputants who have "less sharpened the *wits* than the *hearts* of men against each other," Pope seems to appropriate some of his predecessor's phrases—including "clear" and "consistent"—in characterizing his "Design" in the *Essay* to reduce the "science of Human Nature . . . to a *few clear points*" in order to form "a *temperate* yet not *inconsistent* . . . system of Ethics" (p. 7).

Pope probably read Sykes's *True Foundations*. Sykes is objecting specifically to the immoderate rhetoric of an antagonist, Daniel Waterland, whose "whole structure of thought" reminds Douglas White of Pope's characterization of human reason in the *Essay*. White astutely notes that by restricting his *Essay* to the "Natural" and thereby eschewing the "Reveal'd," Pope sacrificed the "key conclusion of Waterland's whole system": the necessity of divine rewards and punishments to restrain a predominantly self-loving creature. Instead, Pope chose what White describes as a "middle road" making self-love and social benevolence identical, "so that present fulfillment, not future rewards, is the motivation" for moral action.[36]

The argument of Waterland and Sykes over the respective ethical roles of reason and passion drew in many other vindicators during the early 1730s. In 1732, the year before Pope's *Essay* anonymously celebrated the sociability of self-love, William Dudgeon published *The State of the Moral World Considered. Or, A Vindication of Providence in the Government of the Moral World*, "the design of it being," Dudgeon stated, "to assert the universal goodness of God in the government of the world, by making all creatures to be proportionately more or less happy as they practice virtue, which tendeth to the good of the *whole* as well as the good of every *individual*."[37] As Pope concludes Epistle III, self-love wakes the virtuous mind to social love as the human soul rises from "*Individual* to the *Whole*" (III:362; italics added). Now lost to literary history, Dudgeon is a perfect example of a writer who clearly belongs in the tale of Pope's text. After Crousaz blasted Pope's impiety, Dudgeon quickly responded with *A View of the Necessitarian or Best Scheme: Freed from the Objections of M. Crousaz, in his Examination of Mr. Pope's "Essay on Man"* (1739). Even so, in the thin contextual descriptions accorded *An Essay on Man*, William Dudgeon disappears entirely; no critic so much as mentions his name.[38]

Because of his fame and his relationship with Pope, Edward Young should be more difficult to ignore. Yet despite the instant popularity of Young's *A Vindication of Providence: Or, A True Estimate of Human Life. In Which the Passions are Considered in a New Light* when it appeared in 1728, no critic has mentioned the work in connection with Pope's use of "vindicate." Neither of the two recent book-length studies of the *Essay* mentions Young at all, much less the *Vindication*; and the introduction to the Augustan Reprint Society's facsimile of the *Vindication* (1984) makes no mention of the *Essay* either. Literary history situates Young, if at all, as a posttext to Pope, seeing *Night Thoughts* as a pious Christian supplement to *An Essay on Man*.[39]

As Harold Bloom notes, great poets have a way of appropriating their predecessors so that their precursors seem to be imitating them.[40] Thus it seems strange now to read that Young was one of those to whom the *Essay* was attributed before Pope acknowledged his authorship. There seems no reason to doubt that Pope knew his friend's *Vindication*. In November of 1727 Young was distributing early copies to his acquaintances; and in December, on Pope's behalf, he visited Richard Savage in prison and gave him money.[41] Certainly Young gave Pope a copy of his treatise which, he informs the reader, has a "design . . . of great consequence, and, I think, new." That design is to vindicate providence from the "prevailing and inveterate" allegations, nurtured by "the pride, the ill-nature, and melancholy, and vice of mankind," that the world is necessarily a scene of suffering. After asking Queen Caroline to "patronize and vindicate a Vindication of Providence," Young concludes his preface by requesting the reader's indulgence for the "great length" of his *Vindication*, a paragraph that may be alluded to when, in his own "Design," Pope justifies his choice of verse over prose as allowing greater brevity: "nothing is more certain, than that much of the *force* as well as the *grace* of arguments or instructions, depends on their *conciseness*."[42] Publishing the *Essay* in the wake of the popularity of Young's prose treatise, Pope might well have anticipated that his substitution of the word "vindicate" for Milton's "justify" would be sufficient bait for some readers to attribute the *Essay* to his ephebic friend; and Pope was delighted when his poem was initially attributed to a number of "inspired" divines, including Edward Young.

ESTABLISHING PRIORITY

The dissemination of "vindicate" in Pope's Miltonic sixteenth line has, thus far, drawn four unnoticed prose writers into the story of Pope's text: Sherlock, Sykes, Dudgeon, and Young. The transition from prose vindication to poetry leads to a more important precursor and an even more surprising example than Young of Pope's attainment of priority over his predecessor; and, again, "vindicate" begins what turns out to be Pope's extended allusion to a prior text: Sir Richard Blackmore's *Creation*.

In the preface to his consciously anti-Lucretian philosophical poem, Blackmore contrasts the zeal of the "learned Gassendus . . . to vindicate the honor of Epicurus, and clear his character from the imputation of irreligion" with the atheistic Epicureanism "kept alive and propagated by the famous poem of Lucretius."[43] In his *Discourse Concerning the Divine Providence*, Sherlock proposed "a noble Argument to prove the Being and Providence of God . . . from the Works of Nature, and the Wise Government of the World": "It would give us a very delightful entertainment, to view all the Curiosities and surprising Wonders of Nature; with what beauty, art and contrivance, particular Creatures are made, and how the several parts of this great Machine are fitted to each other, and made a regular and uniform World; How all particular Creatures are fitted to the use and purposes of their several Natures, and yet are made serviceable to one another, and have as mutual a connection and dependence, as the Wheels of a Clock. What an equal and steady Hand governs the World, when its motions seem most excentrick and exorbitant, and brings Good out of Evil, and Order out of Confusion, when things are so perplext, that it is impossible for any one, but a God, to disentangle them."[44] This argument became the agenda for the Boyle lecturers; and the polymathic Blackmore undertook to render physico-theology sublime in a poetic antidote to Lucretius.

In *Creation* Blackmore undertakes to confute two types of atheists: those who deny the existence of God and those who allow God's existence but insist that "he showed no wisdom, design, or prudence, in the formation, and no care or providence, in the government of the world" (p. 326). His method is precisely that recommended by Sherlock and attempted earlier by others in prose.[45] Blackmore acknowledges that his arguments are "none but what have been produced before by many writers, even from the eldest days of philosophy" but justifies his work because it is a poem: "The harmony of numbers engages many to read and retain what they would neglect if written in prose" (p. 331). Pope subsequently justifies his use of poetry analogously: precepts in verse "both strike the reader more strongly at first, and are more easily retained by him afterward" (p. 7).

In 1712, just as Pope was beginning his literary career, Blackmore published his poetic vindication. It was enthusiastically praised and imitated by both old Miltonists like John Dennis and new Augustans like Joseph Addison. At the same time that he was discharging his critical blunderbuss against young Pope's *An Essay on Criticism*, Dennis voiced the contemporary consensus when he described Blackmore's *Creation* as "an admirable Philosophical Poem which has equall'd that of LUCRETIUS, in the Beauty of its Versification, and infinitely surpass'd it, in the Solidity and Strength of its Reasoning."[46] Although *Creation* is now obliterated from literary history, when Pope began his *Essay on Man* his primary precursor was not Milton's biblical epic but Blackmore's anti-Lucretian "Philosophical Poem." Extravagantly praised for uniting the excellencies of poetry ("Beauty of Versification") and philosophy ("Solidity and Strength of Reasoning"), Blackmore's *Creation* was the pretext Pope had to subsume before Du Resnel could say that it was "an Honor reserved" for Pope alone to unite the "Flights of the Poet, and the Argumentation of the abstracted Reasoner."[47]

In his extensive ridicule of Sir Richard between *An Essay on Criticism* and *An Essay on Man*, Pope had left *Creation* virtually untouched, possibly because it alone among Blackmore's works enjoyed lavish praise, possibly because its piety made it off limits to the ordinary critical canons, and possibly because Pope admired and was to emulate so many of Blackmore's techniques. The resemblances in argument, imagery, and diction between *Creation* and the *Essay* are indisputable, significant, and pervasive, from the summary of the "arguments" that begins both poems to the "Hymn to the Creator of the World" that concludes *Creation* but that Pope wrote but omitted, reportedly upon the advice of George Berkeley. Textual juxtapositions suggest how powerfully Pope's poetic superiority overturns the tyranny of time and almost makes a reader believe that Blackmore (1712) is imitating Pope (1733).

Pope's deliberate allusiveness is nowhere more stunning than at the beginning of the *Essay*. Pope's "vindicate the ways of God to Man" consciously links Pope's undertaking to Milton's in *Paradise Lost*. Blackmore revered Milton and frequently imitated his works. Although written, as the *Essay* was to be, in heroic couplets, *Creation* begins with an invocation to Milton's "Celestial Dove," which Blackmore implores to help him "soar":

How abject, how inglorious, 'tis to lie
Groveling in dust and darkness, when on high
Empires immense, and rolling worlds of light,
To range their heavenly scenes, the Muse invite!
I meditate to soar above the skies,
To heights unknown, through ways untry'd to rise.
(p. 340)

"Heights unknown" occurs in line eleven of *Creation*; in line eleven of *An Essay on Man* Pope proposes to follow

> The latent tracks, the giddy heights explore
> Of all who blindly creep, or sightless soar;
> Eye Nature's walks, shoot Folly as it flies,
> And catch the Manners living as they rise;
> Laugh where we must, be candid where we can;
> But vindicate the ways of God to Man.

In the final sentence of his preface, Blackmore "demands only a candid temper in the reader," although like Pope he reserves the right to ridicule when folly takes flight. In verses with analogues both in the *Essay* and the *Dunciad,* Blackmore laughs at Epicureans soaring above the limits of human reason:

> Above the clouds while they presum'd to soar,
> Nature's trackless heights ambitious to explore,
> And heaps of undigested volumes writ,
> Illusive notions of fantastic wit;
> So long they Nature search'd, and mark'd her laws,
> They lost the knowledge of th' Almighty Cause.
> (p. 252)

In his third verse paragraph, speaking of the Miltonic Dove, Blackmore elaborates the height/depth metaphor:

> Thou dost the full extent of nature see,
> And the wide realms of vast immensity:
> Eternal Wisdom thou dost comprehend,
> Rise to her heights, and to her depths descend. . . .
> Order from thee, from thee distinction came,
> And all the beauties of the wondrous frame.

Pope's second verse paragraph conflates the identically numbered lines from Blackmore with a later passage from *Creation*:

> Thro' worlds unnumber'd tho' the God be known,
> 'Tis ours to trace him only in our own.
> He, who thro' vast immensity can pierce,
> See worlds on worlds compose one universe,

Observe how system into system runs,
What other planets circle other suns,
What vary'd being peoples ev'ry star,
May tell why Heav'n has made us as we are.
But of this frame the bearing, and the ties,
The strong connections, nice dependencies,
Gradations just, has thy pervading soul
Look'd thro'? or can a part contain the whole?
(1:21–32)

"Vast immensity" traditionally has sent allusion-hunters scurrying to *De Rerum Natura* as preliminary to identifying Lucretius as Pope's "uniform Original." Yet "vast immensity" occurs in line twenty-one of *Creation* and line twenty-three of Pope's *Essay.* Similarly, "frame" is in line thirty-one of *Creation* and line twenty-nine of the *Essay.* Another "vast immensity" passage from *Creation* provides the clearest semantic and stylistic parallel to Pope's passage. In Book II Blackmore explains that no human sight is sufficiently comprehensive to grasp "this mighty system" wherein our world is but one of myriads:

All these illustrious worlds, and many more,
Which by the tube astronomers explore;
And millions which the glass can ne'er descry,
Lost in the wilds of vast immensity;
Are suns, are centres, whose superior sway
Planets of various magnitude obey.
(p. 349)

Bringing Sherlock or Young or Blackmore into the narrative of the making of Pope's text is not a new way of putting Pope in his place but is rather an attempt to question the possibility and desirability of situating him at all. There are many stars in the Gutenberg Galaxy; but the search for the one "centre whose superior sway" Pope's *Essay* must obey is futile and frustrating; and, too frequently, when the textual suns and planets proliferate, we blame our interpretive vertigo on Pope. Yet every bit of evidence suggests, as some deconstructionists allege, that the greatest writers have already anticipated whatever we can do to reduce their works to more manageable dimensions. In this regard, what are we to make of Pope's appropriation of Sir Richard? So successfully has Pope obliterated poor Blackmore from the history of the generation of texts—including *An*

Essay on Man—that the most felicitous phrases in *Creation* seem pale imitations of a poem published twenty years later:

[1] 'Tis but a part we see, and not a whole.
An Essay on Man

. . . to the universal whole advert;
The Earth regard as of that whole a part.
Creation

[2] Man, like the gen'rous vine, supported lives;
The strength he gains is from th' embrace he gives.
An Essay on Man

Observe its parts link'd in such artful sort,
All are at once supported and support. . . .
The creeping ivy, to prevent its fall
Clings with its fibrous grapples to the wall.
Thus are the trees of every kind secure,
Or by their own, or by a borrow'd power.
Creation

[3] And if each system in gradation roll,
Alike essential to th' amazing whole;
The least confusion but in one, not all
That system only, but the whole must fall.
An Essay on Man

For should a void Nature's monarchy invade,
Should in her works the smallest breach be made,
That breach the mighty fabric would dissolve.
Creation

[4] Ask for what end the heav'nly bodies shine,
Earth for whose use? Pride answers, "'Tis for mine."
An Essay on Man

We may pronounce each orb sustains a race
Of living things, adapted to the place.
Were the refulgent parts, and more refin'd,
Only to serve the dark and base design'd?
Were all the stars, whose beauteous realms of light,
At distance only hung to shine by night,
And with their twinkling beams to please our sight?
Creation

[5] Presumptuous Man! . . .
Snatch from his hand the balance and the rod,
Re-judge his justice, be the GOD of GOD!
An Essay on Man

Presumptuous race!
Who would the Great Eternal Mind displace;
Take from the world its maker, and advance
To his high throne.
Creation

THE GIDDINESS OF THICK DESCRIPTION

These examples are but a sample of resemblances. The subtle and blatant strategies by which Pope appropriates the energies of Blackmore's text would require a Quintilian to catalog; but, pervasive as the resemblances between the two texts are, no reduction of Pope's poem to Blackmore's would warrant our interpretation of the *Essay* as authoritative. How much less adequate then are searches for the hermeneutical key of Pope's "uniform Original" that ignore Blackmore entirely? Blackmore is not mentioned in the introduction to the Twickenham Edition of the *Essay* (1950); nowhere in White's *Context* (1970) is Blackmore or *Creation* ever referred to; and Nuttall's study (1984), despite a section on Pope's "sources," is also innocent of any awareness of Blackmore. Bernhard Fabian, writing "On the Literary Background of the *Essay on Man*" (1980), advances claims for the predominant influence of Lucretius but shows no awareness of Pope's popular anti-Lucretian predecessor.[48] In a subsequent study, Brean Hammond (1984) goes to ingenious lengths to destroy Fabian's argument for Lucretius and to reinstate Bolingbroke as Pope's primary source.[49] Predictably, there is no mention of Sir Richard or *Creation*. In fact, no modern critic of the *Essay* has so much as mentioned the relationship between *Creation*—the most popular philosophical poem in English in the early eighteenth century—and Pope's poem. It is odd that the searchers after Pope's "source" for the *Essay* are the very ones who have abetted Pope in writing *Creation* out of literary history; what is arguably the most significant poetic precursor of *An Essay on Man* has been obliterated from interpretation.

This omission of Blackmore's *Creation* is thin description with a vengeance.[50] Yet the seductiveness of thin description is easily understandable. Thick description is messy. When the abyss of textual dissemination yawns, where do we plant our interpretive feet? With the regress of allusion into allusion, where can we confidently erect our interpretive borders and halt the disorienting intertextual play? The answer, of course, is that we cannot, that any place we erect our hermeneutical fences is but our arbitrary stay against an uncontrollable proliferation of possible contexts. Pope's art is impossibly long, and our critical lives pathetically short. How much world enough and time would be required to track Pope to the recesses of his reading when, Samuel Johnson assures us, there was probably not a fortuitous image or phrase in all of English poetry prior to Pope that he had not worked in some way into his translation of Homer?[51]

Nor is this intertextual abyss an aberration of line sixteen; it is a richness that inheres in every line. Consider the first image in that same initial verse paragraph:

> Let us (since Life can little more supply
> Than just to look about us and to die)
> Expatiate free o'er all this scene of Man;
> A mighty maze! but not without a plan.
> A Wild, where weeds and flow'rs promiscuous shoot,
> Or Garden, tempting with forbidden fruit.

Pope's comparison of this "scene of Man" to a "mighty maze" dazzles our critical eyes with allusions. The history of interpretive analogues cataloged in Mack's edition includes Blount, Gould, Sheffield, Garth, Thomson, and Hill. But surely, we think, these are fry too small for the ocean of the *Essay;* and given line sixteen which ends the paragraph, *the* allusion—also perpetuated in the Twickenham Edition—is to Milton's description of the idle discussions held by the fallen angels in Book II of *Paradise Lost* (II:557-61):

> Others apart sat on a Hill retir'd,
> In thoughts more elevate, and reason'd high.
> Of Providence, Foreknowledge, Will, and Fate,
> Fixed Fate, Free will, Foreknowledge absolute,
> And found no end, in wand'ring mazes lost.

And yet, following yet another cited analogue, might not Dryden's *Religio Laici* be a likelier source? In style and genre Dryden's poem is undeniably the closer progenitor. Moreover, Dryden's referent is even the contending philosopher's theories of happiness that will be the focus of Pope's *Essay*:

> Thus, *anxious Thoughts* in *endless Circles* roul,
> Without a *Centre* where to fix the *Soul*;
> In this wilde Maze their vain Endeavours end.[52]

Eureka! Pope's "mighty maze" of line six becomes in line seven "A Wild." Unmistakably Pope has appropriated Dryden by sundering his mentor's adjective ("wilde") from his noun ("Maze"); and, in a clever typographical clue, Pope has reversed the capitalization so that his "maze" is lower case and his "Wild" is capitalized, a significant "inconsistency." "Viva la bagatelle," he snickers to Swift and to us—now that we are in on the joke.

And yet, Pope's very next line—"Or Garden, tempting with forbidden fruit"—brings the eternal note of Milton back in. Frustrating. Just when we thought we were really in control, univocally on Pope's wavelength and ready to interpret, his polysemous rhetoric betrays us. Yet wait; if we choose another analogue from the Twickenham notes, we can have "maze," "wild," and "fruit" in the same passage. Joseph Addison's *Cato* warns us:

> The ways of Heaven are dark and intricate,
> Puzzled in *Mazes* and perplex'd with errors:
> Our understanding traces 'em in vain,
> Lost and be*wild*er'd in the *fruit*less search.[53]

We remember that at Addison's invitation the young Pope wrote the prologue for *Cato*. What greater warrant could there be that this text, finally, is *the* longed-for interpretive key? Manifest parallels between Pope's "system of Ethics" and Addison's personification of Stoic ethics in Cato blossom before our imagination.

And yet, what of the analogues not identified in the Twickenham or in any other edition? The Morgan Library manuscript of Epistle I shows that Pope originally addressed "Memmius" in the first line, only later substituting "Laelius" for the first two anonymous editions and, finally, "ST. JOHN" (BOLINGBROKE) ever after. The manuscript Memmius is also the name of the friend Lucretius praises in the opening of *De Rerum Natura*. Since Dryden translated portions of Lucretius's poem, Pope would certainly have rifled that repository; and the parallels of tone and situation with the opening of the *Essay* are striking when Dryden translates Lucretius's praise of philosophic retirement at the beginning of Book II:

But much more sweet thy lab'ring steps to guide,
To Vertues heights, with wisdom well supply'd,
And all the *Magazines* of Learning fortifi'd:
From thence to look below on human kind,
Bewilder'd in the Maze of Life, and blind.

Our earlier surmise that Pope playfully reversed the capitalization of Dryden's "wilde Maze" works equally well with "Bewilder'd in the Maze"; and Dryden's "blind" becomes Pope's "sightless." Strengthening this hypothesis is Pope's earlier appropriation of Dryden's phrase in *An Essay on Criticism* where "Bewilder'd in the Maze of Life" (Dryden) becomes "bewilder'd in the Maze of Schools" (Pope).

And yet the anti-Lucretians also knew the use of mazes. In urging a "fuller Vindication of the Justice of Providence," Sherlock notes that nothing "excites in us a greater Admiration of God, than to see great and glorious things brought to pass by a long and winding Labyrinth of surprising and perplex'd Events, which we know nothing of, nor whither they tend, till we see where they end." Addison's *Cato* narrates the "winding Labyrinth of surprising and perplex'd Events" that befall his hero but does not presume to assess the "ways of Heaven . . . Puzzled in Mazes." Blackmore anticipates Addison by castigating the Lucretians as "Degenerate minds, in mazy error lost."[54] Usually, however, Blackmore uses the labyrinth image to demonstrate "the existence of a God from the marks of wisdom, design, contrivance, and the choice of ends and means, which appear in the universe" (p. 381), thereby reinforcing the argument from design, as Sherlock recommends. Thus the heavens are psalmist to the divine order:

In beauteous order all the orbs advance,
And in their mazy complicated dance,
Not in one part of all that pathless sky,
Did any ever halt, or step awry.
(p. 346)

This cosmic order, so transcending human understanding, demands our awe:

The mind employ'd in search of secret things,
To find out motion's cause and hidden springs,
Through all th' ethereal regions mounts on high,

Views all the spheres, and ranges all the sky;
Searches the orbs, and penetrates the air,
With unsuccessful toil, and fruitless care;
Till, stopp'd by awful heights, and gulphs immense
Of Wisdom and vast Omnipotence,
She trembling stands, and does in wonder gaze,
Lost in the wide inextricable maze.

(p. 348)

Thus are we back, by another image, to the openings of Epistles I and II of *An Essay on Man* that now seem a conflation of allusions to Blackmore's *Creation:* "vindication," "vast immensity," "frame," "maze," the whole of which we see but part, Newtonian intellect unable to trace "one motion" of the maze that is its own mind.

For an instant only let us, self-seduced by the parallels with *Creation,* situate Pope's poem differently than ever before. What seemed to all earlier critics a univocal allusion to *Paradise Lost*—"vindicate the ways of God to Man"—we now interpret as one of many allusions to the anti-Lucretian, servilely Miltonic invocation of Sir Richard Blackmore's enormously popular philosophical poem. Given this hermeneutical key we suddenly see the twofold way that Pope has made intertextual space for his own philosophical poem. Stylistically, every allusion to Blackmore's *Creation* is an invitation to compare the fashionings of a genius to a dunce, a device reminiscent of his earlier belittling comparison in the *Guardian* of his own pastorals to those of Ambrose Philips. The manifestly greater art of the *Essay* simply subsumes its predecessor; and, priorities reversed, Blackmore's original can only be read as an anemic, bombastic, servile imitation of Pope. And that reversal is possible only as long as anyone reads *Creation* at all, for the final triumph is for Pope to cause all his allusion-hunters to forget that one Blackmore ever wrote. The tyranny of time is finally rectified when, in the archives of literary criticism and history, Blackmore is nowhere to be found.

That alone, however, is not enough. As Pope acknowledges in his preface to the *Iliad,* original invention is the highest accomplishment; therefore, even sublime improvements are insufficient for greatness. Fortunately, Blackmore's poem specifically invites such originality. The "deists of the present time," Blackmore asserts in his preface, have not adequately "drawn or published any scheme of religion, or catalogues of the duties they are obliged to perform, or when such obligations arise"; but such a work "would give great satisfaction, and remove the objections of those that charge them with direct irreligion" (pp. 332–33). Pope accepts the challenge, and, appropriating whatever he finds useful from *Creation,* he makes textual room for himself by providing an ethics for deism. Concerned to "*vindicate the Scripture*" against its deistic critics, Sykes did not see, in *True Foundations of Natural and Reveal'd Religion* (1730), how the deists could ever "get out of the *Labyrinth* they are in" (his italics).[55] "A mighty maze," Pope replies, "but not without a plan" (1733).

We may leave others to write the residue of our interpretive tome. The objection to this hypothetical study is not a betrayal of insecurity concerning the importance of Blackmore's neglected *Creation* to the genesis of Pope's *Essay.* Nor is it an objection to hierarchies of textual influence. Milton, Horace, and Lucretius seem less important to Pope's text than Dryden, Shaftesbury, Pascal, Montaigne, Charron and—probably—Bolingbroke's correspondence and conversation. More important still is the general milieu of discussion of natural religion and naturalistic ethics including works by Bishops William Sherlock, William King, and Joseph Butler. Close to the tip of the pyramid of influences would be Aristotle, Cicero, and the wisdom books of the Hebrew scriptures, especially Job, Blackmore's *Paraphrase* of which Pope made notorious a few years earlier in *Peri Bathos.* But for Epistle I especially and despite the fact that no twentieth-century interpreter of the *Essay* has so much as hinted that Blackmore's poem influenced Pope, no single prior work seems more significant in the genesis of *An Essay on Man* than Sir Richard Blackmore's *Creation.*

What is objectionable about our proposed "source" study is the temptation to read the *Essay* as a posttext to *Creation,* as a text to be assessed in terms of its resemblances and differences to a prior text. Fortunately, we are saved from folly by the inherent absurdity of translating Pope into Blackmore. Lord Hervey suggested Shaftesbury as perhaps being the "uniform Original" planet for Pope's "hodge-podge" satellite; but even such an inveterate enemy would never propose the rumbling Sir Richard, writer to the rhythm of his carriage wheels. But the folly remains seductive because it erects those longed-for interpretive borders; it limits dissemination; it situates Pope's text. *An Essay on Man* becomes our oyster which we with hermeneutical key will open. The correspondences between *Creation* and the *Essay* are touchstones for an elaborate architecture of textual sympathy and antipathy, of imitation and parody, of appropriation and innovation. The free play of signifiers is, if not wholly ceased, mightily diminished. Giddiness recedes; our interpretive feet grasp solid ground.

The error of much criticism that emphasizes Pope's allusiveness as a key to interpreting *An Essay on Man* is to pervert two complementary methodologies in a manner that makes them mutually exclusive. A text is both an autonomous work different from any other work and a matrix of intertextual convergences. Thus, both of these utterances are true: each text is unique, and all texts are made up of other texts. Each utterance manifests itself in a methodology: textual criticism interprets the unique text in isolation, and structuralism stresses its reinscription of a "deep structure" it shares with other texts. The isolationist inclinations of classic New Criticism have, thus far, posed no interpretive threat to Reuben Brower's Poet of Allusion; but the conflating inclinations of Intertextuality have made the *Essay* unreadable.

Intertextual description has an intrinsic interest as one variety of literary history and can furnish invaluable information relevant to the interpretation of individual works. However, the situational heresy—the compulsion to put Pope in his place—occurs when intertextual description becomes the primary tool of textual interpretation. In fact, most of the interest over Pope's "indebtedness" to Leibniz or Shaftesbury or Bolingbroke or, recently, to Lucretius is not primarily an interest in textual history but an act of placement preparatory to interpretation and evaluation. To know what Pope says or fails to say, we first identify the *Essay*'s "uniform Original." Since these dominant prior texts are almost always works of philosophy, Pope's philosophical poem is literalized into propositional prose, any superfluous "poetry" or "rhetoric" being relegated to the outland of "nonserious discourse."

This use of a prior text to erect interpretive borders is thin intertextual description. A thick intertextual description, in contrast, shows dissemination at work across texts, generating at many points new interpretive possibilities. It resists univocation—the false belief that there is one truth to be uttered and that the researcher's assignment is to isolate and announce that truth. In Pope, perhaps above all authors, every text resonates with energies converging from many other texts; and to read even as direct an allusion as line sixteen of the *Essay* as a univocal reference to *Paradise Lost* is a weary capitulation to misreading. This conclusion implies that to some extent textual meaning and authorial intention are forever inaccessible: "No meaning can be determined out of context," Jacques Derrida asserts, "but no context permits saturation."[56] In other words, no description can ever be thick enough. That need not, I believe, disable the critic. Some descriptions are thicker than others; and even if, pressed to the frontiers of theory, we are forced to admit that all intertextual description is but the shadow of a greater richness, we can still characterize good intertextual description.

First, from a sense of its own ultimate inadequacy to describe all possible textual disseminations, good intertextual criticism resists monumentalization—the erection of one or a small group of dominant "influences" or "sources" or "pretexts" as the parameters making interpretation possible. Good intertextual description refuses to discipline randomness into order by disfiguring the text. Joseph Warton asserts that line sixteen proves that Pope "intended his poem for a defence of providence, as well as Milton" (1782). Two hundred years later (1984), Nuttall reinscribes the assertion, adding that the philosophical term "for the justification of God is *theodicy*" and that it is according to the canons of theodicy that the *Essay* must be vindicated or—in his case—damned. A work of many voices is made univocal; randomness is regulated; disseminations are disciplined to the predictabilities of received literary history. Good intertextual description, in contrast, does not coerce.

Second, good intertextual description is thick description. With no vested interest in leaving anything out, it embraces dissemination. Fecundity rather than fixity is its aim. It supplements rather than desiccates. Aware that no context can be fully recapitulated, it does not aspire to close the book on the *Essay* but to stimulate new interpretive possibilities. The more texts that it can bring to bear on Pope's text the better, for every new text is insurance against disfiguration, monumentalization, and the alienating closure of literary history's last word. Good intertextual description recognizes the author's power, in Roland Barthes's words, "to mix writings, to counter the ones with the others, in such a way as never to rest on any one of them."[57]

Good intertextual description respects Pope's right to "steer betwixt" texts, a right he powerfully establishes in the first thirty-two lines of the *Essay* with multiple allusions to two prominent pretexts: Milton's pious *Paradise Lost* and Lucretius's pagan *De Rerum Natura*. The addition to those same lines of Blackmore's Miltonic and anti-Lucretian *Creation* gives us additional reason to talk about a text that refuses to settle out of creative strife into the closure of definitive allegiance. Good intertextual description does not simplify our task as interpreters. "Bewilder'd in the Maze" of allusions "without a *Centre* where to fix" our interpretive borders, our eyes dazzle indeed at Pope's mightily wrought "Maze." We are right to be dazzled, for sometimes—with the greatest works—our only alternative is willful blindness.

God cannot endure a Logician.

—Joseph Hall (1606)

THREE

The Self as Aporia

INCE THE PUBLICATION of *An Essay on Man* its critics have sought to deconstruct the poem into inconsistency. In that enterprise Pope's "sources" are used against him to prove either that he is an uncomprehending, incoherent imitator of greater "uniform Originals" or that he is an indiscriminate eclectic, oblivious to his argumentative inconsistencies. In criticism of persona and tone within the *Essay,* the identical impulse is at work.

Philosophical poetry promises to bring a larger repertoire of human responses to bear on philosophical questions than is usual in propositional prose: the emotional, the aesthetic, and the ethical as well as the logical. Such poetry presents the Crousazian logician with a difficulty, for whereas constative propositions are discredited if they can be shown to be contradictory, emotional, aesthetic, or ethical responses may conflict without contradiction. Consequently, the Crousazian insists that the infection of subjective utterance be translated out of the text prior to its assessment as "philosophy." As Hume famously says, if propositions concern neither matters of fact nor relations of ideas, they do not belong in a work of philosophy. Hume is discouraging "school metaphysics" and making room for a richer discussion of ethical and aesthetic matters.[1] In contrast, the Crousazian insists that however rich or revealing other types of utterance may be, if they are neither empirical statements nor logical arguments, they are philosophically "meaningless."

Historically, this implicit subjective-objective dichotomy has structured discussion of persona and tone in *An Essay on Man*. Critics tend to divide into two broad groups: philosophers and phenomenologists. Philosophers insist on excising the emotive in order to assess the internal logic of Pope's poem whereas phenomenologists ransack the poem for emotive evidence of Pope's "real" beliefs. Both groups reduce *An Essay on Man* to a pretext, but in different ways. Crousazian philosophers translate all of the persona's utterances into univocal logical propositions and then assess their own translation for consonance to empirical reality and mathematical logic. As early as 1734 critics undertook to liberate readers from Pope's rhetorical chains by laying before them "in plain and genuine colours" Pope's philosophy "undisguised by any *Arts*, unassisted by the *Magic* of his *Numbers*."[2] Phenomenologists, in contrast, treat the poem as one evidence of the deep structure of Pope's consciousness; the *Essay* is pretext to proving/disproving that Pope is/is not a Roman Catholic/a Christian/a deist/a pantheist/an atheist. "No man ever . . . entertained a firmer persuasion of the truths of Christianity," early biographer Owen Ruffhead asserted; Lord Chesterfield countered, "He was a deist believing in a future state."[3]

In effect, phenomenologists are interested in what the *Essay* tells us about Pope and are willing to leave the poem itself to the philosophers. What philosophers do with the *Essay* is archetypally illustrated by their objection to the self-contradiction of the opening and closing verse paragraphs of Epistle I. Section I of the first epistle limits the sphere of possible knowledge: "Say first, of God above, or Man below, / What can we reason, but from what we know?" A note Pope added in 1735 dispels any ambiguity caused by the utterance being cast as a question: "he can reason only from *Things Known*, and judge only with regard to his *own System*" (p. 14). As Locke argued earlier, human reflections must be warranted by human sensations; or as Hume said slightly later, our ideas can legitimately extend no further than our perceptions. Pope's initial anti-metaphysical empiricism, Crousazians complain, is blatantly contradicted by his conclusion:

> All Nature is but Art, unknown to thee;
> All Chance, Direction, which thou canst not see;
> All Discord, Harmony, not understood;
> All partial Evil, universal Good:
> And, spite of Pride, in erring Reason's spite,
> One truth is clear, "Whatever IS, is RIGHT."
>
> (1:289-94)

If we can only reason from what we have experienced first-hand, critics from Crousaz to Nuttall consistently object, how could a non-omniscient Pope know that nature is art rather than accident or that "Whatever IS, isn't WRONG"?[4] The a posteriori empiricism of the opening is alleged to contradict the a priori rationalism of the conclusion; while Section I asserts the impossibility of metaphysics, Section X asserts a metaphysics of Leibnizian rational optimism. Pope is discredited by self-contradiction, for, as Charles Williams succinctly says, Pope "denies his perceptions for the sake of his philosophy."[5] Pope is torn, in William Bowman Piper's formulation, between his "empiricist devotion to living experience and his nostalgic hanker for Platonic Simplicities."[6]

Discrediting his argument impugns the authority of the author; and there is a strong ad hominem strain in most criticism of Pope's handling of persona and tone in the *Essay.* In proving the poem's inconsistency, Crousaz intends to expose Pope's philosophical ineptitude: "*Man,* says Mr. *Pope, is perfect as he ought.* Whence arises this profound knowledge? Has he forgot the *Weakness, Littleness,* and *Blindness of Man*? *Can a Part contain the Whole*? Has his Soul pervaded and look'd through the Universal System?"[7] Johnson similarly finds self-contradiction everywhere: "Having exalted himself into the chair of wisdom, [Pope] tells us much that every man knows, and much that he does not know himself."[8] Within a year of the *Essay*'s publication, hostile commentary was objecting to the inconsistency not only of Pope's arguments but of his tone as well, one anonymous author contrasting Pope to the more "uniform" Shaftesbury who was "no peevish Satyrist, no proud Dictator."[9] Joseph Warton also criticized Pope's tonal inconsistency: "Surely such strokes of levity, of satire, of ridicule, however poignant and witty, are ill placed and disgusting, are violations of that propriety which Pope in general so strictly observed."[10]

Reuben Brower condemns the same mixture of tones: "Pope had been tempted—perhaps by Bolingbroke—to write in Horace's manner a kind of philosophic poem that is contrary to the genius of the style."[11] There are "many shifts of narrative tone" in the *Essay,* Simon Varey observes, especially between the poet as philosopher and the poet as satirist.[12] Rarely, a phenomenological critic discusses the different voices and tones in the *Essay* empathetically as in Dustin Griffin's examination of how the "warring impulses within Pope" turn the poem into "a kind of psychomachia,"[13] but inevitably such interpreters focus on Pope's psyche outside the poem rather than on the dynamics of the text. Most commentary, however, is condemnatory, as in Martin Price's contention that Pope's "two voices" in the *Essay* are reflections of his inability to resolve "central contradictions."[14] "Is there not a case to be made," Richard Striner writes approvingly of Felicity Rosslyn's devaluation of the *Essay,* "that the writing of the *Essay on Man* might have been a troubled exercise in which—with very great struggle indeed—Pope unsuccessfully tried to talk himself into an abstruse system of ideas (the venerable doctrine of the Great Chain of Being) that could not sustain his unqualified allegiance however much he wanted to believe in it—or *thought* that he wanted to believe in it?"[15]

This chapter questions the consensus view that Pope's pervasive inconsistency invalidates the poem as philosophy. By resurrecting Pope's characterization of human nature from the intellectual trash heap of imitated commonplaces, the chapter seeks to reinterpret utterances that critics have deconstructed into self-contradiction as, in fact, complementary. S. L. Goldberg usefully hypothesizes that Pope's "confusions" are the source of "any poetic life" in the *Essay,* that the poem's central and energizing contradiction comes from "an attraction in Pope towards chaos, disorder, and eccentricity, quite as powerful as that towards order, form, and moral rationality."[16] This chapter acknowledges and attempts to characterize this dual perspective, arguing that it is far from being the result of any "confusion" on Pope's part.

THE PROFUNDITY OF SELF-CONTRADICTION

In stark contrast to the "self-doubt" and sense of irony that Richard Rorty sees as the intellectual consequence of our realization that we cannot, after all, hold the mirror up to nature and speak with the authority of a final vocabulary, logocentric Crousazians demand that the poet-who-would-be-a-philosopher speak the word that correlates perfectly with the world.[17] Crousazians confidently denounce "confusion" and "contradiction" as perverse or ignorant deviations from the ideal of unqualified univocal statement, as the inability of the literary text to mirror flawlessly the great text of nature; they reinscribe Crousaz's frustration that Pope's is "not the stile of a Philosopher; it is the language of Homer."[18] Pope's early biographer William Ayre accurately points out that Pope had full advantage of all such criticisms of *An Essay on Man* yet saw no reason "to alter one Sentiment," being unmoved by "any Arguments which were ever urg'd against it."[19] Incessant reinscriptions notwithstanding, nothing new has been objected to the *Essay* since Pope's death. To understand why allegations of fundamental inconsistency left Pope unmoved, we must take seriously Pope's conception of human nature and its implications for the persona of the philosophical poet.

With "Whatever IS, is RIGHT" resonating as the last line of the previous epistle, Pope opens Epistle II with the Delphic and Socratic admonition to "Know Thyself" before eloquently delineating the human predicament in one of the most frequently anthologized fragments in literature:

Know then thyself, presume not God to scan;
The proper study of Mankind is Man.
Plac'd on this isthmus of a middle state,
A being darkly wise, and rudely great:
With too much knowledge for the Sceptic side,
With too much weakness for the Stoic's pride,
He hangs between; in doubt to act, or rest,
In doubt to deem himself a God or Beast;
In doubt his Mind or Body to prefer,
Born but to die, and reas'ning but to err;
Alike in ignorance, his reason such,
Whether he thinks too little, or too much:
Chaos of Though and Passion, all confus'd;
Still by himself abus'd, or disabus'd;
Created half to rise, and half to fall;
Great lord of all things, yet a prey to all;
Sole judge of Truth, in endless Error hurl'd:
The glory, jest, and riddle of the world!

This "doubtful" duality bewilders the literal-minded author of *Common Sense:* "Man is sole Judge of Truth, and yet is made to wander in an endless Maze of Error, which is making him no Judge of it at all." Perhaps, this archetypal anonymous critic concludes, Pope "had no other End in this than in being inconsistent, which seems to be his Rule of Writing, for he never deviates from it."[20]

In fact, Pope's epistemology correlates perfectly with his methodology. Pope's intention in the "Design" to "steer betwixt the extremes of doctrines seemingly unlike" is entirely appropriate to a being who "hangs between" in "a middle state." Moreover, a being "Created half to rise, and half to fall" is the proper subject for a poet exploring both the "latent tracks" and the "giddy heights" of all who "blindly creep, or sightless soar" (I:12). Pope's *via media* methodology correlates with an epistemological moderation that characterizes "ignorance" both as thinking "too little" (those who "blindly creep") "or too much" (those who "sightless soar").

Pope's determination to "steer betwixt" extremes is his metaphorical characterization of the *Essay* as an intertext. Analogously, his genre—the philosophical poem—is also an intertext, negotiating as it does between the codes of philosophy and poetry. Thus his methodology both gives him imaginative room to create an original work and provides a popular sanction for his approach. Pursuing the via media serves as sanction in several ways: it encapsulates an ideal of the dialectical determination of truth; it endorses a standard of ethical behavior; and it acknowledges the dualistic psychology of human nature as a "Chaos of Thought and Passion, all confus'd."

As Stanley Jaki contends, this "instinctive middle" was unobtrusively dominant in the writings of Newton and his major intellectual forebears.[21] In fact, Pope possibly alludes with his "steering betwixt" metaphor to Henry Pemberton's recommendation in 1728 that scientists who aspire to emulate Newton must "steer a just course between" contending methodologies.[22] A closer analogue, however, may be Dryden's advice to the parliamentarians assembled in Oxford in March 1681: "'Tis Wisdoms part betwixt extremes to Steer"; and this is certainly the stance Dryden adopts in *Religio Laici*. After hearing contending fanatical arguments, he resolves to "wave each Extreme," a moderation applauded by the Earl of Roscommon in his commendatory verses: "What then have honest thinking men to doe, / But chase a mean between th' usurping two?" In assuming the moderate persona of an "honest thinking man," Pope follows Sherlock's advice in his *Discourse Concerning the Divine Providence*. In phrases anticipatory of Pope's *Essay*, Sherlock warns against dogmatism in interpreting "the submission we can owe to God" and in discharging "the duties which belong to that state" in which providence has placed us. "This ought to be carefully considered," the Bishop warns, "because there are dangerous extremes on both sides."[23]

As Aristotle warns in the *Nicomachean Ethics*, virtue requires extraordinary character and care because the mean is a delicate balance of contending forces and "men are bad in countless ways, but good in only one."[24] On the Morgan Library manuscript of Epistle II, Pope wrote: "Arist. Eth. 1.7 reduces all ye Passions under Pleasure and Pain as their universal Principles. The mean between opposite Passions makes Virtue, ye Extremes Vice." Other authoritative precursors include the Academics

Cicero and Plutarch. Philosophers like Cicero, Pope's contemporary Conyers Middleton affirms, "held the proper medium" and kept their intellectual balance "in an equal poise between the two extremes."[25] Similarly, the title page of William Wollaston's very popular *Religion of Nature Delineated* (1724) quotes Plutarch: "Some in order to avoid superstition, have fallen into the widest and most obstinate atheism, and trampled upon that piety which lies between either extreme."[26]

Pope's via media is also sanctioned by the "common sense" of mankind, an identification the hostile author of *Common Sense a Common Delusion,* quoted above, contests. Contemporaries routinely invoked this authority. As one of his four proofs of the existence of God in *The Principles and Duties of Natural Religion,* John Wilkins argues that all cultures universally assent to the proposition;[27] and John Tillotson, arguing for the reality of moral distinctions, invokes "the general Vote and Consent of Mankind."[28] These appeals are, of course, to the *Sensus Communis,* which the Earl of Shaftesbury recommends as that "greater Community" that acts as the "disinterested" antidote to the polarization of contending enthusiasms.[29] So pervasive was this appeal to the mean that it often dictated the format of works of philosophy and theology, both those intended for a broad popular audience like Isaac Watts's "The Strength and Weakness of Human Reason: or the important Question about the Sufficiency of Reason to conduct Mankind to Religion and future Happiness, argued between an inquiring Deist, and a Christian Divine: And the Debate compromised and determined to the Satisfaction of both, by an Impartial Moderator"[30] and those addressed to more subtle and ironic readers like Hume's *Dialogues Concerning Natural Religion.* During Pope's lifetime the dialogue was a major genre of philosophical and religious writing.[31] Thus Pope's stance as "honest thinking man" and "Impartial Moderator" had an august heritage, an instinctive popular appeal, and the rhetorical appearance of a "disinterested" pursuit of truth.

Contextualizing Pope's methodology and persona, as we have just attempted to do, has a deleterious effect. Having historicized the *Essay* into a "period piece," we have unintentionally put Pope in his place again; and it takes imaginative effort to see anything more profound in his poem than exploded epistemologies with their antiquated models of the psyche. However, emboldened by Pope's admonition that a very few profound truths "serv'd the past, and must the times to come" (II:52), we may find it more generative to sympathetic interpretation to see parallels between the epistemology of *An Essay on Man* and modern discussion of the same matters. In *The Nature and Destiny of Man,* for example, Reinhold Niebuhr's characterization of human duality is indistinguishable from Pope's, as is his chiding of the all-too-human propensity to pride oneself on a capacity for self-transcendence, the alleged ability to overcome one's subjectivity and assume a cosmic, "objective" point of view.[32]

However, the most revealing parallel to Pope's analysis of humanity's "middle state" occurs in a number of works by contemporary philosopher Thomas Nagel, especially *Mortal Questions.* Like Pope, Nagel argues that we are unable to answer definitively certain very important philosophical questions because of our dual nature: because of the ineradicable opposition between our subjective and objective perspectives. "We cannot live human lives without energy and attention, nor without making choices which show that we take some things more seriously than others," Nagel explains in characterizing our subjective perspective. "Yet we have always available a point of view outside the particular form of our lives, from which the seriousness appears gratuitous." These two inescapable perspectives "collide in us," Nagel argues, and make life absurd: "It is absurd because we ignore the doubts that we know cannot be settled, continuing to live with nearly undiminished seriousness in spite of them." On such fundamental questions as the existence of God, the meaning of life, and "the mind-body problem," we generate two contradictory answers—one from our internal, subjective perspective and another from our external, objective perspective. Because apodictic certainty is impossible, our task is to accept the polarity "without allowing either of its terms to swallow the other. . . . The coexistence of conflicting points of view, varying in detachment from the contingent self, is not just a practically necessary illusion but an irreducible fact of life."[33]

An Essay on Man is an ethics for just such a composite creature as Niebuhr and Nagel describe, a creature who "hangs between; in doubt." Ultimate questions are undecidable because the aporia—the point of doubt—in the world's great text is human nature itself. The self is an interpretive impasse, source of opposing and incompatible perspectives. The subjective self (Self-Love or Passion) gives one answer and the objective self (Thought or Reason) another. Unless it arbitrarily chooses to privilege one perspective over another, the honest self must speak against itself in, literally, "self-contradiction."

Those hostile authors who have paraphrased the *Essay* into self-contradiction are probably the critics least sympathetic to a Derridian deconstruction that painstakingly, even pedantically, teases out the contradictory or alogical elements in a text that, because it is a text, inescapably embodies "a clash of incompatibles which grates, twists, or bifurcates the mind."[34] Yet to maintain Pope's laudatory balance between the "usurping two," our mental bifurcation must inhere in deliberate dualities of voice, tone, argument, and image rather than be written out according to the univocal style manual of logocentrism.

Pushing the parallel with both Nagel and Derridian deconstruction further, we can argue that Pope has already deconstructed his own text. Because of the nature of human perception all texts are "knowingly or unknowingly" already deconstructed, J. Hillis Miller contends, insisting that the greatest writers know this fact.[35] Pope's characterization of the duality of human nature, we can argue, amounts to a "knowing" deconstruction; and, consequently, he would find narrowly logocentric readings of the *Essay* unsubtle, uninteresting, and trivial. Jonathan Culler argues that deconstruction is merely a systematic demonstration that the logic used to defend a position will, when pushed to an extreme, actually contradict that position: that deconstruction is reading and writing "attuned to the aporias that arise in attempts to tell us the truth."[36] Paradoxically, perhaps the most truth is told by simultaneously asserting and eschewing extremes.

By seeing the self as the matrix of doubt—as the aporia of undecidability between conflicting viewpoints—Pope gives that distinctive doubleness of tone to his *Essay* that critics like Warton and Brower have censured as a defect of self-contradiction. But in the *Essay* both subject and author are simultaneously "glory" and "jest" (II:18), simultaneously members of "Man's imperial race" and "Vile worms" (I:209, 258), both "God" and "Beast," "lord" and "prey" (II:8, 16). Hayden White suggestively notes that aporia, as a rhetorical figure signaling a real or feigned disbelief in the truth of one's own statements, is "the favored stylistic device of Ironic language."[37] Analogously, Richard Rorty advocates the stance of the "ironist" who has "radical and continuing doubts about the final vocabulary she currently uses" but acts in hopefulness nevertheless.[38]

Similarly, Thomas Nagel argues that our awareness of our dual perspective as both participant and observer does not cause us to forgo having beliefs or from acting on them but it does lend those beliefs "a peculiar flavor." The incompatibility of our two perspectives causes us to "return to our familiar convictions with a certain irony and resignation. . . . Our seriousness is laced with irony." Thus Nagel, with no thought of Pope, perfectly characterizes the tone of the *Essay*. In a letter purportedly written to Addison in 1713 but first published in 1735 just after the *Essay*, Pope anticipates Nagel's formulation: "Great God! What an incongruous animal is Man. . . . What is Man altogether, but one mighty Inconsistency. . . . What a bustle we make about passing our time, when all our space is but a point? What aim and ambitions are crowded into this little instant of our life. . . . Who that thinks in this train, but must see the world and its contemptible grandeurs lessen before him at every thought? 'Tis enough to make one remain stupify'd, in a poize of inaction, void of all desires, of all designs, of all friendships. But we must return (thro' our very condition of being) to our narrow selves, and those things that affect our selves: our passions, our interests, flow in upon us, and unphilosophize us into meer mortals."[39] Pope's awareness that one's concerns must at the same time appear both sublime and ridiculous—that man is "Created half to rise, and half to fall" (II:15)—pervades his text with conscious irony.

"IS, IS": RESIGNATION AND JOSEPH BUTLER

"Irony and resignation," Nagel says. The resignation comes from knowing there is no way out of the aporia; the "impasse of interpretation" makes it impossible ever to get beyond signs to the true nature of the signified, out of text into truth.[40] Our awareness of this impasse constitutes skepticism. As Hume writes in his *Treatise of Human Nature* only six years after Pope's initial epistle was published, a "true sceptic," because he is aware of the limits of human perception "will be diffident of his philosophical doubts, as well as of his philosophical conviction."[41] In other words, his seriousness will be laced with irony.

Nagel and the current jargons of semiotics and deconstruction reinscribe presuppositions shared by Pope, Hume, and Kant and suggest why, wakened from his "dogmatic slumbers" by Hume, Kant found Pope a greater philosopher than Leibniz.[42] All three certainly saw the nature of human intellect as the aporia terminating all metaphysical ambitions. In interpreting the world's great text, we are constrained by the nature of human knowing: our knowledge of phenomena, Kant asserts, provides no avenue to the noumenal. The self-contradictory categories of human intellect can never provide a coherent account of reality. Kant's antinomies of the human mind categorize our interpretive impasse.

In writing the *Essay* Pope assumed general acknowledgment of an epistemological aporia. The great works of Hobbes, Locke, Berkeley, Joseph Butler, Hume, David Hartley, and numerous, now-forgotten tomes of other philosophers and theologians are epistemologies demonstrating the limitations of human intellect, often as the first step toward some other end: pious for Berkeley and Butler, pragmatic for Hobbes and Hume. Locke, for example, describes *An Essay Concerning Human Understanding* as an inquiry into "the original, certainty, and extent of human knowledge," which would be preliminary to his authorship of a systematic ethics. Locke never wrote his ethics; but in writing his, Pope presupposes Locke's conclusions on the limits of human knowledge and assumes that his readers will have at least a general, "formulaic" knowledge of them.[43]

By the time the *Essay* was published it was a commonplace that all human knowledge was subjective, dependent on sense experience and, consequently, limited. Condillac writes: "Ideas in no way allow us to know things as they actually are; they merely depict them in terms of their relationships with us, and this alone is enough to prove the vanity of the efforts of those who pretend to penetrate into the nature of things."[44] Condillac is writing in 1754; but Bolingbroke anticipates the Frenchman phrase for phrase in an essay to Pope probably written during the composition of the *Essay on Man*. In discussing "the Nature, Extent and Reality of Human Knowledge," Bolingbroke writes: "Our ideas are the foundations, or the materials . . . of all our knowledge." Therefore, human knowledge is "not complete, nor absolute, because our ideas, concerning which alone human knowledge is conversant, are inadequate to the nature of things."[45] The "thing in itself" is outside our ken; consequently, as Hume concludes "Of the Understanding," Book I of the *Treatise:* "Human Nature is the only science of man." Pope anticipates Hume by asserting that "the proper study of Mankind is Man" (II:2) and by concluding the *Essay* with his ringing aphorism that "All our Knowledge is, OURSELVES TO KNOW" (IV:398).

The limits of human knowledge was a rhetorical sword in the hands of the orthodox and the heterodox alike. Surrounded every second by incomprehensible mysteries, Pascal piously argued that our only certitude lay in revelation. Locke, in contrast, opposes "enthusiastic" revelation and asserts the primacy of "Natural Revelation"; and Bolingbroke fulminates against "the presumptuous habits of theology" that authorize Christian apologists in invoking "the plan which they suppose infinite wisdom to have formed, as if they viewed it from an higher stage of intelligence and knowledge."[46] Pope shares his friend's contempt for "high priori" travelers like Samuel Clarke who, in their Boyle Lectures, "presume [to scan] God" (II:1) for the edification of an enlightened status quo.

Pope's epistemology resembles the anti-dogmatism of earlier French skepticism—including Montaigne, Charron, and Bayle—much more than that of the dogmatic deists attacked in Berkeley's *Alciphron* or discredited by Philo in Hume's *Dialogues*. Their shared distrust of "first philosophy" or metaphysics derives from the logocentric coerciveness of its a priori reasoning, whether Christian, deist, or atheist. In this attitude Montaigne and Pope superficially resemble Pascalian divines who abuse reason to exalt revelation. In his *Ethics* Spinoza complains against the distinction enjoyed by those divines who carp most eloquently against the defects of human reason. Robert Jenkins rose to be Cambridge Professor of Divinity by such carping. "Before Men venture upon making Objections against the Scriptures," he warns in *The Reasonableness and Certainty of the Christian Religion* (1715), "they would do well, first, to consider the Compass and Strength of their own Parts and Faculties." Trotting out a series of mind-bewildering paradoxes, Jenkins representatively concludes that "our Faculties were never design'd" for metaphysical speculation but for our "Use and Welfare" in the world of "Sense." Sense speaks of things as they appear to us; for the reality of "things in themselves," our only "*Certainty* [*is*] *the Christian Religion*."[47] The "last extent of human thought," Job concludes in Edward Young's 1719 *Paraphrase on Part of the Book of Job*, is to recognize that "man was not made to *question* but *adore*."

Perhaps the most striking analogues to Pope's epistemology in a Christian apologist are found in another work ignored by Pope scholars: Joseph Butler's sermon "Upon the Ignorance of Man," the fifteenth in a collection published shortly before *An Essay on Man*. Buttressed with citations from Job, Solomon, and Saint Paul, Butler invokes science and logic to demonstrate that even "the wisest and most knowing cannot comprehend the works of God, the methods and designs of his providence in the creation and government of the world." Both Pope and Butler assume that finite reason cannot reach infinity. "Can a part contain the whole?" Pope asks rhetorically; Butler asserts, "Parts cannot be comprehended without the whole." Pope chastises:

> Presumptuous Man! the reason wouldst thou find,
> Why form'd so weak, so little, and so blind!
> (II:35–36)

The same answer is to be given, Butler insists, "why we are placed in these circumstances of ignorance, as why nature has not furnished us with wings; namely, we were designed to be inhabitants of this earth." Pope writes:

> Why has not Man a microscopic eye?
> For this plain reason, Man is not a Fly.
> (1:193–94)

"I am afraid we think too highly of ourselves; of our rank in the creation and of what is due to us," Butler writes. Pope's "Design" is to show us "what *condition* and *relation* man is placed in"; Butler argues that we "forget our nature and condition" when we lose sight of "the circumstances man is placed in."[48]

The plenitude of verbal and argumentative resemblances between Butler's sermon and Pope's poem culminates in a shared rhetorical thrust toward a concern with conduct and away from any connection between philosophical or scientific knowledge and the existence and providence of God—the primary aim of physico-theological works like Blackmore's *Creation* or any of the prose tracts with titles analogous to John Ray's *The Wisdom of God Manifested in the Works of Creation*. Lecturers like Richard Bentley, Samuel Clarke, and William Derham received the bounty of Natural Philosopher Robert Boyle's bequest mandating an annual recitation of which of God's new glories science had enabled us to comprehend. In contrast, Butler suggests that "the difficulty of learning nature may be the reason of Solomon's dealing mainly with conduct." Our proper study, he concludes, is not Natural or Supernatural Knowledge but "the science of improving the temper, and making the heart better"; virtue rather than knowledge is "demonstrably the happiness of man." The last verse paragraph of Epistle I of Pope's *Essay* concludes with a summons to submission:

> Know thy own point: This kind, this due degree
> Of blindness, weakness, Heav'n bestows on thee.
> Submit. (1:283–85)

Similarly, Butler's last paragraph exhorts us "in all lowliness of mind" to "form our temper to an implicit submission to the Divine Majesty; beget within ourselves an absolute resignation to all the methods of his providence, in his dealings with the children of men."[49]

Discovering another of Pope's unrecognized precursors can enrich our sense of Pope's rhetorical strategies. Recognition of our ignorance of both Natural and Supernatural Knowledge, Butler argues, should lead to "resignation"; Nagel analogously describes the "irony and resignation" that come from our recognition of the incompatibility of our dual perspectives. The addition of irony to resignation exactly characterizes the difference between Butler's and Pope's rhetoric; and it accounts for Warton's discomfort with Pope's purported violation of rhetorical decorum. Like Butler, Pope uses the limits of reason to abate "self-esteem"; and, again like Butler, this demonstration of metaphysical incompetence is preparatory to an ethics. But, unlike Butler, Pope does not clear intellectual ground to make room for Christian dogma. Butler's sermon expatiates on a sacred text and is studded with concurring citations from other biblical texts whereas Pope's *sermones* deliberately avoid any invocation of biblical authority, as detractors eagerly and Christian friends uneasily noted.

Unlike Jenkins and Butler and Pascal before them, Pope does not return to the "Certainty" of the Christian religion but remains "in doubt"; and it is that difference which, in Nagel's phrase, laces his "seriousness . . . with irony." What substitutes for Christian dogma at the conclusion of the first epistle of the *Essay* is the sense of awe encouraged by the contrast between finite human reason and the seemingly infinite copia of creation.[50] Butler's final sentence is from Revelation: "Great and marvelous are thy works, Lord God Almighty! just and true thy ways." The same Jobian mixture of awe and resignation animates the last section of Epistle I with its much-quoted concluding couplet:

> And, spite of Pride, in erring Reason's spite,
> One truth is clear, "Whatever IS, is RIGHT."

Auditors of sermons like Butler's reasonably expected that Pope would follow his denigration of "erring Reason" with a return to the closure of Christian orthodoxy, and it became biblical scholar Warburton's burden to prove exactly that from a recalcitrant text that Pope refused to alter to include even a single reference to a distinctly Christian dispensation. Unsatisfied with Pope's delineation in the paragraph immediately following of the inevitability of human "doubt," coercive readers forced the text to fulfill their expectations by interpreting lines written to abate self-esteem as the positive metaphysics which the entire first epistle denies the possibility of attaining. Crousaz's massive tomes are sniffings out of the latent Leibnizian "first philosophy," which he was convinced must, in a very inconsistent manner, undergird Pope's ideology.

One of the more curious misreadings of literary history is the appropriation of Voltaire as a denigrator of *An Essay on Man*. Both Voltaire's *Lisbon Earthquake* and *Candide* have been used to reinforce Crousaz's reading of "Whatever IS, is RIGHT" as jejune Leibnizian rational optimism. In fact, Voltaire viewed Pope as a fellow deist.[51] In the preface to his poem on the Lisbon disaster, Voltaire explains that Pope's famous line has been misinterpreted and that he is attacking Pope's misreaders and not Pope's great poem. Similarly, in the initial chapter of *Candide* in a ludicrous phrase precursive of Heidegger and Derrida, Voltaire has his "metaphysico-theologo-cosmolo-nigo-logist" Professor Pangloss disassociate himself from Pope's famous maxim. Pangloss glosses: "It follows that those who maintain that all is right talk nonsense; they ought to say that all is for the best." Pope scholars have ignored both Voltaire's criticism of Pope's misreaders and his distinction between "all is right" (Pope's *Essay*) and "all is for the best" (Leibniz's *Theodicee*). After asserting that Pope's method of vindicating God is "to prove that the scheme of the universe is the best of all possible schemes," the entry on *An Essay on Man* in the *Oxford Companion to English Literature* concludes: "Pope's attempts to prove that 'Whatever is, is right' recall the efforts of Pangloss in Voltaire's *Candide*."[52]

Using *Candide* to conflate Pope and Leibniz is especially ironic because the German philosopher was for Pope's circle the epitome of the anthropomorphizing "high priori road"; and they, like Voltaire, ridiculed him. In this respect Pope is the heir of the empiricism of Hobbes and Locke in contrast to the strain of rationalism that culminates in Leibniz. In criticism of Thomas White's argument "that the existing world is the best of those creatable," Hobbes writes: "In this question I freely confess my ignorance. . . . It suffices . . . that God created this world and not another one. From this we gather that no other world had pleased Him more. If anyone philosophizes beyond this point, he speculates beyond his own powers of comprehension."[53] In the same vein Bolingbroke writes to Pope that Locke's inquiry into the limits of human intellect is the true corrective to Leibniz: "LOCKE . . . grounded all he taught on the phaenomena of nature. He appealed to the experience and conscious knowledge of everyone, and rendered all he advanced intelligible. LEIBNITZ, one of the vainest, and most chimerical men that ever got a name in philosophy, and who is so often so unintelligible that no man ought to believe that he understood himself, censured LOCKE as a superficial philosopher. What has happened?"[54]

This hostility to Leibniz's logocentrism, which Pope shared with Bolingbroke, and their sympathy with Locke's more modest epistemology should make critics circumspect about conflating the *Essay* and the *Theodicee*. Moreover, there seems to be a strong possibility that even the famous "Whatever IS, is RIGHT" is a direct link not between Pope and Leibniz but between Pope and Locke. Scholars have made nothing of the fact that the phrase occurs in quotation marks in Pope's text; but, knowing Pope's meticulousness with typographical details, we should attend to that clue. In Locke's *Essay,* while attacking the emptiness of rationalistic metaphysics based on the tautological law of identity, Locke uses the phrase "What is, is" as the paradigm of a "trifling" proposition that does not add to our "real knowledge" (IV:7.2). This discussion leads into Locke's anti-enthusiastic discussion "of our knowledge of the existence of a god." Locke uses a similar phrase—"Whatsoever is, is"—in opposing innate ideas (I:1.4).

In writing to Pope, Bolingbroke varies Locke's phrase to "Whatever is, is"; and Pope's own correspondence proves that the phrase was habitual with him. What happens after death cannot trouble him, he writes to Swift, for "whatever is, is right" (2 April 1733). In a late letter to the Earl of Orrery he attributes the phrase: "Whatever is, is right. It was the saying of Socrates" (10 December 1740). Putting the phrase in quotation marks in the *Essay* suggests that Pope is quoting, and he is certainly rephrasing a Socratic sentiment. After receiving sentence of death in the *Apology,* Socrates characterizes the events of his trial and condemnation with resignation: "I suppose that these things must be regarded as fated,—and I think that they are well."[55] It seems likely that Pope's precise phrase is his conflation of Locke's representative tautology with the use Butler makes of Socrates at the conclusion of his sermon "Upon the Ignorance of Man." After quoting Job and Ecclesiastes, Butler adds: "So . . . Socrates was not the first who endeavoured to draw men off from laboring after, and laying stress upon other knowledge, in comparison of that which related to morals."[56] In *The History of Philosophy* owned by Pope, Thomas Stanley cites Cicero and others to characterize Socrates both as the embodiment of "Irony" and as one who eschewed "things above the reach of Man, . . . esteeming speculative knowledge as far only as it conduceth to practice."[57]

A number of recollected biblical passages could have supplied the "RIGHT" to Locke's tautology ("the ways of the Lord are right," Hosea 14.9). What seems to have occurred is this: in his peroration to Epistle I, drawing upon the empiricist ridicule of "high priori" rationalism succinctly encapsulated in Locke's "what is, is," Pope blended it with the sermonic rhetoric of chastisement, awe, and resignation with which Butler concludes. The shared stress of all four persons—Socrates, Locke, Butler, and Pope—is on epistemological limits as a means to redirect human energies from metaphysics ("sightless soaring," I:12) to ethics ("Virtue is demonstrably the happiness of man," Butler, 231 / "VIRTUE only makes our Bliss below," Pope, IV:397). Thus two separate philosophical and theological traditions of stressing the limits of human intellect are merged in Pope's memorable "quotation": "Whatever IS, is RIGHT." Frustrated at not finding the comforting dogma that usually accompanied such sermonic rhetoric, some of Pope's contemporaries insisted on extrapolating from his lines a Leibnizian metaphysics manifestly at odds with his Lockean epistemology and, thereby, initiated the ridicule of Pope's "self-contradiction," which modern commentary uncritically perpetuates.

"A *DIALECT*, MORE BECOMING SHORT-SIGHTED MORTALITY"

The irony of reading Epistle I of Pope's *Essay* as Leibnizian metaphysics seems all the stranger since scholars have commented perceptively on Pope's distrust of any system-building that goes beyond the evidence of immediate experience.[58] Another root of the misreading whereby Pope is metamorphosed into a system-builder is Warburton's defense of the *Essay* against critics like Crousaz who impugned its piety. Revealingly, Warburton praises exactly those images censured by the Crousazians as Leibnizian or fatalistic by lauding Pope's "Art of converting Poetical Ornaments into Philosophical Reasoning; and of improving a *Simile* into an *Analogical Argument*."[59] Like the Crousazians, the Warburtonians translated "Poetical Ornaments" into "Philosophical Reasoning," "*Similes*" into "*Analogical Arguments*," but now the metaphysical context was Christianity rather than Continental rationalism. In the years immediately preceding Pope's *Essay,* a heated controversy raged over analogical versus empirical reasoning.[60] Both sides agreed that we have not "the *Least glimmering* Idea of things purely Spiritual." In contrast to the empiricists, however, analogists like Peter Browne and George Cheyne saw an avenue to metaphysics in "the noble art of just analogy"; and it is in the camp of the analogists that Warburton aspires to situate explication of Pope's *Essay.*

Theologians who acknowledged the epistemological limits described in Locke's *Essay* typically tried to save access to the divine either by deference to the Bible as a supernatural supplement to the human perspective or by authorizing an analogical reading of the great text of nature—that book, as Thomas Paine argues, that only a god could write. Without some access to the divine will, theologians argued, we are disoriented by insoluble mysteries and ignorant of our duty. In *Religio Laici* Dryden defends the authority of the Bible by arguing that God would not leave humans so bewildered; but partly as a result of exploration and mercantile expansion, Pope's contemporaries were faced increasingly with the fact of the diversity of revealed scriptures, each claiming to be the only true Word. During the fifty years between *Religio Laici* and *An Essay on Man,* the Lockean and latitudinarian tendency to deemphasize supernatural revelation led to increased reliance by Christian theologians on the argument that God's mind must bear a strong analogy to our own. Bishop Browne's twin tomes *Procedure, Extent and Limits of Human Understanding* (1728) and *Things Divine and Supernatural Conceived by Analogy with Things Natural and Human* (1733) are representative. Although God is "out of the reach of all human Imagination," Browne contends, yet through analogy with "our greatest Excellencies" we may know something "of his incomprehensible Perfections."[61] Unless we analogize from human perceptions to metaphysical properties, John Balguy insists, we are "cutting the knot" that links us to the divine.[62] Fortunately, Browne argues, analogy allows "the greatest Enlargement of human Understanding," providing a way out of our doubtful state into certain knowledge.[63]

Browne and Balguy both published major works advocating analogy in the year *An Essay on Man* appeared; but, Warburton's misreading notwithstanding, Pope was having none of it and remained consistently skeptical of such reasoning throughout his life.[64] Analogists aspire to speak the dialect of divinity, attempting, as Bolingbroke complains to Pope, to expatiate on the eternal plan "as if they viewed it from an higher stage of intelligence, and knowledge."[65] The self's dilemma is that although it has a text to interpret it knows that its faculties are inherently inadequate to the language of the text. Patricia Meyer Spacks astutely notes that in the *Essay* "man's power to abstract exemplifies the limitless possibilities of intelligence" whereas "the ineluctable facts of the concrete embody his limitations."[66] The self's conjunction of its Lockean capacities for sensation and reflection is both its power and its prison: it knows something but not everything, a part but not the whole. A metaphysical dialect is out of the question.

Joseph Glanvill asserts in the *Vanity of Dogmatizing*, "Did we but compare the miserable scantiness of our capacities with the vast profundity of things, both truth and modesty would teach us a *dialect*, more becoming short-sighted mortality." The dialect Pope adopts to characterize human duality in the first verse paragraph of Epistle II is that of Pascal's *Pensées*. The Frenchman's popularity in England was at its height when Kennet's translation was published in 1727.[67] John Caryll recommended the *Pensées* to Pope while he was composing the *Essay*; but Pope responded that he had already been there (6 February 1731). In fact, the first paragraph of Epistle II is Pope's rhetorical appropriation of Pascal's delineation of "the strange Contrarieties discoverable in Human Nature, with regard to Truth and Happiness." Pope coins powerful epigrams from Kennet's clear prose: Kennet's "The study of man is the proper employment and exercise of mankind" Pope alchemizes to "The proper study of Mankind is Man."[68]

In a passage closely paralleling Pope's first paragraph, Pascal explicitly characterizes the dualistic rhetoric obligatory to authors who would effectively address human nature. "What a confused Chaos! What a subject of Contradiction!" Pascal observes of the human condition: "A profess'd Judge of all Things, and yet a feeble Worm of the Earth; the great Depository and Guardian of the Truth, and yet a mere Huddle of Uncertainty; the Glory and the Scandal of the Universe. If he is too aspiring and lofty, we can lower and humble him; if too mean and little, we can raise and swell him." Such a dual dialect of inspiration and ridicule, Pascal suggests, acts as an antidote to the influence of univocal philosophers who have "never furnished Men with Sentiments agreeable to these two Estates."[69]

Although man seems fashioned "for the Knowledge of Truth," Pascal observes, "yet when he endeavours to lay hold on it, he is so dazzled and confounded, as never to be secure of actual Possession." To obliterate our anxiety, Pascal speculates, philosophy split our "Huddle of Uncertainty" into two contending univocal dialects: the Pyrrhonians and the Dogmatists, the first sect convinced of the impotence of reason, the second convinced of its omnipotence. The Pyrrhonic Skeptics "would utterly deprive man of all Truth," Pascal writes, while the Dogmatists offered such "impossible Reasons, as only to increase our Confusion and Perplexity." Thus both the "pure Grandeur" inspired by the Dogmatists and the "mere Abjectness" inculcated by the Pyrrhonians lead to inappropriate extremes: "the double Danger to which [human nature] is always exposed, of Despair and of Pride." A balanced philosophy and a wise rhetor, in contrast, will steer between extremes, teaching us "how to doubt where we ought, to rest assured where we ought, to submit where we ought. He who fails in any of these Respects is unacquainted with the Power of Reason," a faculty whose final wisdom "is to discover, that there's an Infinity of Things which utterly surpass its Force."[70] Like Joseph Butler's admonition to "form our temper to an implicit submission to the Divine Majesty," Pascal urges us "to submit" to the Roman Catholic Church. "To reason right," Pope admonishes, "is to submit."

PERVERSIONS OF A DUAL PERSPECTIVE

The "dismembered fragments" of Pascal's dialectic between his skeptical and his Christian self all conduce to orthodoxy.[71] Understandably, readers of Pascal like Pope's friend Caryll expected him to follow the great mathematician's lead out of the dialect of doubt into the certitudes of Christianity and were perplexed when he refused. However, Pope's admonition to "Reas'ning Pride" is not to submit to revelation but to acknowledge the limits of its competence. In spite of its aporias the human "Huddle of Uncertainty" longs for a sense of cosmic centrality that will negate its despair at its insignificance in the face of infinitude. Thus when the Christianity that has traditionally provided both centrality and certainty is threatened, "Reas'ning Pride" claims consubstantiality with the divine and rationalizes its presumption with both a priori and a posteriori arguments for God's being and humanlike attributes. Both rationalism's "high priori" road and the aspiring "Evidences of Christianity" documented by physico-theology are the "tricks to shew the stretch of human brain" Pope characterizes as the "equipage of [intellectual] Pride" (II:43–48); they are perversions of logic and science to serve our egocentric ends. For at the same time that science was putting the human condition into cosmic perspective and thereby undermining revealed religion's comforting myth of the self's centrality, it also encouraged a counter-tendency: the confidence that the unknown was merely the as-yet-undecoded and that Newton's "godlike" intellect was proof that human intellect would eventually grasp the scheme of things entire.[72] Thus that reason which according to Nagel allows the objective detachment necessary "to counter the egoistic distortion of a purely internal view, and to correct the parochialism engendered by the contingencies of [an] over-specific nature and circumstances" is perverted into a tool for interpreting the universe to fit our fancy.[73]

The obliteration of the occult in natural science led writers like John Toland to attempt to rid religion of mystery, now redefined as "superstition." Traditional theologians like Richard Willis, Bishop of Winchester, responded to Toland's argument in *Christianity Not Mysterious* by stressing our inability to interpret "the various methods of the Providence of God." In surveying the universe, he argues, "we find a vast Scene of Difficulties and Objections, which the wisest Men in all Ages have not been able to answer; and indeed no other wise answer can be given, but that *God's ways are not our ways, nor his thoughts our thoughts*."[74] But avant-garde theologians like the Boyle lecturers were temperamentally allied with the progressive ideology of their benefactor—chemist Robert Boyle—and looked inward to human intellect as the key to a theological interpretation of the great text of nature. With his twelve a priori and abiblical proofs that God is a being of infinite goodness, justice, and truth, Samuel Clarke epitomizes the rationalistic strain; and although he acknowledges that we cannot adequately comprehend the essences of things—including God and gravity—the popularity of his projections of human desires into divine attributes depends on the presumed consanguinity of created and creator.

Rather than creep up slowly, "a posteriori, to a little general knowledge," Bolingbroke writes to Pope, the likes of Leibniz and Clarke "soar at once as far, and as high, as imagination can carry them. From thence they descend again armed with systems and arguments a priori, and regardless how these agree, or clash with the phaenomena of nature, they impose them on mankind." Such a "preposterous method" of searching for certainty "out of the bounds of human knowledge" simply panders to "their prejudices, their passions, and their interest" by substituting "that which is imaginary in place of that which is real."[75] Theologians like Clarke have "platonized and corrupted the truth," Pope told Joseph Spence.[76] As Pope has his metaphysician address the Queen of Dulness in *The Dunciad:*

> Let others creep by timid steps, and slow,
> On plain Experience lay foundations low,
> By common sense to common knowledge bred,

And last, to Nature's Cause thro' Nature led.
All-seeing in thy mists, we want no guide,
Mother of Arrogance, and Source of Pride!
We nobly take the high Priori Road,
And reason downward, till we doubt of God.
(IV:465–72)

Pope's "gloomy Clerk" (pronounced "Clarke"), a "Sworn foe to Myst'ry yet divinely dark," aspires to

Make God Man's Image, Man the final Cause,
Find Virtue local, all Relation scorn,
See all in *Self,* and but for self be born.
(IV:477–80)

Pope's ridicule of Leibnizian "platonizing" should not suggest that he is more sympathetic to the pretended a posteriori reasoning of physico-theology. In fact, those who survey nature and see in the herding instinct of animals evidence of God's particular concern that humans dine well clearly presuppose what they pretend to prove: the centrality of self. "Since the argument from innate ideas [to prove the existence of God] hath been laid aside by some, and less insisted on by others," Phillips Gretton acknowledged in 1726, "Reasons drawn from the Works of Creation and Providence, have been chiefly used, and with great success."[77] Some writers—not including Pope—celebrated the a posteriori interpretations of physico-theology as empirical correctives to rationalistic distortion. In *Creation* Blackmore defines his Argument from Design in contrast to those a priori philosophers who

Consum'd their fruitless hours in eager chase
Of airy notions, through the boundless space
Of speculation, and the darksome void,
Where wrangling wits, in endless strife employ'd,
Mankind with idle subtleties embroil,
And fashion systems with romantic toil;
These, with the pride of dogmatizing schools,
Impos'd on Nature arbitrary rules;
Forc'd her their vain inventions to obey. . . .
Above the clouds while they presum'd to soar . . .
They lost the knowledge of th' Almighty Cause.

In *The Dunciad* Pope characterizes Samuel Clarke's God as indistinguishable from "such as Lucretius drew" (IV:484); Blackmore similarly admonishes the "Lucretian tribe" to abandon their empty a priorism and instead

> gaze on Nature's face,
> Remark her order, and her motions trace,
> The long coherent chain of things, we find,
> Leads to a Cause Supreme, a wise Creating Mind.

"Tho' Man's a fool," Pope concludes Epistle II, "yet GOD IS WISE."

Blackmore's rhetoric is precursive of Pope's criticism of the "high priorists" in the *Essay* and the *Dunciad*.[78] Where they differ unmistakably is in their approach to arguments a posteriori. Blackmore repeatedly cautions against overinterpretation, against placing humankind at the center of God's design; but his whole poem is, disclaimers notwithstanding, just such an exercise in anthropocentrism. Just as a priorists inevitably projected human attributes onto God, so the method of the physico-theologists forced them into organizing nature around a human center. Green was the predominant color in nature, they reasoned, because as the middle color of the human spectrum it was most pleasing to our eyes, clear proof that God had us in mind in leaving the trees. All nature conspired, they concluded, to pamper God's favorite creature. Thus was theological argument back again, by the low a posteriori road, to us as the final cause of creation.

To counter this "enormous faith of many made for one" (III:242), Pope adopts both Blackmore's argument against the rationalism of the Lucretians and the Lucretians' own objections to the imperfections of the universe. Blackmore typically counters the Lucretian objection that the universe is often actively hostile to us with a strategy Pope subsequently uses for his own ends: the insistence that we and our Earth are but "of the whole a part." Blackmore asks rhetorically:

> Were all the stars, whose beauteous realms of light,
> At distance only hung to shine by night,
> And with their twinkling beams to please our sight?

Pope's appropriation of this passage illustrates his divergence from Blackmore's physico-theologizing:

> Ask for what end the heav'nly bodies shine,
> Earth for whose use? Pride answers, "'Tis for *mine*:
> "*For me* kind Nature wakes her genial pow'r,
> "Suckles each herb, and spreads out ev'ry flow'r;
> "Annual *for me,* the grape, the rose renew
> "The juice nectareous, and the balmy dew;
> "*For me,* the mine a thousand treasures brings;
> "*For me,* health gushes from a thousand springs;
> "Seas roll to waft *me,* suns to light *me* rise;
> "*My* foot-stool earth, *my* canopy the skies."
> (1:131–40, italics added)

Pride's physico-theological *me-ism* immediately receives Pope's ironic rebuttal:

> But errs not Nature from this gracious end,
> From burning suns when livid deaths descend,
> When earthquakes swallow, or when tempests sweep
> Towns to one grave, whole nations to the deep?
> (1:141–44)

Metaphysical pride responds with the stock rationalization for physical evil which Pope turns against him when he inconsistently objects to moral evil. Pope's playful ridicule of metaphysical answers to life's most perplexing questions anticipates Voltaire's similar theme in *The Lisbon Earthquake* and *Candide* and suggests the appropriateness of Voltaire's defense of *An Essay on Man.* In definitive rebuttal of the "absurdity *of* [*man's*] *conceiting himself the* final cause *of the creation*" (Argument of the First Epistle), Pope says to the physico-theologist: "If the great end be human Happiness, / Then Nature deviates" (1:149–50). The only way out of the maze of metaphysical rationalizations is to limit Right Reason to the sphere of sense, as Rochester recommends in "A Satyr Against Mankind." Metaphysics, Pope concludes, is "erring Reason" (1:293) whereas "to reason right is to submit" (1:164). Metaphysics, personified as "Presumptuous Man" (1:34) and "Pride" (1:132), pimps for our ego and, thereby, becomes the butt of Pope's epistemological and anti-metaphysical Epistle I. Epistle II opens with the admonition to leave metaphysics alone: "presume not God to scan." Ever alert to Pope's self-contradiction, the author of *Common Sense* objects that Pope "forbids us to do what just before he was doing himself, and teaching us to do."[79]

Pope's "presume not God to scan" invites comparison with Raphael's reply to Adam's metaphysical inquiries in Book VIII of *Paradise Lost*. The great architect will "*not* divulge / His secrets *to* be *scan*ned by them who / Ought rather admire," the angel counsels. The ways of God transcend human reason deliberately so "that earthly sight / If it *presume*, might err in things too high" (VIII:72–75, 119–21, 173–74, italics added). Yet few words in the *Essay* so richly distill disseminations from a variety of other texts dealing with "Natural Religion" as does Pope's use of "presume." Consequently, it is not surprising that Pope scholars have frequently misread the *Essay* just as intellectual historians in general have oversimplified and distorted the "spectrum of attitudes" that Pope's age had toward physico-theology.[80] The parallel to *Paradise Lost* assumes Milton's authority without committing the *Essay* to his biblical theology, and, in fact, characterizing the divine Architect by analysis of his architecture was consistently objected to as anthropocentric by writers without a theological agenda from Bacon to Hume.[81] Bolingbroke's objections to "first philosophy" recapitulate Bacon's warnings against presuming to trace the phenomena of nature back to "first causes." The third limitation on human knowledge Bacon recommends in the *Advancement of Learning* is that we "do not presume by the contemplation of nature to attain to the mysteries of God."

Man easily convinces himself that "the highest link of nature's chain must needs be tied to the foot of Jupiter's chair," but Bacon warns that all such speculations are "vain philosophy." Pope shares Bacon's image and idiom when he demands of "Presumptuous Man":

> Is the great chain, that draws all to agree,
> And drawn supports, upheld by God, or thee?
> (I:33–35)

In *Lectures on Philosophical Theology*, Kant warns against the same "subtle anthropomorphism," and his argument can be read as his explication and paraphrase of Pope's image. "If I went so far as to ask why God created me, or mankind in general, this would certainly be presumptuousness," Kant insists, "for it would be as much as to ask why God completed and joined together the great chain of natural things through the existence of a creature like man. Why did he not instead leave a gap? Or why didn't God make man an angel instead?"[82] As Pope asserts:

> In Pride, in reas'ning Pride, our error lies;
> All quit their sphere, and rush into the skies.

> Pride still is aiming at the blest abodes,
> Men would be Angels, Angels would be God.
> (I:123–26)

The topos of presumption was preparatory to many different kinds of argument. Bishop Sherlock characterizes presumptives as those who, "ignorant to such a degree, as not to know they are ignorant, . . . find a great many Faults in God's Government of the World"; and he ridicules them to reassert the Christian status quo.[83] Bishop Browne cautions against metaphysical presumption in using his analogical method. Out of its sphere, he warns, our reason "sinks into Weakness and Infirmity. . . . So that in all its noblest Efforts and most lofty *Flights*, it must ever have a steady *Eye* to the *Earth* from whence it took its Rise; and always consider that it mounts upward with *Borrowed* Wings: For when once it presumes upon their being of its own *Natural* growth, and attempts a *Direct* Flight to the heavenly Regions; then it falls Headlong to the Ground, where it lies *Groveling* in Superstition or Infidelity."[84] Less distinctively Christian, Blackmore attacks the latter-day Lucretians as "vain philosophers! presumptuous race!" with the aim of discrediting their nihilistic fatalism.[85]

What all criticisms of presumption share initially, however, is an opposition to the vanity of dogmatizing. Bishop Butler invokes Solomon's characterization of intellectual presumption as vanity, and perhaps the closest English analogue to Pope's use of presumption is in his friend Matthew Prior's now little-known philosophical poem *Solomon*. Prior's image for man's duality is Pope's "isthmus" (II:3): "Amid two seas on one small point of land / Wearied, uncertain, and amaz'd we stand." To assuage our anxiety, Prior argues, we compel the text of the world to bear our interpretation:

> Can Thought beyond the Bounds of Matter climb?
> In vain We lift up our presumptuous Eyes. . . .
> The little which imperfectly we find,
> Seduces only the bewilder'd Mind
> To fruitless Search of Something yet behind.
> Various Discussions tear our heated Brain:
> Opinions often turn; still Doubts remain . . .
> How narrow Limits were to Wisdom giv'n?
> Earth She surveys: She thence would measure Heav'n.[86]

This is the measuring metaphysician of Pope's first epistle who presumes to snatch from God's hand "the balance and the rod" (I:121).

The dialect shared by Pope and Prior probably derives most directly not from contemporary Christian apologetics but from Charles Cotton's three-volume translation of Montaigne's *Essays*. Pope carefully read and annotated his copy; and in opposing anthropocentrism, Maynard Mack judges, Pope "unmistakably draws on Montaigne's delineation of human arrogance in supposing the universe only made for man."[87] Montaigne's *Essays* anticipate most of what was said against presumption in debates a century later. Not only does Montaigne devote a separate essay to "Presumption" but much of his ambitious "Apology for Raymond Sebond" is a cataloging of commonplaces on the limits of reason. "O presumption, how you hinder us!" he laments. To the self-projecting analogical argument he objects that nothing is "more vain than to try to divine God by our analogies and conjectures," and he characterizes the arguments from design offered in Sebond's *Natural Theology* as compensatory wish-fulfillment. "Indeed," he disparages, such "philosophy is but sophisticated poetry."[88]

Montaigne is especially suggestive in achieving the same doubleness of tone found in Pope's *Essay*: an engaging coexistence of aggressive Solomonic wisdom with radical Socratic doubt. Presumption is always metaphysical, Montaigne implies, because presumption insists on dominating from one of two human perspectives. If we dominate the objective world from our subjective perspective, we become metaphysical mythmakers telling ourselves what we want to hear; on the other hand, if our subjective perspective is swallowed up by our cosmic objectivity, we simply make mechanistic and fatalistic myths of another kind. The "double Danger" of presumption, as Pascal suggests, is "of Despair and of Pride." Christian theology traditionally opposes hope to the double dangers of despair and presumption, more narrowly defined.[89] Modern theologian Jurgen Moltmann reverses the formulation in a way that parallels Pascal and Pope: "hopelessness can assume two forms: it can be presumption, *praesumptio*, and it can be despair, *desparatio*." Both are sins against hope. "Presumption is a premature, selfwilled anticipation of the fulfillment of what we hope for from God," Moltmann says. "Despair is the premature, arbitrary anticipation of the non-fulfillment of what we hope for from God."[90]

Anthropocentric religion mythologizes its dual presumptions into a hell and a heaven, as Pope says in his natural history of religion in Epistle III: "Fear made her Devils and weak hope her Gods" (III:256). Pope's alternative to both premature projections is to "Hope humbly" (I:91); like Montaigne but unlike Pascal, Pope refuses the closure of Christian dogma that seemed the solution to many of his pious contemporaries. Stage-hating Jeremy Collier, for example, offers essays to combat either malady. Against the presumptives he fulminates "Upon the Weakness of Human Reason," and for those requiring Christian comfort, he writes "Against Despair."[91] Despair and presumption, then, were the extremes of the self's oscillations between conceiving itself as "a God, or Beast" (II:8), and each extreme made itself a metaphysics.

Much has been written about the philosophical implications of Pope's use of the great chain metaphor, but almost nothing has been said about its rhetorical effectiveness in diminishing presumption and consoling despair. Warburton and Rousseau each have it half right: Rousseau praises Pope's *Essay* for the consolation it gives him, and Warburton lauds its success in mortifying "that *Pride,* which occasions the impious Complaints against Providence."[92] In fact, Pope does both simultaneously. As Pope told Spence, he adopted the "cant" metaphor of a "scale of beings" because of its currency in the *Spectator* where it was one of Addison's favorite phrases.[93] In Epistle I Pope utilizes the metaphor to force us to become objective spectators to our relatedness to other beings in the "gen'ral frame" of nature, "frame" being an alternate, popular biblical metaphor for the same human connectedness to a larger creation.

"By viewing ourselves from a perspective broader than we can occupy in the flesh," Thomas Nagel contends, "we become spectators of our own lives. . . . By feigning a nebula's-eye view, we illustrate the capacity to see ourselves without presuppositions, as arbitrary, idiosyncratic, highly specific occupants of the world, one of countless forms of life."[94] Pope's energetic image creates exactly this effect:

> See, thro' this air, this ocean, and this earth,
> All matter quick, and bursting into birth.
> Above, how high progressive life may go!
> Around, how wide! how deep extend below!
> Vast chain of being, which from God began,
> Natures aethereal, human, angel, man,
> Beast, bird, fish, insect! what no eye can see,
> No glass can reach! from Infinite to thee,
> From thee to Nothing!
>
> (I:233–41)

Pope uses the metaphor to displace metaphysical man out of his anthropocentrism. For humans—but one element in "this dread ORDER"—to expect special treatment is the "Madness, Pride, and Impiety" of a "Vile worm!" (I:257–58). Pope is not offering an argument from design but, in

Bacon's words, is disabusing those "who presume" to trace "nature's chain" to "Jupiter's chair."

This "objective" perspective Pope offers of humans as one of a myriad of species riding a smallish planet circling a minor star poises us precariously in those dreaded Pascalian spaces between the Infinite and Nothingness. Having made us a minor part in the drama of the cosmos, Pope immediately, in compensation, shifts from his mechanical metaphor of a chain of being to a consoling, organic metaphor of the consanguinity of all creation:

> All are but parts of one stupendous whole,
> Whose body Nature is, and God the soul; . . .
> To him no high, no low, no great, no small;
> He fills, he bounds, connects, and equals all.
> (1:267–68, 279–80)

To his "objective" metaphor of subordination of parts within a whole, Pope adds the subjectively satisfying pantheistic metaphor that abolishes the particularity of the parts in one, perfect unity of reciprocal energy.

An identical dual rhetoric of chastisement and consolation determines Pope's handling of human reason. Used metaphysically it is "erring Reason"; in its proper sphere it is the distinctive mark of "Man's imperial race" (1:209). Pope's reading of Montaigne may have suggested to him an apt embodiment of the simultaneous blindness and insight of human reason. In his "Apology"/Indictment of physico-theologist Raymond Sebond, Montaigne illustrates the limits of human reason by considering "man in his highest estate," by characterizing "that small number of excellent and select men who, having been endowed with fine and particular natural ability, have further strengthened and sharpened it by care, by study, and by art, and have raised it to the highest pitch of wisdom that it can attain."[95]

For Pope's audience one man epitomized human intellect in its highest estate. Job had cowed abashed when God demanded, "Canst thou bind the sweet influences of the Pleiades?" Isaac Newton, in contrast, seemed to his contemporaries competent to bind them with the power of his intellect, having "discovered the fundamental law of the heavens" and given, in his *Principia,* a mathematical formulation of the divine mind.[96] Pope's famous epigram characterizes Newton's birth as a second creation:

> Nature and nature's laws lay hid in night;
> God said, "Let Newton be," and all was light.

Awed by Newton's accomplishments, even Voltaire turned physico-theologist and argued against blind chance based on the manifest difference between Newton and a mule's droppings.

But even the consensus genius of the age could be viewed from two perspectives simultaneously. Certainly from our human perspective, *Spectator* No. 635 observes, Newton "seems like one of another Species"; yet from a wider perspective "how narrow is the Prospect even of such a Mind? And how obscure to the Compass that is taken in by the Ken of an Angel." Prior expands this topos in *Solomon* by having the wisest of biblical figures conclude "that as to Human Science, ALL IS VANITY." Similarly, in the second verse paragraph of Epistle II, Pope belittles the metaphysical pretensions of the "wond'rous Creature" Man to "mount where Science guides." With an Aristotelian empiricism matched to his ethics, Pope ridicules those who would "soar with Plato to th' empyreal sphere / To the first good, first perfect, and first fair" (II:19–24). Pope's following paragraph uses Newton to illustrate the futility of "first philosophies":

> Superior beings, when of late they saw
> A mortal Man unfold all Nature's law,
> Admir'd such wisdom in an earthly shape,
> And shew'd a NEWTON as we shew an Ape.
> Could he, whose rules the rapid Comet bind,
> Describe or fix one movement of his Mind?
> Who saw its fires here rise, and there descend,
> Explain his own beginning or his end?
> (I:31-38)

Even the greatest human intellect, Pope dramatizes, has no certain knowledge, either epistemological ("his Mind") or metaphysical ("his own beginning, or his end"). Consequently, a "Modest Science" is the only sane option for a "being darkly wise" (II:43, 4).

Pope's use of Newton puts univocalist critics in a rage. Thomas Bentley, writing in 1735, is near the fount of a long lineage of interpreters who cannot decide how to read Pope's use of Newton: "Are you *mocking* those same *superior Beings*, for regarding NEWTON in no better light than we do a *Baboon*? Or are you *Satirizing* the Philosopher for presuming to pry into *them*?"[97] Warburton objects to a satiric reading and misreads Pope into having written "a higher compliment to the great *Newton*, as well as a more ingenious, than was ever yet paid him by any of his most zealous Followers."[98] Using the same terms to debate the same distinction over a century later, Mark Pattison acknowledged that critics were still uncertain whether the "superior Beings" admire Newton's "aspiring intelligence, or ridicule the presumption of man." He concludes, with dissatisfaction, that the "words are open to either interpretation."[99]

It is precisely this interpretive openness that irritates critics yearning for univocal closure and a decorous consistency of tone. "There are Starts and Flights of Poetry very fine," Bentley objects in discussing the Newton passage, "but you *prove* nothing. When we fancy we are going to learn some valuable thing, you fly off, and leave us in a Smoak." Nuttall varies the disparaging metaphor only slightly when he complains that "Pope is writing in a kind of mist. Perhaps he felt a certain unclarity might provide protection as he proceeded to undermine the greatest scientific intelligence the world had so far seen, Sir Isaac Newton."[100] The denigration of Pope's writing as a "Smoak" (1735) or "mist" (1984) illustrates the 250-year dissatisfaction with the *Essay*'s deviation from the logocentric ideal of transparency, a univocal and anti-rhetorical ideal of perfect correspondence between words and things.

In *Gulliver's Travels* a scientist hostile to interpretive openness eschews words entirely and, when he wishes to communicate, pulls things from his gigantic backpack and just points. Swift's ridicule of the Royal Society's ideal of identity between *res* and *verba* with its consequent abolition of irony, metaphor, and ambiguity remains applicable to our contemporary ambitions to replace untidy words with the stable symbols of mathematical logic. The misreadings of critics are partly attributable to this hostility to "words open to either interpretation" but are strengthened by the thinness of descriptions of Pope's rhetorical context. In fact, Pope's use of Newton is anything but vague, as the analogues from Montaigne, the *Spectator*, and *Solomon* attest. "The wisest and most knowing," Joseph Butler argues alluding to Newton, "cannot comprehend the ways and works of God" for human intellect perceives only effects but never first causes: "What are the laws by which matter acts upon matter, but certain effects; which some having observed to be frequently repeated, have reduced to general rules."[101] Blackmore makes the identical point about gravity ("attractive virtue"):

The masters form'd in Newton's famous school,
Who does the chief in modern science rule,

> Erect their schemes by mathematic laws. . . .
> Yet these sagacious sons of science own,
> Attractive virtue is a thing unknown.[102]

Despite the antagonistic tone of those from Bentley to Nuttall who undertake to defend Newton from Pope's ambiguous abuse, the real Isaac Newton would never have felt abused by his dual rhetorical role as exemplar of humanity's "highest estate" and inhabitant of a tiny isthmus of intellect surrounded by mysterious seas. The celebratory strain documented in Marjorie Hope Nicolson's *Newton Demands the Muse* coexisted with a cautionary strain that Newton himself encouraged. Newton warned Boyle lecturer Richard Bentley against suggesting that he understood gravity: "You sometimes speak of gravity as essential and inherent to matter. Pray do not ascribe that notion to me, for the cause of gravity is what I do not pretend to know."[103] Whatever he might seem to some of his contemporaries, Newton insisted, he seemed to himself to have described but a few pebbles on the shore while the great ocean of nature roared unexplained beyond him. Revealingly, Newton's metaphor derives from the same tradition Pope presupposes. In an essay "Against Confidence in Philosophy," Joseph Glanvill—author of *The Vanity of Dogmatizing*—said of his own discoveries, "When I look back upon the main Subject of these Papers, it appears so *vast* to my Thoughts, that me-thinks I have drawn out a *Cockle-shell* of Water from the *Ocean:* Whatever I look upon, within the *Amplitude* of *Heaven* and *Earth,* is evidence of Humane *Ignorance.*"[104]

On . . . occasion a poet may be allowed to be obscure,
but inconsistency never can be right.

—*Johnson on Pope*

FOUR

Optimism and Pessimism

OCKE'S WIDELY ACCEPTED DELINEATION of the limits of human perception made the classical distinction between knowledge and opinion useful to Pope's contemporaries. The fuller title of Glanvill's most famous work, for example, is *The Vanity of Dogmatizing: or Confidence in Opinions. Manifested in a Discourse of the Shortness and Uncertainty of our Knowledge* (1661). The difficulty Gulliver has in explaining "Opinion" to his masters the Houyhnhnms satirically encodes a skeptical consensus argued by Bacon and articulated most fully by Hume. "No light of nature," Bacon says, "extendeth to declare the will and true worship of God." Science may create "wonder, which is broken knowledge" and thereby stimulate an awe at the immensity and complexity of creation that "sufficeth to convince atheism, but not to inform religion."[1] As Dryden concurs in *Religio Laici*, nature and reason afford at best a glimmering light that may guide us upward to the specifically Christian "sun" of supernatural revelation. Pope agrees with Bacon and differs from Dryden in that we may look "thro' Nature, up to Nature's God" but must be "Slave to no sect" for human intellect has no access to certitude (IV:331–32). "Various Discussions tear our heated Brain," Prior's Solomon laments: "Opinions often turn; still Doubts remain."

"AN *IF* INSTEAD OF A *SINCE*"

In *An Essay on Man* because we "hang between; in doubt," we may see or say nothing definitively. Presumption strives to see other than through a glass darkly and makes a metaphysical creed. Man as god and man as worm—Christianity and atheism—are the dogmatic poles of presumption: premature fulfillment and premature despair of what we hope. Both philosophies presume to overcome our doubtful state by putting "Confidence in Opinions" and indulging the "Vanity of Dogmatizing." Similarly, dogmatic certitude (Christianity, atheism) and dogmatic incertitude are also opposed poles of presumption. It is equally an escape from our middle state to presume full knowledge ("the Stoic's pride") or to deny the possibility of any knowledge ("the Sceptic side").

The tone mandated by consciousness of our uncertain state is exemplified brilliantly in Pope's knowing deconstruction of our hope for an afterlife: another contentiously debated section of Epistle I. To Christians eternal life is both apology and incentive: an afterlife both redresses present grievances against God's distributive justice and rewards adherence to church dogma. All the evidences of human ignorance marshaled in Butler's sermon "no way invalidate that which is the *conclusion of the whole matter: Fear God, and keep his Commandments.*" Butler adroitly shifts attention to our "present state" by insisting that "Virtue is . . . happiness," but the biblical sanctions of heaven and hell inevitably exert their rhetorical power.[2] In contrast, when Pope asserts that "Virtue alone is Happiness," he specifically praises the individual who refuses allegiance to any religious "sect" (IV:310, 331).

Butler and Pope share a rhetoric opposing speculative metaphysics (Pure Reason) and advocating ethics (Practical or "Right" Reason), but Pope, unlike Butler, accepts the full consequences of their shared epistemology and refuses to dogmatize. "Almighty power exerted in the creation and government of the world" is entirely beyond human faculties, Butler insists. "What would be the consequence, if we could get an insight into these things, is very uncertain; whether it would assist us in, or divert us from what we have to do in this present state."[3] Pope's adaptation of Butler's "present state/future state" dichotomy has presented problems for almost every interpreter of the *Essay:*

> Heav'n from all creatures hides the book of Fate,
> All but the page prescrib'd, their present state;
> From brutes what men, from men what spirits know:
> Or who could suffer Being here below?
> The lamb thy riot dooms to bleed to-day,
> Had he thy Reason, would he skip and play?
> Pleas'd to the last, he crops the flow'ry food,

And licks the hand just rais'd to shed his blood.
Oh blindness to the future! kindly giv'n,
That each may fill the circle mark'd by Heav'n;
Who sees with equal eye, as God of all,
A hero perish, or a sparrow fall,
Atoms or systems into ruin hurl'd,
And now a bubble burst, and now a world.
Hope humbly then; with trembling pinions soar;
Wait the great teacher Death, and God adore!
What future bliss, he gives not thee to know,
But gives that Hope to be thy blessing now.
Hope springs eternal in the human breast:
Man never Is, but always To be blest.

(I:77–96)

The "self-contradictory" doubleness of tone in these lines and those following has usually been evinced as proof of Pope's indecisiveness and intellectual confusion. Hovering dangerously and unintentionally "on the edge of irony," a recent critic says, Pope is "obscurely ill-at-ease. The idea of heavenly bliss lay outside the scope of his poem. . . . But here the idea of an after-life presses for admission to the argument, and Pope seems not to know exactly how it should be handled."[4]

Pope knows what he is doing. As he said to Spence, "Some wonder . . . how the immortality of the soul came to be omitted [from the *Essay*]. The reason is plain, [it] lay out of my subject, which was only to consider man as he is, in his present state, not in his past or future."[5] In fact, outside the *Essay* Pope speaks of personal immortality as "a Grand Peut-être," frequently using some variant of his "Socratic" "Whatever IS, is RIGHT" to characterize his resignation.[6] Within the *Essay* an afterlife is similarly uncertain: at best a possibility, at worst an illusory attempt to dominate the universe from our human perspective. Pope acknowledged the uncertainty in a letter to his Catholic friend John Caryll in commenting on lines 73–76:

If to be perfect in a certain sphere,
What matter, soon or late, or here or there?
The blest today is as completely so,
As who began a thousand years ago.

Still pretending in his correspondence to be ignorant of the authorship of the *Essay,* Pope admits the poem "has merit in my opinion, but not so much as they give it; at least it is incorrect and has some inaccuracies in the expressions; one or two of an unhappy kind, for they may cause the author's sense to be turned, contrary to what I think his intention a little unorthodoxically. Nothing is so plain as that he quits his proper subject, *this present world,* to insert his belief of *a future state* and yet there is an *If* instead of a *Since* that would overthrow his meaning. . . . I want to know your opinion of it after twice or thrice reading."[7]

Pope subsequently told Spence that he intentionally excluded a "future state" from the poem; here he tells Caryll that the author of the *Essay* includes "*a future state*" but "incorrectly" introduces the afterlife with the hypothetical "*If*" rather than the conclusive "*Since.*" Needless to say, Pope never corrected his "mistake." For Pope, "*If*" functions logically as an hypothetical, introducing opinion rather than certain knowledge. As Douglas Patey astutely notes, Pope was no stranger to hypothetical reasoning, for "the whole of the *Essay on Man* is a hypothetical argument resting on the protasis introduced at the beginning of Epistle I: 'Of Systems possible, *if* 'tis confest.'"[8] In reading Epistle I, where this syntactic structure recurs, Pope's deconstructive hint to Caryll is enormously significant, alerting us not to misread hypotheticals as axiomatic, as critics unfailingly have. For example, Douglas White quotes

> Of Systems possible, if 'tis confest
> That Wisdom infinite must form the best,
> Where all must full or not coherent be,
> And all that rises, rise in due degree,

with the condemnatory comment that "a great deal is 'confest' in these lines, but it is evident that Pope regards the propositions as a priori truths."[9] Leopold Damrosch quotes White's assessment with approval, adding that "the entire poem, in fact, is a series of deductions from these axioms, whose plausibility is never subjected to scrutiny."[10]

Clearly the interpretative tradition, by forcing Pope's deliberate hypotheticals to function as unexamined a priori axioms, is not reading—as Pope requires in *An Essay on Criticism*—"With the same Spirit that its Author *writ.*" This fundamental misreading necessarily blinds the critic to Pope's rhetorical virtuosity because it transforms inherently ambiguous propositions into dogmatic assertions. Thus, merely by rhetorically deploying the doctrine of the "best" and its plenitudinarian rationalisms in hypothetical form ("if 'tis confest"), the avowedly anti-metaphysical Pope becomes a Rational Optimist indistinguishable from Leibniz. When White juxtaposes his interpretation of the *Essay*'s "a priori truths" with Pope's recurrent "scoff[ing] at system-building that goes beyond the evidence of immediate experience," he politely concludes that Pope "is not entirely consistent."[11]

Pope's deliberately dense rhetoric gave interpreters fits from the beginning. "We are born for Immortality," Crousaz writes, "and Mr. Pope insinuates our future Existence in the strongest Terms." The "smoak" of Pope's "insinuating" rhetoric makes him a slippery, inconsistent adversary, Crousaz continually complains.[12] Pope's advocates were equally troubled by his ambiguity. Caryll, Young, and Warburton repeatedly urged him to include unambiguous assertions of his belief in an afterlife. In effect, they wanted a univocal meaning and tone for passages like "The soul, uneasy and confin'd at home, / Rests and expatiates in a life to come" (1:98–99). A year before his death Pope altered the preposition in the first line from "at home" to "from home," apparently at the urging of friends to whom the original reading seemed to exclude a future existence, as, "to speak the plain truth," Joseph Warton insists, "it was intended to do."[13]

Indicatively, Pope's alteration does not "speak the plain truth" any less ambiguously than the original reading; in fact, Pope may have revised in order to make univocal, "excluding" readings less tenable. Pope probably drew the metaphor of the soul "at home" from Kennet's translation of Pascal: "For 'tis undeniably certain, that the Soul of Man is here incapable of Rest and Satisfaction. . . . [T]o make her exquisitely miserable, nothing more is required but the engaging her to look into her self, and to dwell at Home." Pope's revision to "from home" decreases his resemblance to Kennet's translation and, thereby, to Pascal's piety. Moreover, the second line retains what Nuttall calls a "dangerous indefinite article." By having us expatiate in *a* life to come rather than in *the* life to come, he argues, Pope unwittingly "almost implie[s] . . . a proto-Freudian theory of religion as a compensatory illusion."[14]

For interpreters seeking a play-free paraphrase of Pope's doctrine, his way of saying one thing but "almost implying" another is maddening. The verses immediately following the problematic couplet are indicative:

Lo! the poor Indian, whose untutor'd mind
Sees God in clouds, or hears him in the wind;
His soul proud Science never taught to stray
Far as the solar walk, or milky way;

> Yet simple Nature to his hope has giv'n,
> Behind the cloud-topt hill, an humbler heav'n;
> Some safer world in depth of woods embrac'd,
> Some happier island in the watry waste,
> Where slaves once more their native land behold,
> No fiends torment, no Christians thirst for gold!
> He asks no Angel's wing, no Seraph's fire;
> But thinks, admitted to that equal sky,
> His faithful dog shall bear him company.
> (1:99–112)

Virtually every interpreter of this passage for the last 250 years has accused Pope of an inconsistency tantamount to intellectual incompetence. Seeking to prove Pope's *Essay* "ridiculous, impious . . . and the chief cause of the formidable Growth of Vice among Christians," one author finds this passage paradigmatic of Pope's confusion: "A little before, that he may for ever be inconsistent, he owns that God put into Men the Hopes of Immortality and future Happiness, which I think is a Hope of being like immortal Gods, whom he (not improperly) calls Angels (Ep.i.1.90.). But still he allows the humble Choice of the ignorant *Indian* (ibid. 1.95.), who aspires not at the Happiness of Angels, nor desires any better Company than his Dog, in a very homely Elysium, at the back of some Mountain, or in a dark Wood, to be wiser than that of Jesus Christ and his Followers, because he thinks there is less Pride in it. But this humility of the *Indian* is like the Humility of a Hog when he wallows in the Mire, it is founded on Ignorance or want of a nicer Taste, and better Sense, and therefore, I think, can have no great Merit in it."[15]

Convinced that the immediate future of Christianity depended on Pope's univocal pronouncement on Hope and the Grand Perhaps, early commentary seethes with suspicion of Pope's impiety. Modern commentary retains all of this animus against the ambiguity of the text without its sectarian markings. Modern critics still demand that Pope speak definitively on hope as either instinctual warrant of immortality or self-flattering illusion, that he pronounce not on the psychology but on the ontology of hope. In an article on the *Essay* indicatively entitled "Reasoning But to Err," Charles Williams concludes that "Hope comes out of the poem very badly. Is hope really a divine comfort or a silly deception? . . . Pope never quite made up his mind whether he said 'hope' as a prayer or a sneer."[16] R. D. Stock finds a confusing "tension" between the Indian as an ideal of innocent humility and as a "*reductio ad absurdum* of those ignorant of true happiness." Believing

Pope to be unaware of his self-contradiction, Stock judges the *Essay* "a congerie of moods, all finely executed but spasmodic and unharmonized. Pope's view of the holy, like his view of the 'poor Indian,' is shifty."[17]

The invariable assumption from Crousaz and Johnson to Williams and Stock is that Pope is not deliberately ambiguous on the question of personal immortality but is unconsciously inconsistent, artful certainly ("finely executed") but ultimately illogical ("spasmodic and unharmonized"). As a result of their shared logocentric dislike of "a dialect more becoming shortsighted mortality," they misread a passage that is primarily ethical as though it were primarily metaphysical. By definition a "Grand Peut-être" is undecidable, and Pope says that Death is the "great teacher" in the matter, not himself. What Pope does do is put the concept of hope under erasure (*sous rature*), using it but acknowledging its problematic status. He does the same with a wide variety of words, including "soul" and "God," that are powerful but, without stipulative definitions, inherently ambiguous. By contradistinguishing his poem from Milton's biblical reinscription, Pope shakes loose all the traditional theological terms from their Christian moorings. The absence of the "Word," which discomforted and disoriented early Christian readers of the *Essay*, persists today in reinscriptions of the identical logocentric objections they made.

Far from indicating argumentative inconsistency, Pope's doubleness of tone is his consistent working out of a rhetoric suited to man's middle state. Clearly the Indian's vision of the afterlife contrasts positively with more grandiose Christian ambitions. However, Pope's closing description of the Indian's desire to meet his dog in heaven strikes critics as condescending. "The Indian is patronized, commended and obscurely envied all at once," one critic complains. "When the Indian crops up again, however, at IV, 177, it is as an object of simple contempt!"[18] The exclamation point marks the critic's irritation at Pope's wanting to have it both ways, and yet that is the essence and excellence of Pope's polyvalent rhetoric. Complexity is not confusion, however, and Pope uses the Indian for two purposes that are distinct but complementary.

Those philosophers "who make imaginary excursions into futurity" are "presumptuous," Bolingbroke wrote to Pope; and the poet uses the Indian to chastise such "excursions into futurity" in two ways. Pope simultaneously praises the Indian's "humbler heav'n" in contrast to the Christian's greed for golden streets and disparages the Indian's view as naively anthropomorphic, a criticism made explicitly in the later passage alluded to:

Weak, foolish man! will Heav'n reward us there
With the same trash mad mortals wish for here?
The Boy and Man an individual makes,
Yet sigh'st thou now for apples and for cakes?
Go, like the Indian, in another life
Expect thy dog, thy bottle, and thy wife.
(IV:173–78)

As Pope told Spence twice, "Our flattering ourselves with the thoughts of enjoying the company of our friends here when in the other world, may be but too like the Indians thinking that they shall have their dogs and their horses there."[19]

Pope's doubleness of response—at once empathetic and derisive—is appropriate to a being necessarily inhabiting more than one perspective. Analogously, there is an appropriate rhetorical doubleness to the Indian as a cautionary tale of childishness ("The Boy" with his cakes "like the Indian" with his dog) and as a Primitivist ideal ("simple Nature," "no Christians," "no Angel's wing . . . But . . . His faithful dog"). Reconstructing his rhetorical context, we see that Pope's use of the Indian presupposes two opposed traditions of Christian argument: heathen religious dogmas that had Christian analogues could be either dismissed as ignorant superstitions or invoked as "concurring beliefs." Moreover, whether the resemblance between heathen and Christian doctrine was used to discredit or reinforce Christianity's special revelation depended on the intention of authors as different as Montaigne and Isaac Watts.[20]

Pope steers betwixt this double doubleness. That the Indian and the European both "expatiate in a life to come" at first suggests, in Dryden's phrase, that "concurring heathens prove the story true," that belief in the afterlife is warranted by what Archbishop John Tillotson designated the "general consent" of different ages and cultures. Immediately, however, Pope tellingly contrasts the Indian's humility to the vainglorious, other-worldly colonialism of Christians, a contrast heightened in four lines of the first edition which Pope later omitted.[21] Thus, suddenly, the difference rather than the resemblance in beliefs makes Pope's point. At the conclusion of the verse paragraph, expectations are overturned again. The patronizing poignancy of the "poor Indian's" compensatory dream that in the democracy of death ("that equal sky") even "His faithful dog shall bear him company" undercuts the authority of "concurring belief" and leaves the reader uncertain of the significance of the resemblance between the pagan and the Christian beliefs. Pope leaves the ontological question undecided while focusing on the psychological significance: that "excursions into futurity" are presumptuous projections and that when we quit our sphere and "rush into the skies" (1:124), we neglect the moral action appropriate to our "nature and state."[22]

CONSTATIVE AND PERFORMATIVE SPEECH ACTS

Pope's rhetoric is not exclusively constative, and this fact confuses interpreters who are heirs of the simplistic tradition. J. L. Austin criticizes: "It was for too long the assumption of philosophers that the business of a 'statement' can only be to 'describe' some state of affairs, or to 'state some fact,' which it must do either truly or falsely."[23] Austin's distinction between constative utterances, which describe a state of affairs and are true or false, and performative utterances, which actually do the action to which they refer and cannot appropriately be described as true or false, correlates suggestively with the distinction between philosophical and poetic discourse because, as Stanley Fish suggests, "the properties that supposedly distinguish constatives from performatives—fidelity to preexisting facts, accountability to a criterion of truth—turn out to be as dependent on particular conditions of production and reception as performatives."[24]

The logocentric Crousazian tradition treats Pope's performative utterances as failed constatives and complains that his philosophy is "infected" by his poetry. Thus Pope's ridicule of "excursions into futurity" is marginalized as an ambiguous distraction from the "argument" of the poem. It is possible to invert this hierarchy and treat the constative as one aspect of the performative, a generative idea in interpreting an ethics. Of Kant's three fundamental human questions—What may I know? What may I hope? What should I do?—we should expect an ethics to subordinate the epistemological and the theological to the ethical. Therefore, since Pope is writing a "System of Ethics," we should expect the constative function of language to be ancillary to the directive function. The special performative challenge of philosophical poetry as a genre, I will suggest later, is to make potentially conflicting functions of language complementary; but our presumption in interpreting an ethics should be that Pure Reason will be subordinate to Practical Reason, a rhetorical corollary to Joseph Butler's praise of Socrates and Solomon for subordinating the pursuit of knowledge to the practice of virtue.

Pope's epistemological Epistle I, therefore, simultaneously restricts the legitimate province of constative statement to human perception ("What can we reason, but from what we know?") and demonstrates the impossibility of constative theological or metaphysical statements ("thy own point . . . this due degree / Of blindness"). These limitations are essential preliminaries, as Pope's "Design" says, to any person attempting "to prove any moral duty" or "to enforce any moral precept." There can be no doubt about what Pope intended in this regard because he told Spence that "the rule laid down at the beginning of the *Essay on Man* of reasoning only from what we know is certainly a right one, and will go a great way toward destroying all the school metaphysics. As the church-writers have introduced so much of those metaphysics into their systems, it will destroy a great deal of what is advanced by them too."[25] Oblivious to Pope's pre-Heideggerian "destructive" strain, philosophical interpretation beginning with theologian and logician Crousaz wrenched primacy from the directive function by translating all utterances into constatives. For example, at the conclusion of the poor Indian passage, Pope admonishes Presumptuous Man: "Go, Wiser thou, and in the scale of sense / Weigh thy Opinion against Providence" (1:113–14). Critics routinely deconstruct Pope's couplet into contradiction by arguing that if Man cannot comprehend the universal order then Pope is unwarranted in presuming a Providence himself. Thus, critics decode as constative (A providential order exists!) an utterance that is directive (Cease making metaphysical pronouncements!).

As we saw in the previous chapter, in opposing "first philosophy" Pope draws heavily on the rhetoric of "church-writers" like Sherlock and Butler who, in contradiction to their own anti-metaphysical arguments, presuppose a specifically Christian providence; but he takes their epistemology without their theology to fashion his two rhetorics of chastisement correlated with our dual nature. To rational presumption Pope opposes the limits of reason and the naturalistic basis of all knowledge. This rhetoric leaves all supernatural questions undecidable and hope possible. To passionate presumption—the self's insistence on cosmic centrality—he opposes the contingency of the human species, reducing us "who here seem principle alone" to dwarfish insignificance in "one stupendous whole" (1:57, 267). The last paragraph of Epistle I places us in the perspective of an awesome, incomprehensible chaos-cosmos:

> Cease then, nor ORDER Imperfection name:
> Our proper bliss depends on what we blame.

Know thy own point: This kind, this due degree
Of blindness, weakness, Heav'n bestows on thee.
Submit. . . .

(I:281–85)

The predominantly directive nature of Pope's rhetoric is clear: "Cease . . . nor . . . name," "Know," and "Submit" are all directive verbs controlling sense and syntax.

Like Butler, Pope creates a context that "abates self-esteem" and encourages "lowliness of mind"; but the "submission" and "absolute resignation" they both counsel resonate differently in the context of a Christian sermon and in a philosophical poem from which everything distinctively Christian is excluded. Without the supplementary warrant of supernatural revelation, hope deconstructs to opinion, and Pope effectively vacillates between the worldly and the otherworldly codes of our objective and subjective perspectives. Hope is *sous rature* because always conditioning the theistic code is the cynical code so aptly encapsulated in La Rochefoucauld's maxim: "Hope, utter charlatan though she be, at least lures us to life's end along a pretty road." Pope perfects the sentiment in his knowing deconstruction of hope at the end of Epistle II:

Mean-while *Opinion* gilds with varying rays
Those painted clouds that beautify our days;
Each want of happiness by Hope supply'd,
And each vacuity of sense by Pride:
These build as fast as *knowledge* can destroy;
In Folly's cup still laughs the bubble, joy;
One prospect lost, another still we gain;
And not a vanity is giv'n in vain.

(II:283–90)[26]

Pope discredits the possibility of a supernatural moral sanction in order to make way for his naturalistic and nonsectarian ethics; Butler discredits metaphysical reasoning to reinforce supernatural belief. Butler exemplifies a conservative variant of John Herman Randall's contention that in creating the "sciences of man" eighteenth-century philosophers, including Voltaire, used an initial empiricist analysis "wholly in the destructive work of clearing the ground" but constructed their own systems in a thoroughgoing rationalist fashion.[27] Whereas the philosophers made room for their systems by criticizing earlier systems as a priori rationalisms and then elaborating new systems from their own arbitrarily invoked axioms, Butler discredits all rationalisms and then invokes a preexisting Christianity. Pope does not defer to a preexisting system, and when he uses the diction and imagery of theism (God, Providence, Hope) or of rationalism (Order, Harmony) they are either radically problematized or put under erasure.

Pope's rhetoric, critics complain, is "fraught with an inner duplicity" that "is tolerated—or even welcomed—as an invigorating ironic tension on a small scale [but] is much harder to accept at the major level of the argument. It becomes, indeed, mere contradiction."[28] At the "major level" of argument where logocentric critics demand constative propositions, Pope chastises, comforts, cajoles, kids, performs, plays, pokes fun, dictates, ridicules, and ravishes; and most of his constatives are coded in a dualistic, paradoxical dialect becoming short-sighted mortality but mortally offensive to Crousaz and his kind.[29] Thus a recent critic's complaint that "Probably [Pope] mentally juggled with both ideas, spent little energy on any attempt to distinguish them and very considerable energy on the production of a smooth and acceptable set of couplets" (1984) merely reiterates Crousaz's complaint that Pope's "is not the Stile of a Philosopher; it is the Language of Homer" (1738).[30]

In this instance it is the language of the Book of Job. That text, Butler argues, illustrates our incapacity to comprehend "the designs and methods of Providence."[31] Job's questions anticipate those of Pope's Presumptuous Man just as the reasonings of Job's misguided comforters anticipate the rationalizations of "high priori" metaphysicians. Much of the epistemological groundclearing in Epistle I is destruction of those rationalizations by repeated use of *reductio ad absurdum*. In this Pope's aggressive didacticism resembles nothing so much as Dryden's characterization of the stance of the author of *De Rerum Natura:* "the distinguishing character of Lucretius . . . is a certain kind of noble pride, and positive assertion of his opinions. . . . [H]e seems to disdain all manner of replies, and is so confident of his cause that he is beforehand with his antagonists; urging for them whatever he imagined they could say, and leaving them as he supposes, without an objection for the future. And this too, with so much scorn and indignation, as if he were assured of the triumph before he entered into the lists" (preface to *Sylvae,* 1685). Butler's repeated use of "we" in his sermon "Upon the Ignorance of Man" downplays the element of kerygma or proclamation fundamental to the genre in favor of an emphasis on shared incapacity. Pope, in contrast, alternates between Butler's comfortable consanguinity ("Let *us* . . . What can *we* . . .") and an aggressively didactic, sermonic rhetoric ("Go, wiser *thou*! . . . Know *thy* own point . . . ").

Pope's dismissive and demeaning ridicule of the "vile worm" presuming to make a critique of the cosmos unites the "scorn and indignation" of Lucretius with the kerygmatic voice of God rebuking his servant Job. Pope's "inconsistent" alternation from an intimate to a mythologizing persona, in fact, correlates with the human alternation from a subjective to an objective perspective.

Even Newton can be seen in a diminishing perspective, and the lines from Job that Pope interlineated on the manuscript of Epistle II were a commonplace of both theological and epistemological works. Browne's *Human Understanding* quotes Isaiah on the title page: "As the Heavens are higher than the Earth, so are my Ways higher than your Ways; and my Thoughts than your Thoughts." Like Pascal and Butler and the Book of Job, Browne's anti-rationalism is in Christian service. "Since then it appears the Ideas of Sensation are the only subject matter which the mind hath to work upon," he argues, revelation is essential as an ethical guide to the good life.[32] Not so Pope. Nowhere in the bible is "the uncertain and equivocal position of man" more profoundly stated than in Job, and Pope's Christian contemporaries, including Blackmore and Young, were constantly publishing paraphrases of it.[33] But Pope adopts Job's "uncertain and equivocal" delineation of the human condition without the expected turn to the certain and univocal closure of Christian revelation.

Pierre Bayle had astutely warned Christian apologists against arguing in the manner of Leibniz or Samuel Clarke. In the war against impiety, theologians must abandon "all the reasons a priori, as the outworks of a place, which may be insulted, and cannot be maintained" and, instead, emulate God's rebuke to Job: "Shall the thing formed say to him that formed it, why hast thou made me thus?"[34] Invoking the precedents of Saint Paul, Solomon, and Job, Bacon had earlier cautioned against three abuses of reason: (1) "that we do not so place our felicity in knowledge, as [to] forget our morality"; (2) "that we make application of our knowledge to give ourselves repose and contentment, and not distaste and repining"; and (3) "that we do not presume by the contemplation of nature to attain to the mysteries of God." These are all three topoi of Pope's *Essay*: (1) "VIRTUE only makes our Bliss below" (IV:387); (2) "WHATEVER IS, IS RIGHT" (IV:394); and (3) "all our Knowledge is, OURSELVES TO KNOW" (IV:398). Bacon and the Book of Job are powerful precedents anticipating the physico-theological pitfall of presuming to know God through study of nature while simultaneously celebrating the wonder of nature. The contemplation of nature can never yield knowledge of the supernatural,

Bacon says, but it stimulates "wonder which is broken knowledge."[35] As the Book of Job asserts, although we study the "wondrous works of God," human intellect "cannot comprehend" (37:14, 5). Pope creates the same sense of wonder at the "Order" and "vast immensity" of the cosmos as a naturalistic invocation of the awe Job experiences when God chides him for searching into matters "too wonderful" to understand. Pope's affirmation of the ineffable is an argument from awe silencing metaphysicians and theologians alike. No one, not even a Newton, was present when the foundations of the earth were laid.

HORATIAN LAUGHTER AND LUCRETIAN GLOOM

In a revealing misreading of the *Essay,* a recent critic notes a parallel between Job and "Presumptuous Man" but turns Pope into one of Job's false comforters, figures "who sometimes reason like eighteenth-century theologians." Instead of adopting "a fully Jobian position: that God's action is wholly incomprehensible," Pope "begins to work within the eighteenth-century version of the cosmic chain of being and at once . . . he is involved in metaphysics, presumptuously rationalizing God's scheme, violating his own prescription of humility."[36] This either-or objection interprets Pope's argument, persona, and tone as interdependent in their inconsistency. Argumentatively, it alleges that man cannot/Pope can reason metaphysically, that a part cannot/a part can contain the whole. Persona shifts correspondingly from Job's blindness to God's omniscience, and tone alters from humble submission to oracular pronouncement. Having deconstructed Pope's persona and tone into a binary opposition of ignorance and all-knowingness and according sole authority to univocal utterance, this line of interpretation pins Pope wriggling to the wall as just another inconsistent eighteenth-century empiricist-rationalist of the kind John Herman Randall criticizes.

The remedy for this coercive simplification begins with more careful attention to the text itself and acknowledgment of the multiple tones and rhetorical stances it deploys, from celebration to satire, from consanguinity to contempt. One of the *Essay*'s greatest admirers, Robert Dodsley, found the poem confusing initially and only with repeated readings came to appreciate its subtlety and profundity; and Pope urged his friends, including Caryll, to read it over "two or three times" before attempting interpretation. Those readers had the advantage of a dense rhetorical context, which modern criticism can achieve only with great effort and only then by fits and starts. Nevertheless, as a shortcut it is a therapeutic distortion to analyze the binary opposition presupposed by hostile commentary. Such a simplification exposes the bias of univocal criticism and is not dangerous if we do not reify our dichotomy and forget that Pope's poem speaks with many voices drawing on multiple linguistic codes.

The poles of this opposition are illustrated succinctly by two recent interpreters. Robert Uphaus contends that in the *Essay* "Pope occupies the role of God's spokesman: he simply elaborates 'Heav'n's first law.'"[37] Dustin Griffin, in contrast, sees the *Essay* as "in some sense a metaphor for Pope's self, an attempt by an acutely self-conscious, self-centered poet to work out . . . a coherent view of some aspects of his life and nature that most disturbed him."[38] This dichotomy into the prophetic (Pope as Leibnizian rational optimist, as one of Job's comforters, as God) and the personal (Pope as "troubled" poet, as Job, as "vile man who mourns"), which is evidence for univocal criticism of Pope's "self-contradiction," correlates exactly both with Pope's characterization of human nature as a dualistic "Chaos of Thought and Passion" and with Nagel's objective and subjective points of view. In Nagel's terminology two "conflicting points of view" collide in us. Necessarily the "self-center" of our subjective universes, we simultaneously see ourselves as cosmic ephemera. Using terms primarily from the last section of Epistle I and the first section of Epistle II, we see Pope's elaboration of this inevitable tension:

Human Nature
"isthmus"
"middle state"
"Chaos"
"riddle"

"Thought"	"Passion"
"God"	"Beast"
"Mind"	"Body"
"lord"	"prey"
"Truth"	"Error"
"knowledge"	"weakness"
"half to rise"	"half to fall"
"wond'rous creature"	"fool"
"glory"	"jest"

Poet chastising presumption	"Presumptuous Man"
"Submission"	"Pride"
Cosmic "whole"	Anthropocentric "part"
Objective perspective	Subjective perspective
"Order"	"Imperfection"
"Direction"	"Chance"
"Harmony"	"Discord"
"Good"	"Evil"
"bliss"	"blame"
Contempt	Compassion
Censure	Consolation
Satire	Sentimentality
Optimism	Pessimism.

Observing the "ambiguous value of perception" in the *Essay*, Patricia Meyer Spacks argues there is a tension between "the poem's philosophical optimism" and its "personal pessimism."[39] In an equally astute commentary, Thomas Edwards finds the poem interesting "as an expression of a conflict between Pope's views of reality as excitingly terrible and as ultimately orderly and peaceful."[40] Similarly, Wallace Jackson argues that "although the relationship between 'I' and 'you' may be objectified into a discourse ('virtuous teacher' and 'erring student'), it exists far more potently as an internal dialogue."[41] All three critics, however, read as phenomenologists interested in the poem "not as philosophy," as Edwards candidly admits, but as psychohistory. In Crousazian fashion Edwards agrees that Pope's "terms and implications clash with the doctrine" in a manner that discredits it as philosophy; but if we ignore the *Essay*'s "jumble of claims," we see Pope "as a man whose strong sense of the value of order makes experienced disorder a dreadful thing to consider, and who yearns for an imaginative myth of cosmic immutability to sustain and console him." We miss the point, Edwards argues, "if we simply judge Pope a bad philosopher and the poem therefore faulty. . . . Something significant has happened. A poet's mind lets us see what it is doing—making poetry out of lumps of philosophy that resist becoming poetry."[42]

Although Edwards's phenomenological and aesthetic emphasis does nothing to rehabilitate the *Essay* as philosophy, it does insightfully locate the poem's power in the unresolved tension between its optimistic and pessimistic perspectives. In contrast, most critics who acknowledge the poem's mixture of tones and do not simply disparage Pope's inconsistency usually privilege one voice or tone as more predominant, sincere, or authentic, thus moving toward interpretive univocality. Thus critics who stress Pope's satiric certainty are balanced by critics who stress his "usually inconclusive or despairing . . . endings."[43] Few resist univocality and value the comic-satiric and the tragic-sentimental as equally sincere, and such interpreters are invariably literary critics who accept the Crousazian assessment of Pope's philosophy as incoherent and inconsistent. Representatively, Fredric Bogel describes the tension of epic and satire he perceives in the *Essay* as "a structure of knowledge [that] embodies a double movement: toward a form of apocalyptic vision and toward a humanizing of the poet that qualifies the authority, the absoluteness, of that vision."[44] No matter how perceptive, such subtle readings are deconstructed easily by blunt-edged Crousazians: a "structure of knowledge" that claims visionary power while simultaneously resisting "the absoluteness of [its] vision" may be dismissed as intellectual muddle. A sometimes subtle reader, Rebecca Ferguson does the Crousazians' work for them when she correlates Pope's "curious blend of declamation and satire, optimism and reservation" with his genius as a poet and his incompetence as a philosopher. Poetry is the "medium in which the tensions embodied in the *Essay* could be kept alive," she contends. "Within the terms of Pope's philosophy, however, it is evident that it is not finally possible to smooth out, or fully counterbalance, many of the difficulties and contradictions which pervade his optimistic 'doctrine.'"[45]

The problem in rehabilitating the *Essay* is not that all critics have failed to appreciate Pope's intentional duality but that no critic has related convincingly that duality of voice and tone to Pope's philosophical argument. The tonal duality was an inherited classical ideal, which Boileau reinscribed in his *Art of Poetry*, translated by Dryden as "Happy, who in his verse can gently steer / From grave to light, from pleasant to severe!" Bowing to and improving his predecessors' diction, Pope concludes Epistle IV by reiterating two of the major metaphors with which he began: "the Muse now stoops, or now ascends / To man's low passions, or their glorious ends . . . happily to steer / From grave to gay, from lively to severe" (IV:375–80). The rising and falling metaphor correlates with man's mixed soaring and sinking state; and the steering metaphor makes explicit the link between variation of voice and tone and Pope's methodology of "steering betwixt the extremes of doctrines seemingly opposite."

In his letters Pope contrasts the predominant tones of Horace and

Lucretius, and it seems clear that those two were his conscious mentors for the major tonal shifts in the *Essay*. Remembering the Juvenalian catalogue of vanities from Epistle IV, we know that the Lucretian and the Horatian by no means exhaust the repertoire of voices alive in the poem, and Howard Weinbrot has argued intriguingly that Pope's preeminence is linked to his virtuosity with a variety of satiric voices alive in the same text.[46] Nonetheless, in *An Essay on Man* Pope's Horatian good humor frequently alternates with his Lucretian scorn as he moves between a companionable *humanitas* ("gay" and "lively") and a sermonic *gravitas* ("grave" and "severe"). Thus it is Pope's own contrast of the predominant voices in the *Essay* that so strikingly anticipates Nagel's characterization of our two "conflicting points of view." When we shift from our "highly specific and idiosyncratic" subjectivity to an objectivity that allows us to reconceptualize ourselves with "that detached amazement which comes from watching an ant struggle up a heap of sand," our response is at once "sobering and comical," a duality lending our life its peculiar character of "seriousness . . . laced with irony."[47]

"THE VERY NADIR OF AUGUSTAN POETRY"

Pope's adaptations from Montaigne and Pascal are sufficient to show that applying Nagel's recent philosophical analysis of our middle state to the *Essay* is not anachronistic. But perhaps it is Hume and Kant who provide the most provocative anticipation, for our purposes, of Nagel's belief that our awareness of the undecidability of ultimate questions does not cause us to abandon an absurd existence but instead to return to our familiar convictions with a certain ironic resignation. An uncompromising philosophic skeptic in his closet, Hume lives his "common life" in humanistic fellowship, an ironist who dies with a resignation befitting his skepticism. The clearest anticipation of Nagel's terminology, however, may be Kant's *Critique of Judgment*. Unable to generate a satisfactory synthesis from the thesis and antithesis of a priori and empirical perspectives, Kant concludes that we can have no warranted beliefs on ontological or metaphysical matters. Nevertheless, since we must act we make judgments. Such a judgment, however, "remains *reflective*, not determinant, that is, acts on a subjective ground, and not according to an objective principle of the possibility of things in their inherent nature."[48]

When action is necessary or desirable—as in science—and the intellect is unable to resolve its conflicting perspectives, Kant argues, we are justified in adopting a hypothesis that usefully organizes what we know so long as we remain aware that our hypothesis is reflective rather than determinant, suspect rather than certain. Here, as in his lectures on philosophical theology, Kant is concerned with teleological judgments. Thus, the double awe Kant felt at the vast immensity outside himself and the moral law within go some way toward accounting for his admiration for Pope's eloquence on both in the *Essay*. It is equally important that Kant found in the *Essay* unwavering opposition to the flawed anthropocentric reasoning whereby both the Leibnizian a priorists and the physico-theologists sought to make their "reflective" judgments "determinant."

Jeffrey Barnouw defends Leibniz as a theodicist in an interesting way. Given a flawed world, according to Leibniz, we can only be reconciled to the will of God if we attain "a rational faith which entails a rejection, or severe qualification, of reasoning from empirical event to the purposes or attributes of God." The sad spectacle of the world cannot prove providence whatever physico-theologists or advocates of "Natural Religion" aver. Consequently, Leibniz relies on "formal rational argument in order to justify the persistence of moral striving even in the face of apparent futility." Rather than presuming to "prove" anything, Barnouw suggests, Leibniz's "vindication of the ways of God is meant to nurture trust and hope as the contexts of ongoing efforts."[49] This more subtle interpretation of Leibniz transforms him from the presumptuous *bête noire* of Bolingbroke and Pope into an ally of Pope in convincing us that "Our proper bliss depends on what we blame" (1:282).

Rather than adopt the dogmatic demonstrative mode of Leibniz's downward reasoning, however, Pope insistently embeds the hypothetical "if," "may," and "perhaps" of reflective rather than determinant rhetoric:

> Respecting Man, whatever wrong we call,
> May, must be right, as relative to all.
> (1:51–52)

"May" anticipates the hypothetical construction of lines 57–60:

> So Man, who here seems principal alone,
> Perhaps acts second to some sphere unknown,
> Touches some wheel, or verges to some goal;
> 'Tis but a part we see, and not a whole.

This possibility of transcendent order and purpose is the "Hope" that Pope subsequently evokes and puts *sous rature*, as doubtful rather than determinant. Although Pope's naturalistic ethics in later epistles does not necessitate a supernatural sanction, most of his audience, as Bolingbroke stresses, need to feel a connectedness to a transcendent order for their lives to seem meaningful. Attitude is all important for sustained moral striving. Thus, there is a double meaning in the initial lines of the last section of Epistle I: "Cease then, nor ORDER Imperfection name: / Our proper bliss depends on what we blame." Existence, even with its imperfections, is the sole source of happiness; and as Pope pessimistically ridiculed the rational optimism of the physico-theologist in asserting the world was made to pamper us, he now stresses the usefulness of a providential hypothesis to human happiness. Earlier he pointed out that plague and earthquake prove that "Nature deviates" from the "gracious end" of nurturing us; now he asserts that "All Nature is . . . Art." The pessimistic judgment coexists with and conditions the optimistic judgment. "Whatever is, is" regardless of our judgments; but an attitude of "Whatever IS, is RIGHT" sustains us even though our reflective judgment is not rationally warranted: "*un*known to thee," "which thou canst *not* see," "*not* understood" (1:289–91).

Writing to Voltaire, Rousseau defends both Leibniz and Pope. *An Essay on Man* "softens my ills and brings me patience," Rousseau testifies, even though "it is very evident that no man would be able to give direct proof for [Whatever IS, is RIGHT] or against it; for the proof depends on a perfect knowledge of the constitution of the world and the intention of its Author, and this knowledge is undeniably above human intelligence." Ultimately, Rousseau argues, all metaphysical reasoning deconstructs to a chain of unprovable hypothetical propositions that we accept or reject without the luxury of certitude: "If God exists, he is perfect; if he is perfect, he is wise, powerful and just; if he is wise and powerful, all is good; if he is just and powerful, my soul is immortal; if my soul is immortal, thirty years of life are nothing for me and are perhaps necessary to the maintenance of the universe. If I am granted the first proposition, the subsequent one can never be shaken; if it is denied, it is unnecessary to argue about its consequences." Because the existence of God is intellectually undecidable, Rousseau condemns both dogmatic atheism and any "superstition which disturbs society." "Religion which sustains society," in contrast, cannot be respected enough.[50]

It is revealing that Rousseau's praise of Pope is not a defense of an argument but of an attitude. Reason can never decide between the antinomies of "if"/"if not," of optimism/pessimism, of theism/atheism, of cosmos/chaos; but as reflective judgments for ongoing activity they may be distinguished as alternatively "sustaining" or "disturbing." Kant makes the same point in *Lectures on Philosophical Theology* but takes it a suggestive step further. Looked at rationally the "sum of sorrow and the sum of good" in the world "might very well just about balance each other," making it "difficult to know it for the best." However, we are justified in accepting the providential hypothesis for it has a utility for us comparable to the usefulness of the teleological hypothesis in science. "The same law," Kant says, "is valid also for organized creatures and for the mineral kingdom, for the sake of the necessary harmony in which everything is combined under the supremely necessary principle of unity. For reason's sake, therefore, we can and must assume that everything in the world is arranged for the best, and that the whole of everything existing is the best possible one. This doctrine has the same influence on morality as it has on natural science. . . . If the world *is* the best one, then my morality will stand firm and its incentives will retain their strength."[51]

The semantic and syntactic resemblances between Pope and his admirers show a shared hypothetical dialect:

> Of Systems possible, *if* 'tis confest
> That *Wisdom* infinite must form the *best*.
> Pope, 1:43–44
>
> *If* he is *wise* and powerful, all is *good*.
> Rousseau on Pope to Voltaire
>
> Respecting Man, whatever wrong we call,
> *May, must* be *right*, as relative to all.
> Pope, 1:51–52
>
> For reason's sake, therefore, we *can* and *must*
> assume that everything . . . is arranged for the *best*.
> Kant

All three authors presuppose that their propositions are unknowable and hypothetical: "reflective" rather than "determinant" in Kant's terminology. Such propositions are neither rational deductions nor empirical generalizations but are instead ways of productively organizing human experience in the context of continued striving.

Voltaire, who composed a philosophical poem in emulation of the *Essay*, shares the dialect, and that is the point of his having Professor Pangloss discredit the ethicist Pope and affirm the rationalist Leibniz:

. . . in erring Reason's spite,
One truth is clear, "Whatever IS, is *RIGHT*."
Pope, 1:293–94

It follows that those who maintain that all is *right*
talk nonsense; they ought to say that all is for the *best*.
Pangloss in *Candide*

Pope ignored contemporary allegations of his "inconsistency" in concluding Epistle I with a chain of a priori propositions because the allegation that they are a priori, while true, is irrelevant, for their force is not determinant (constative propositions of Pure Reason) but reflective (directive propositions guiding Pragmatic and Practical Reason). They are not evidence but incentive.

This shared hypothetical dialect with its assumption of the limitations and dualisms of human perception confuses and infuriates univocal interpreters of *An Essay on Man*, as we see most vividly in criticism of the brilliant and beautiful conclusion of Epistle II. Steering between Hobbesian-Mandevillean selfishness and Lockean-Shaftesburian benevolence, Pope subsumes both under a biblical paradox earlier evoked by Montaigne in his skeptical critique of human intellect:

Whate'er the Passion, knowledge, fame, or pelf,
Not one will change his neighbor with himself.
The learn'd is happy nature to explore,
The fool is happy that he knows no more;
The rich is happy in the plenty giv'n,
The poor contents him with the care of Heav'n.
See the blind beggar dance, the cripple sing,
The sot a hero, lunatic a king;
The starving chemist in his golden views
Supremely blest, the poet in his muse.
See some strange comfort ev'ry state attend,
And Pride bestow'd on all, a common friend;
See some fit Passion ev'ry age supply,
Hope travels thro', nor quits us when we die.
Behold the child, by Nature's kindly law,
Pleas'd with a rattle, tickled with a straw:
Some livelier play-thing gives his youth delight,
A little louder, but as empty quite:
Scarfs, garters, gold, amuse his riper stage;

And beads and pray'r-books are the toys of age:
Pleas'd with this bauble still, as that before;
'Till tir'd he sleeps, and Life's poor play is o'er!
Mean-while Opinion gilds with varying rays
Those painted clouds that beautify our days;
Each want of happiness by Hope supply'd,
And each vacuity of sense by Pride:
These build as fast as knowledge can destroy;
In Folly's cup still laughs the bubble, joy;
One prospect lost, another still we gain;
And not a vanity is giv'n in vain.
Ev'n mean Self-love becomes, by force divine,
The scale to measure others wants by thine.
See! and confess, one comfort still must rise,
'Tis this, Tho' Man's a fool, yet GOD IS WISE.
(II:259-94)

As with the "Socratic" "Whatever IS, is RIGHT," which ends the first epistle, Pope concludes the second with an aphoristic appropriation of Montaigne's use of "the foolishness of God is wiser than men" from I Corinthians. Montaigne is ridiculing theologians who market their dogmas by "hopes appropriate to our mortal appetites."[52] Similarly, harking back to earlier themes, Pope further deconstructs Hope into Opinion, reducing it by parallelism with Pride to just another sustaining vanity. Even the Sophoclean-Shakespearean stages-of-life paragraph diminishes Catholic rosaries and Anglican rituals ("beads and pray'r-books") into "toys of age," mere "baubles" to lure us, as La Rochefoucauld says, "to life's end along a pretty road."

Pope marries perspectives by including himself among the self-deceived. No longer the scornful satirist exempt from the folly of his fellow creatures, Pope personalizes his pronouns:

Hope travels thro', nor quits *us* when *we* die.

Mean-while Opinion gilds with varying rays
Those painted clouds that beautify *our* days.

One prospect lost, another still *we* gain;
And not a vanity is giv'n in vain.

Thus are the mad alchemist and the author of *An Essay on Man* consubstantial:

> The starving chemist in his golden views
> Supremely blest, the poet in his muse.

Pope presents himself as the final exemplar. The effect of this dual vision—satirist as objective observer and satirized as subject observed—is twofold. First, the lines have that "peculiar flavor" of irony and resignation that Nagel argues accompanies "the collision between the seriousness with which we take our lives and the perpetual possibility of regarding everything about which we are so serious as arbitrary, or open to doubt."[53] Second, this dual perspective allows no univocal determination of ultimate questions. As with Nagel's example of philosophical skepticism, there is a radical undecidability that forces us to "hang between . . . in doubt" (II:7).

Pope's self-characterized rhetoric of "an *If* instead of a *Since*" signals a perpetual aporia of paradoxically conflicting claims. Thus, "Hope travels thro', nor quits us when we die" is ironic in Hayden White's sense: it asserts and signals disbelief simultaneously. Hope is both La Rochefoucauld's utter charlatan and our instinctual warrant of a life everlasting. Hope is a "strange comfort" (II:271), and Pope's polysemous rhetoric both comforts and estranges. Crousaz misreads Pope as univocally atheist: "I cannot, without Melancholy and Pity, see that Hope, which is so firmly grounded, so strongly supported, and so highly to be valued; that Hope, for which we owe such ardent and frequent acknowledgments to the Goodness of our Creator, rank'd among airy Visions, and wild Chimeras, which are indebted for their influence and Existence to nothing but our Pride and Inattention."[54] Warburton defends Pope as univocally Christian: Hope embodies a "great and noble Thought. . . . But so strongly perverse is [Crousaz] that he will suppose [Pope] to mean anything rather than what the obvious Drift of his Argument requires."[55]

A recent interpretation of the same lines continues the same reductionism, but this time the univocal interpretative template is not atheism or Christianity but the theodicy of rational optimism. The end of Epistle II, Nuttall argues, "is the very nadir of Augustan poetry, a bland sequence of pseudo-universals. Any hack versifier of the time could in some five minutes supply a set of lines, directly opposed to Pope's, just as true and just as false as his." Oblivious that Pope's irony has already done so, the critic condescends to compose two counter-couplets, and then continues his assessment. "Pope proceeds from bad to worse. The blind and crippled, he points out, dance about and sing and must therefore be very happy. Starving geniuses, meanwhile, go mad and become megalomaniacs, so they are all right. We have the right to expect from a great poet a more than ordinary acuteness of perception. . . . Here he has nothing to give but a studied obtuseness." Continuing his pattern of criticizing Pope every time he "neglects" his optimistic theodicy, Nuttall objects that "the prayer-book is seen as an idiot's bauble" and that Pope, "with a backwash of cynicism far deeper than anything in Mandeville," characterizes human happiness as "the giggling of a lunatic." This kind of optimism, he concludes, "is profoundly depressing." Nuttall perceives Pope's duality without knowing what to make of it; consequently, he interprets it variously as confusion, as self-contradiction, as "studied obtuseness," as the kind of thing that gives "poets a bad name with philosophers." "Pope's reaction to a creaking argument is, again and again," Nuttall concludes, "that of the expert rhetorician rather than that of the philosopher."[56] If this is the nadir of modern criticism of Augustan poetry, the fault is not primarily A. D. Nuttall's, for he is simply giving a more audacious rendering of our logocentric impatience with ambiguity and our critical addiction to the vanity of dogmatizing.

Negative Capability, *that is when man is capable of being in uncertainties, Mysteries, doubts. . . .*

—*John Keats (27 December 1817)*

FIVE

Academic Discourse

MODERN CRITICISM cannot read a dialect that Pope shared with his eighteenth-century contemporaries, and because of that disability we can neither read *An Essay on Man* nor understand the enthusiasm of so many great minds for it. This chapter on argument and the next on metaphor attempt to characterize that dialect. To understand why charges that the *Essay* is fundamentally defective as philosophy are wrong or trivial, we must first characterize the worlds of discourse that have dominated judgment of Pope's poem and then describe the alternative.

LOGOCENTRIC REDUCTIONISM

The antagonistic dialects of philosophic and poetic discourse stand opposed most vividly in their differing responses to argument and to figurative language: the nominal components of philosophical poetry. Beginning with the dichotomies structuring initial characterizations of Pope's success or failure in bridging these dialects, the seductive, separatist epistemes are easy to schematize:

Philosophic Episteme	*Poetic Episteme*
Gentleman's Magazine [1734]	
"Nervous Reasoning"	"sublimest Poetry"

Philosophic	Poetic
Dodsley [1734]	
"the Sage's Wisdom"	"the Poet's Fire"
Mémoires de Trévoux [1736]	
"Metaphysics"	"Poetry"
Du Resnel [1736]	
"Argumentation of the abstracted Reasoner"	"Extasies of the Poet"
Silhouette [1736]	
"un philosophe profound"	"un poete sublime"
Crousaz [1737]	
"the Stile of a Philosopher"	"the Language of Homer"
"Natural Philosophy"	"Poetry"
Warburton [1739]	
"Reasoning"	"Rhetoric"
"a *System of Philosophy*"	"a *Poem*"
Bolingbroke [pub. 1754]	
"the philosopher"	"the poet"
"to prove"	"to warm the affections"
"to convince"	"to speak to the heart."

In contrast to the aphorism of the poetic episteme that "Beauty is truth," the motto of the philosophic episteme might well be Boileau's insistence that "Only the truth is beautiful." The contrasting epistemes range philosophers Aristotle, Locke, and Shaftesbury against poets Homer, Addison, and Pope. In the division of the "Operations of the Mind," as Locke designates them in his *Essay* and as Addison quotes them in *Spectator* No. 62, philosophers are accorded judgment and poets wit: "For *wit* lying most in the assemblage of ideas, and putting those together with quickness and variety, wherein can be found any resemblance or congruity, thereby to make up pleasant pictures and agreeable visions in the fancy; *judgment,* on the contrary, lies quite on the other side, in separating carefully, one from another, ideas wherein can be found the least difference, thereby to avoid being misled by similitude, and by affinity to take one thing for another." Judgment with its "exactness," its "clearness," and its "severe rules of truth and good reason," Locke insists, "is a way of proceeding quite contrary to metaphor and allusion; wherein for the most part lies that entertainment and pleasantry of wit." This contrast may explain, he hypothesizes, why "men who have a great deal of wit, and prompt memories, have not always the clearest judgment or deepest reason."[1]

According to this division of the mind's operations, the logocentric philosopher proves by logically ordering literal propositions about the real world; in contrast, the poet persuades by creating a network of artful, bewitching metaphors in literary space. In contrast to the analytic philosopher who discriminates between univocal constative propositions, the synthetic poet analogizes with disseminating, polysemous irony and ambiguity. The philosopher speaks the words that are the objective world; the poet sings the fears and desires that are our subjective selves. Each episteme sanctions a different interpretative authority: the philosopher and the literary critic respectively. Both interpreters are authorized by dialects that define themselves by difference from the other. Consequently, both perceive philosophical poetry as inherently self-contradictory, as generic bastardization or pollution:

Philosophy	*Philosophical Poetry*	*Poetry*
Aristotle's *Metaphysics*	Lucretius' *De Rerum Natura*	Hesiod's Theogony
Newton's *Principia*	Blackmore's *Creation*	*Genesis*
King's *Origin of Evil*		Milton's *Paradise Lost*
Locke's *Essay*	Pope's *Essay on Man*	Sterne's *Tristram Shandy*
Leibniz's *Theodicy*		Voltaire's *Candide*
Shaftesbury's *Moralists*		Addison's *Cato*
Fichte's *Vocation of Man*		Goethe's *Wilhelm Meister*
Kant's *Critiques*		Blake's *Milton*

The philosopher speaks with authority regarding texts in the left column, and the literary critic speaks with authority on texts in the right column.

So problematic are texts in the center that success in philosophical poetry amounts to miracle, and early enthusiasts of the *Essay,* including Voltaire, laud Pope as unique. So unprecedented was a successful marriage of the virtues of philosophy and poetry that the *London Evening Post* credits Pope with having created a new genre (17 March 1733). The default judgment was and remains that crossing discourse borders is contamination. For aesthetic critics like De Quincey, Pope soils Prospero's robe of poetry by wearing it in the muddy miasma of an unimaginative philosophic discourse; for logocentric critics like Crousaz, Pope's philosophy stinks precisely to the extent that it "smells of the poet." While the philosopher interprets logic and the literary critic interprets rhetoric, each disparages or trivializes the other as lack, as either "illogical" (without logic) or "unimaginative" (without images).

The disparagement is unequal and, on the part of literary critics, latent and half-hearted. Both logocentric and aesthetic interpreters concede that the first term of the oxymoron "philosophical poetry" controls the other: whether such a work succeeds or stumbles is always decided according to the canons of philosophical discourse. "From the earliest Years of my Youth," Crousaz revealingly says, "I found in myself a strong Tendency to the Study of LOGIC." Beginning with Warburton's limitation of his defense to the "Reasoning" of the *Essay*—to the *Essay* not "as a *Poem* . . . but as a *System of Philosophy,*" Crousaz's "strong Tendency to . . . LOGIC" has dominated discussion.[2] Even those literary critics who are most appreciative of Pope's disseminating, ironic, paradoxical, and metaphorical play begin by conceding Pope's incapacity for sustained conceptual thinking.

To assess the *Essay* as philosophy, the logocentric critic must first excise its "poemness," translating its "bewitching," "dazzling," disruptive rhetoric into logospeak: an exclusively constative propositional network of complete and consistent rational argument. Logospeak aspires to speak the Logos—the Word that is the world—and the closer the dialect approaches the mathematical afigurality of $E = MC^2$ the better. Pope's "system" must be distinguished from his singing before the logocentric critic can turn "disorder into Order, differences into Identities and words into the Word."[3] This network of constative propositions, its borders policed by logicians wary of rhetorical infiltration, is preparatory to passing judgment on Pope's pretention to write philosophy.

Once the critic's more responsible and rigorous formulation of Pope's "system" is in place, it can be evaluated using the canons of logocentric discourse, the canons constitutive of "philosophy." Pope always fails for the same reasons: (1) obscurity, (2) incoherence, and (3) inconsistency. These flaws are, predictably, the malevolent opposites of logocentric (1) clarity or transparency, (2) coherence around a "first last and main Argument" as befits a "uniform Original," and (3) consistency and univocality, opposites of irony, aporia, figurality—especially of paradox, the epitome of the self-conflictual trope. Ironically, logocentric critics perversely apply Pope's own advice:

> Trace Science then, with Modesty thy guide;
> First strip off all her equipage of Pride,
> Deduct what is but Vanity, or Dress,
> Or Learning's Luxury, or Idleness;
> Or tricks to shew the stretch of human brain,
> Mere curious pleasure, or ingenious pain:
> Expunge the whole, or lop th' excrescent parts
> Of all, our Vices have created Arts:
> Then see how little the remaining sum.
> (II:43-51)

The logocentric critic traces the text by lopping all Derridian "traces." He strips all that is art, all that is poetry rather than philosophy. Poetic discourse is devalued as seductive ornament ("Vanity, or Dress"), as a vicious dialect ("Vice") meant to "bewitch" ("trick"). With the *Essay*'s excrescent rhetoric excised, it only remains for the critic to show "how little the remaining sum."

A THIRD WORLD OF DISCOURSE

Interpretation of philosophical poetry requires another dialect than either the Logocentric or the Aesthetic, and we can discover such a dialect by returning to the first paragraph of Epistle II:

> Plac'd on this isthmus of a middle state,
> A being darkly wise, and rudely great:
> With too much knowledge for the Sceptic side,
> With too much weakness for the Stoic's pride,
> He hangs between.

The third world of discourse lies between what Pope and his contemporaries understood as the Skeptic and Stoic extremes. Commentary has been blind to this third world because instead of seeing the Skeptic and the Stoic as "doctrines seemingly opposite," which Pope intends to steer between, it has separated the two and accounted for them differently. Pope, it is argued, opposes the Skeptics on epistemological grounds and the Stoics on ethical grounds. Representatively, when Maynard Mack speculates briefly on what Pope "may have meant" by steering betwixt doctrines, he opposes Stoicism not to Skepticism but to Epicureanism.[4] By retaining the epistemological focus of the preceding lines, however, we can discover Pope's third world: the dialect of moderated skepticism adopted by the Academics.[5]

In his *Life of Cicero* (1741) Conyers Middleton succinctly distinguishes between Academics, including Cicero, and both Skeptics and Stoics: "the *Academy* held the proper medium between the rigor of the Stoic, and the indifference of the Sceptic: the Stoics embraced all their doctrines, as so many *fixt and immutable truths*, from which it was infamous to depart; and by making this their point of honour, held all their disciples in an inviolable attachment to them. The Sceptics on the other hand, observed a perfect neutrality towards all opinions; maintaining all of them to be equally uncertain . . . thus they lived without ever engaging themselves on any side of a question." The Academics differed from both dogmatisms—apodictic certainty and absolute skepticism—by "adopting *the probable* instead of *the certain*." Thus, Middleton argues, only the Academics "kept the balance in an equal poise between the two extremes; making it their general principle, to observe a moderation in all their opinions."[6]

Perhaps more than any other classical author, Cicero exemplified for Pope and his friends the deliberate union of the philosopher and the rhetorician: the ideal of the good man speaking well by bringing into fruitful conjunction the logical and affective uses of language. Peter Gay contends that Cicero's works shaped the Enlightenment mind "more than any other products of ancient thought," yet critics of the *Essay* have never used Cicero or his Academic colleagues as an interpretive tool.[7] To do so is to understand Pope's contention in the "Design" that his *Essay* is "not *inconsistent*."

Bolingbroke's essays addressed to Pope offer a convenient base from which to approximate succinctly the Academic universe of discourse they share. The Ciceronian moderation that Middleton praises is exactly Bolingbroke's rhetorical stance as he praises Pope for chastising the epistemological presumption that makes theologians and philosophers "dogmatical in the midst of ignorance, and often sceptical in the midst of knowledge."[8] Significantly, in characterizing his own epistemological modesty in contrast to "first philosophers" like Leibniz and Samuel Clarke, Bolingbroke allies with Cicero, Plutarch, Seneca, Montaigne, Erasmus, Bacon, and Locke—all frequent allusive presences in *An Essay on Man.*[9]

The first of Bolingbroke's essays to Pope concerns the "Nature, Extent and Reality of Human Knowledge," and all the essays share the same epistemological assumptions. First, since human knowledge cannot attain certainty, dogmatism is always intellectual error. Instead, "freethinking" is appropriate to the human condition. In support of freethinking he cites Cicero's opposition to dogmatic thinkers "sworn . . . to follow all their lives the authority of some particular school." Second, in Socratic fashion, doubt rather than certainty is the beginning of wisdom. Citing Cicero's *De Natura Deorum* for support, Bolingbroke distinguishes between those who undertake to think for themselves and those who do not. He neither expects nor desires "to see any public revision made in the present system of Christianity"; it is appropriate that the majority who are not freethinkers should "believe in the laws of their country, and conform their opinions and practice to those of their ancestors." In contrast, "those who have the means, and opportunities the others want" should rest on no authority; they should doubt because "Doubt . . . is the key of knowledge." Third, objecting angrily to Leibniz's censure of Locke as a "superficial philosopher," Bolingbroke acknowledges the paradoxical character of human knowledge in what Pope calls our "darkly wise" state. "To speak the truth, tho it may seem a paradox," Bolingbroke asserts, "our knowledge on many subjects . . . must be superficial to be real. This is the condition of humanity. We are placed, as it were, in an intellectual twilight, where we discover but few things clearly, and none entirely."[10]

The dialect for this Socratic uncertainty lay ready to hand in one of the schools that traced its origin back to Socrates himself—Academic skepticism. "The most eminent of all Sects derived from *Socrates,*" Thomas Stanley says in the *History of Philosophy* owned by Pope, "was the *Academick.*"[11] Because the "Academy" embraces so many philosophers over such a long time and because of the substance and methodology of their thought, no succinct, definitive characterization is possible. However, the opposition to both Stoics and Skeptics that Pope and Middleton stress characterizes by contrast the Academic ideology that Cicero, Seneca, Montaigne, and Pope share.[12] The Academic thought that Cicero advocated grew out of the dialectic between the opposed dogmatisms of

Stoicism and Epicureanism on the one hand and the radical skepticism of Pyrrhonism on the other. "There seemeth to be three kinds of Philosophy," Stanley quotes from Sextus Empiricus's *Outlines of Pyrrhonism:* "*Dogmatick, Academick, Sceptick*."[13] Pope liked reading Bayle's *Dictionary* and would have found the identical tripartite division inscribed in Bayle's article on Pyrrho.[14]

Positive and negative dogmatisms are equally wrong; we know less than the Stoics and Epicureans assert and more than the Pyrrhonists deny. Carneades of Cyrene (214–129 B.C.) presents the Academic middle ground in attacking all dogmatic philosophies while maintaining that, although our limited faculties cannot answer ultimate questions, we do have sufficient knowledge to guide our practical and ethical behavior. There are degrees of doubt and probability; thus it is not appropriate to suspend judgment entirely as the Pyrrhonists maintain. However, neither is it appropriate to cease doubting entirely and dogmatize as the Stoics do since "even the highest degree of probability does not guarantee truth."[15] Pope had elaborate treatments of Carneades to hand in both Stanley and Bayle. Quoting from Cicero, Stanley characterizes Carneades as believing "though nothing can be perceived, a wise Man may assent to that which is not perceived; that is, he may *opinionate;* but so as he knoweth himself to opinionate, and that there is nothing which can be comprehended and perceived."[16]

Academics advocated activism in contrast equally to Stoic apathy and Pyrrhonic "*Suspension*" or "*Indisturbance*." In Stanley's *History of Philosophy* Sextus distinguishes "Wherein *Skepticism* differs from the *Academick* Philosophy": "they differ from us, in the dijudication of Good and Evil. For the *Academicks* say, that something is Good and Ill, not after our manner, but as being persuaded, it is more probable, that what they call Good is Good, than the contrary: Whereas we say not that any thing is Good or Ill, as thinking what we say is probable, but without Opinion, we follow the ordinary course of Life, or otherwise we should do nothing. . . . They use in the course of Life, what is Credible, we following Lawes, Customes, and natural Affections, live without engaging our Opinion."[17]

Thus the Academy, like the Enlightenment, has two impulses: one critical and one constructive. The critical impulse is well exemplified by Sextus Empiricus's *Against the Dogmatists*, a title anticipatory of Glanvill's *Vanity of Dogmatizing*. Among the many topoi that this critical strain of Academic thought bequeaths to Montaigne and Pope are the limits of reason and the presumptive folly of anthropocentric teleology. Against Stoic claims for the omnipotence of reason, the Academy marshals a mind-bewildering array of skeptical arguments anticipatory of Pope's Epistle I and Kant's antinomies.

The second, constructive impulse takes over when all positive dogmatisms are down. Directed against negative dogmatism, specifically against the followers of Pyrrho who denied the possibility of any "real" knowledge whatsoever, the constructive strain of Academic thought advocates the "doubtful" system of eclecticism, a commonsense combination of hypotheses from various sources that does not insist dogmatically that only a completely coherent system of absolutely certain knowledge can serve as a basis for action. Anticipating Descartes and Locke, Carneades argues that the clarity and vividness of our sense impressions can give us probable knowledge; further, that probable knowledge is sufficient to formulate a naturalistic ethics superior to any *a priori*, dogmatic ethics. Similarly, Antiochus of Ascalon (130–68 B.C.), who greatly influenced Cicero, advocates an ethical naturalism based on "the things according to nature." Unlike the Stoics, who saw an absolute difference between virtue and other goods, Antiochus maintains that the happy life, although possible through virtue alone, "was completed by bodily and external goods"—Pope's "Health, Peace, and Competence," joys of "Sense" that supplement Virtue (IV:80). Although the natural instincts for self-preservation and self-development are central, Antiochus stresses, the perfection of human nature involves "all parts of it, not only the highest, and also man's relationship to others and to the community"—"Social" as well as "Self-love" in Pope's terminology (IV:396).[18]

The broad characteristics of Ciceronian Academic discourse, then, are these: (1) opposition to epistemological dogmatism in both its guises—claims of certainty (the Stoics) and assertions of absolute ignorance (the Pyrrhonic Skeptics); (2) advocacy of a limited skepticism that pursues practical knowledge through doubt and observation; (3) eclecticism; and (4) ethical naturalism. Critically, their usual method is to "dis-close" the dogmatic pronouncements of their adversaries by demonstrating the impossibility of certain knowledge. Constructively, their method is empirical (not a priori) and eclectic (not dogmatically committed to one "system" or "school"). This is the ideology that tempers the Ciceronian ideal of *humanitas*. "The man who practiced *humanitas*," Peter Gay explains, "was confident of his worth, courteous to others, decent in his social conduct, and active in his political role. He was a man, moreover, who faced life with courageous skepticism: he knows that the consolations of popular religion are for more credulous beings than himself, that life is uncertain, and that sturdy pessimism is superior to self-deceptive optimism." Furthermore, since he has no access to metaphysical certainty, virtue consists in the perfection of his human nature rather than its overthrow or subjection according to dogmatic injunctions either rational (Stoic) or revealed (Christian).[19]

Scholars have argued that Cicero gave the philosophes their philosophy; it is sufficient for our argument that the Academic dialect that Cicero exemplified was a possible mode of discourse for Pope and his contemporaries. There can be no doubt that Pope knew of Academic discourse, as a succinct survey of Pope's admired precursors Erasmus, Montaigne, Charron, and Bayle proves. As Jaroslav Pelikan notes, the pious always suspected that "behind the sarcasm of Erasmus was a basic skepticism about central Christian teachings and an Epicureanism that cloaked itself in Gospel language but was in fact pagan."[20] After *An Essay on Criticism* Pope drew pious criticism for rehabilitating Erasmus, "That *great, injur'd* Name" who became "a lifelong hero for Pope"; he responded to Caryll that his Roman Catholic critics should suffer his praise of Erasmus to pass without objection lest "I should be forced to do that for his reputation which I would never do for my own, I mean to vindicate so great a light of our Church from the malice of past times and the ignorance of the present, in a language which may extend farther than that in which the trifle about criticism is written."[21] In the *First Satire of the Second Book of Horace*, a poem published simultaneously with the *Essay on Man* in 1733 as part of Pope's plan to disguise his authorship, Pope's identification with Erasmus is most aggressively set forth:

> My Head and Heart thus flowing thro' my Quill,
> Verse-man or Prose-man, term me which you will,
> Papist or Protestant, or both between,
> Like good *Erasmus* in an honest Mean,
> In Moderation placing all my Glory,
> While Tories call me Whig, and Whigs a Tory.[22]

Socratic and Ciceronian sympathies are pervasive in Erasmian works popular with Pope's contemporaries. Published in 1725, *Twenty Two Select Colloquies out of Erasmus Roterdamus, Pleasantly representing several Superstitious Levities That were Crept into the Church of Rome In His Days* includes "Reflections upon the Excellencies of *Socrates* and *Cicero*" and praise for the "Purity of Thought" in Plutarch's *Morals*. Tully is such a "*Divine Heathen*," one speaker affirms, that "I had rather lose *all Scotus*, and twenty more such as he, than *one Cicero* or *Plutarch*." Among non-Christians none "came nearer to us, than *Socrates*. . . . What a wonderful Elevation of Mind was this in a Man that only acted by the Light of Nature!" Admiring Socrates' "absolute Resignation of himself to the Divine Will," one speaker exclaims, "*Saint* Socrates, pray for us."[23]

The 1722 preface to *Wit and Wisdom: Or, The Praise of Folly* praises Erasmus for being able to "Polish the roughest *Paradox* with as much Ease and Success as he could *illustrate* the most received *Truth*" and for his successful blend of "Satire and Panegyrick." As modern scholars agree, the voices of Folly and Erasmus are indistinguishable both in their censure of "croaking Stoicks" speaking in the "Mood and Figure" of logic and in their celebration of the Academics: "For all sublunary Matters are enveloped in such a Cloud of Obscurity, that the Short-sightedness of Humane Understanding cannot pry through and arrive at any comprehensive Knowledge of them: Hence the Sect of *Academick* Philosophers have modestly resolved, nothing can be known as *Certain*."[24] Pope wrote to Ralph Allen, "And indeed No true Judgment can be made, here, of any Man or any Thing, with certainty."[25] A year later in his will he bequeathed his own published works and his "eleven volumes of those of Erasmus" to Bolingbroke.[26]

Pope's manifest admiration for Montaigne needs no elaboration here, although it is pertinent to remember that Montaigne explicitly contradistinguishes the Academics from the Pyrrhonians: "The *Academicks* admitted a certain partiality of judgment; and thought it too crude to say, that it was not more likely, that Snow was White than Black, and that we were no more assur'd of the motion of a Stone, thrown by the hand, than of the eighth Sphear. And to avoid this difficulty and strangeness, that can, in Truth, hardly lodge in our Imagination; though they did conclude, that we were in no sort capable of Knowledge, and that Truth is ingulfed in so profound an Abyss, as is not to be penetrated by Human Sight: yet do they acknowledge something to be more likely than others. . . . The *Pyrrhonians* Opinion is more bold, and also more likely."[27] Montaigne illustrates his contrast with a quote from Cicero's *Academica* exactly as Bayle does in his explication of the limited skepticism of Carneades.[28]

In his massive *Dictionary* Bayle defends himself against charges of impiety by contrasting his opinions to the greater skepticism of Montaigne, but Bayle's sympathies are clearly with the Academics, just as the organization of his *Dictionary* is dialectic, eclectic, and doubting. "Neither the Dogmatists nor the Sceptics will ever be able to enter the kingdom of God," Bayle defensively urges, "unless they change their maxims, renounce their wisdom, and make a burnt-offering of their vain systems at the foot of the cross." However, such lip service did little to mitigate his powerful conflation of religion with philosophical dogmatism. "Now I maintain," he writes, "that That Method of the Dogmatists was a bad one . . . for one of their chief Artifices was, to conceal all the Advantages of the Causes, which they opposed, and all the weak Sides of those, which they maintained." In contrast, the "Academics represented the strong and weak Arguments of the two opposite Parties faithfully, and without any Partiality. Religion does not admit of the Character of an Academic; it requires either a Negative or an Affirmative."[29] Bayle includes a long article on Montaigne's friend Pierre Charron and quotes Charron's elaborate interpretation of the engraving that prefaced his *De la Sagesse*. Charron's engraving is the graphic equivalent of Bayle's contrast between Academic wisdom and Stoic or Christian dogmatism. "*Charron* caused *Wisdom* to be represented," Bayle writes, "By a Woman stark naked." To her right are the words "*I know not*, which is her Motto." She stands above four deformed crones representing respectively passion, opinion, superstition, and "false *Science*, an artificial, acquired, and pedantic Virtue, a Slave to Laws and Customs, with a Face puffed up, proud, and arrogant, with lofty Eye-brows, reading in a Book, wherein are these Words, *Yes, No*." The engraving, Bayle slyly says, "seems to favour the *Sceptics*."[30]

Charron himself was more direct, as was evident to Pope's contemporaries in George Stanhope's English translation of *De la Sagesse* as *Of Wisdom*, the third edition of which appeared four years before *An Essay on Man*. Citing Cicero as model, Charron asserts "that while we endure to examine everything . . . yet we yield our Assent to nothing, but what is good and decent, tho' never so universally commended or receiv'd"; consequently the reader should "not look upon all That as Resolved and Determined, and Declared in Favour of, which is only offered to Consideration, Argued and Disputed Problematically, and in the old Academic Way." Subsequently the translator notes that Charron explicitly intends "to write after the manner of the Academick Philosophers; who made it their Business, to represent each side of the Question in its utmost Beauty and Strength, without delivering any decisive Opinion in the case."[31]

Unlike Bayle's *Dictionary* George Stanhope's translation includes Charron's now-famous frontispiece with "*Wisdom* represented by a beautiful Woman. . . . The void space around her signifies Liberty: She looks in a Glass, held by a Hand coming out of a Cloud, at some distance from her, which presents her with the Reflection of her own Face; for Wisdom is employ'd in the Knowledge and Contemplation of her Self." In his subsequent description of the first section in *Of Wisdom,* Charron specifies that wisdom "consists of the Knowledge of a Man's own Self; and the Condition of Humane Nature in general." Citing Socrates as his paradigm, he exhorts us to "*Knowledge* of our Selves. This is in Truth the Foundation upon which all *Wisdom* is built, the direct and high Road to all Happiness." Charron's Academic skepticism and his aversion to Pyrrhonian dogmatism are inscribed beside nude Wisdom: "Upon her Right-side are these Words, *I know not;* not thereby to give Countenance to perpetual Doubt and Skepticism; but arguing, that she is mature and cautious in Deliberating, slow in Determining; not positive or peremptory, but reserving an Ear open for fresh Reasons, and not ashamed to confess, that the best Human Knowledge is still dark and imperfect."[32]

As in his friend Montaigne's essays, presumption is the cardinal vice, the "last and most hideous Line of the whole Picture." Deploying most of the topoi used later by Pascal and Pope, Charron marvels "*That no Creature is more miserable, and yet none more proud than Man. . . .* How then shall we reconcile these Extremes?" Like Montaigne and Pope's "Presumptuous Man," Charron's "*Man* pleases himself, that the Heaven, the Stars, and all that Glorious Movement over our Heads, and indeed the whole Frame and Order of this Material World, was thus created and constituted merely for his sake." The "great instance of humane Presumption," Charron argues, is our dogmatic "believing and misbelieving." This point is illustrated in the frontispiece by the "Four little, deformed, wretched, wrinkled Old Women, bound in Chains" beneath the goddess Wisdom. Passion, Opinion, and Superstition are alike, bound to their dogmatic slumber; but worst and last "there is Learning, which is a counterfeit, artificial, acquir'd, and Pedantic Virtue; a Slave to Laws, and Customs, and Forms; with a swell'd Face, a haughty arrogant Look, bold staring Eyes; and she reads in a Book, wherein is written, *Yea, Nay;* importing the Vanity and Confidence of Learned Men, their Eternal Disputes, and the wide Disagreement of their Notions; and yet the Presumption and Positiveness they betray in the midst of all this Difference and Uncertainty."[33]

The Elwin-Courthope edition of the *Essay* notes the striking parallel between Pope's "The proper study of Mankind is Man" and Charron's "La vraie science et le vrai étude de l'homme est l'homme"; predictably scholars have done nothing to expand the suggestive resemblance.[34] Shortly after citing Socrates as the model for asserting that "the true science and studie of man, is man himselfe," Charron anticipates the "mighty maze" metaphor with which Pope opens the *Essay.* "To consider and understand Man" adequately, Charron says, we must engage in "searching and ransacking every Hole and Corner, every Maze and Labyrinth."[35] There is no question that Pope knew Charron. In his *Epistle to Cobham* "Of the Knowledge and Characters of Men," Pope asks aid of the great experts on human nature:

> What made (say Montagne, or more sage Charron!)
> Otho a warrior, Cromwell a buffoon?
> A perjur'd Prince a leaden Saint revere,
> A godless Regent tremble at a Star?

F. W. Bateson acknowledges that the first half of Pope's epistle is "derived from" the essay that Pope told Spence was Montaigne's best—"Of the Inconsistency of our Actions"; but he sees no evidence in the epistle that Pope knew Charron well "if he read him at all." "No doubt," Bateson concludes, Pope was "merely repeating Bolingbroke's often expressed preference for Charron to Montaigne."

The *Epistle to Cobham* was published on 16 January 1734, another diversion from Pope's anonymous issue of the *Essay;* it is to the *Essay on Man* that Bateson might have looked for Pope's knowledge of Charron. The clues are clear enough. Bateson even quotes Warburton's annotation to Pope's punning tribute to his "sage": "Charron was an admirer of Montaigne; had contracted a strict friendship with him; and has transferred an infinite number of his thoughts into his famous book *De la Sagesse;* but his moderating every-where the extravagant Pyrrhonism of his friend, is the reason why [Pope] calls him *more sage Charron.*"[36] Instead of investigating the shared discourse world that makes the distinction between Pyrrhonism and Charron's more "moderate" and "sage" Academic skepticism, Bateson parallels Warburton's denigration of Charron as an imitator of "an infinite number" of his friend Montaigne's thoughts with Pope as "merely repeating Bolingbroke."

Expanding this shared discourse world, Pope's and Bolingbroke's letters are laced with direct Ciceronian citations, and the Ciceronian analogues noted by editors of the *Essay* could be expanded exponentially. It is more significant that when Pope's poem was initially issued anonymously, the friend to whom the *Essay* was addressed was not "BOLINGBROKE" but "LAELIUS," an encourager of Roman philosophy and an interlocutor in several of Cicero's dialogues; indicatively, *Tully's Laelius: Or, Discourse upon Friendship* was published in 1713. And, of course, Bolingbroke is compared directly to Cicero in Pope's final epistle (IV:240). Moreover, Pope's last verse paragraph perfectly characterizes their shared Ciceronian *humanitas:*

> Come then, my Friend, my Genius, come along,
> Oh master of the poet, and the song!
> And while the Muse now stoops, or now ascends,
> To Man's low passions, or their glorious ends,
> Teach me, like thee, in various nature wise,
> To fall with dignity, with temper rise;
> Form'd by thy converse, happily to steer
> From grave to gay, from lively to severe;
> Correct with spirit, eloquent with ease,
> Intent to reason, or polite to please.
> Oh! while along the stream of Time thy name
> Expanded flies, and gathers all its fame,
> Say, shall my little bark attendant sail,
> Pursue the triumph, and partake the gale?
> When statesmen, heroes, kings, in dust repose,
> Whose sons shall blush their fathers were thy foes,
> Shall then this verse to future age pretend
> Thou wert my guide, philosopher, and friend?
> That urg'd by thee, I turn'd the tuneful art
> From sounds to things, from fancy to the heart;
> For Wit's false mirror held up Nature's light;
> Shew'd erring Pride, WHATEVER IS, IS RIGHT;
> That REASON, PASSION, answer one great aim;
> That true SELF-LOVE and SOCIAL are the same;
> That VIRTUE only makes our bliss below;
> And all our Knowledge is, OURSELVES TO KNOW.

One aspect of this shared Academic skepticism is the "Painful preeminence" of intellect that Pope attributes to Bolingbroke in his catalog of the vanity of human wishes in Epistle IV:

> In Parts superior what advantage lies?
> Tell (for You can) what is it to be wise?
> 'Tis but to know how little can be known;
> To see all others faults, and feel our own.

Momentarily Pope moves from "You" to "our"; but quickly shifts back:

> Painful preeminence! yourself to view
> Above life's weakness, and its comforts too.
> (IV:259–68)

Bolingbroke warned Pope not to show too unequivocally his skepticism toward the comforts of Christianity. You should beware the pious outrage of the "dogmatical," he advises, and safely screen yourself "in the generalities of poetry . . . against any direct charge of heterodoxy," exactly the shared rhetorical stance of Montaigne, Charron, and Bayle.[37]

In another prolix letter to Pope "On the Folly and Presumption of Philosophers, especially in Matters of the First Philosophy," Bolingbroke characterizes the Academics as laudably anti-dogmatic. Unfortunately, "the most absurd system, that is dogmatical, will prevail sooner and longer, and more generally, than that of the second or third academy . . . much sooner than CARNEADES would have persuaded them to lay aside all claim to decision, and to confound true and false in the class of probability." Academics "entertained a perpetual suspension of mind, denied that any certainty was to be had, and disputed at most, about probability," Bolingbroke continues. "Such a man as TULLY [Cicero], who was ostentatious of his eloquence, might very naturally take, as he did, this part upon him." Too soon, however, Platonic rationalism "reassumed the gaudy dress of which it had been stripped in the academy."[38]

Exactly what relation Bolingbroke's essay-letters to Pope bear to the composition of the *Essay* is uncertain. Evidence suggests that Bolingbroke did not begin writing them until he had seen much of the poem and certainly not before the first three epistles were completed; when Bolingbroke's *Fragments or Minutes of Essays* was finally published Pope had been dead ten years. Both Warburton in his excoriating *View of Lord Bolingbroke's Philosophy* (1755) and Maynard Mack in his edition of the *Essay* (1950) assert that any "phrasal influence" between the *Essay* and the *Fragments* is due to Bolingbroke's appropriation of Pope's infectious idiom and not the other way around.[39] What is certain is that when Pope says we must "strip" empty rationalism of its "Dress" (II:44–45) before we can pursue useful knowledge his dialect is one shared with Carneades, Cicero, Charron, and Bolingbroke.

For Bolingbroke the Academics provide the corrective contrast to a metaphysical dogmatism extending from Plato to Leibniz and the British "high priorists." In his formal "letters" to Pope, Bolingbroke is reluctant to describe the Academics as having a "system" and similarly characterizes himself to Pope in a personal letter: "First then I'd assure you, that I profess no System of Philosophy whatever, for I know none which has not been push'd beyond [the bounds] of Nature and of Truth."[40] The same letter quotes from Cicero's *De Natura Deorum*. The web of shared discourse spreads in all directions. While composing the *Essay* in March of 1729, Pope quoted Cicero's *Tusculan Disputations* in a letter to the Earl of Oxford. A few paragraphs after the lines transcribed by Pope, Cicero discusses Apollo's maxim *Nosce te* (know thyself). "Know then thyself, presume not God to scan," Pope begins Epistle II. Socrates avoided "speculation on the so-called 'Cosmos' of the Professors," Xenophon says of the first Academic. "Did these thinkers suppose that . . . it was their duty to neglect human affairs and consider only things divine? Moreover, he marvelled at their blindness in not seeing that man cannot solve these riddles."[41] Pope's "Socratic" "Whatever IS, is RIGHT" immediately precedes "Know then thyself"; and, in the lines immediately following, the "riddle" that is man "hangs between" the Skeptic and the Stoic.

Pope's "Design" informing readers that his focus will be ethical rather than metaphysical suggests another reason why Academic skepticism was an appropriate dialect. "The principle difference between Academic skepticism [the sect of which Valla considers Cicero the spokesman] and Pyrrhonian skepticism [the more radical sect whose principles are preserved in the writings of Sextus Empiricus] is," according to Lisa Jardine, "the *end* it serves." Whereas the Pyrrhonist aims at suspension of all beliefs, the Academic uses the "confrontation between the key beliefs" of different philosophical schools to determine "*levels* of probability in competing systems, and the subsequent ranking is then available as a basis for making specific decisions about conduct."[42] Cicero's *Academica* amplifies this distinction, and in his preface to *De Natura Deorum*, he defends his "Academic method of philosophy," which was "introduced by Socrates." "If it is valuable to follow out a single line of argument, how much more valuable to follow out all of them," Cicero argues. "We in the Academy are not people who will accept *nothing* as true. But we hold that every true perception has in it an admixture of falsehood so similar to the truth that we have no certain criterion of judgement and assent." All we can hope to attain, then, are "probable truths, which although they cannot be proved as certainties, yet may appear so clear and convincing that a wise man may well adopt them as a rule of life."[43] The "Socratic" "Whatever IS, is RIGHT" is just such a hypothetical "rule of life." "I cannot help thinking," Bolingbroke wrote Pope, "that TULLY was more attached to SOCRATES on account of his academical, than his moral character."[44]

Pope was similarly attached to Cicero. When he set aspiring footman and celebrator of the *Essay* Robert Dodsley up as a bookseller in 1735, they named the new shop in Pall Mall "Tully's Head." In 1741, when Pope wanted to give a symbolic remembrance to his revered friend Ralph Allen, he chose his own rare, two-volume folio edition of Cicero's works.[45] Only the rigidity and repetitiveness of the rut that is modern commentary on the *Essay* can explain the wholesale ignoring of the Academic dialect Pope and his circle used with such facility. In his study of the friendship between Pope and Bolingbroke, Brean Hammond mentions a vague "mutual language" of "moderate, antiextremist" views but makes no mention of Cicero or the Academics.[46] Similarly, the best book-length study of the *Essay* does not mention Cicero,[47] and the worst omits Cicero entirely from its section on Pope's "Design and Sources."[48] One explanation for this absence may be that commentary on the relationship between Pope and Bolingbroke has focused almost exclusively on the question of who plagiarized whom rather than on the existence of a shared discourse world with venerable classic roots.[49]

AGAINST DOGMATIC DISCOURSE

Another disincentive for discovering an Academic world of discourse is that it compels us to reconsider traditional intellectual categories that have previously served us as neat pigeonholes. Even against all evidence we want to put Pope in the rationalist hole with Leibniz-Pangloss, distinguished unambiguously from realists like Voltaire and Hume. When a disconcerting contra-indication comes along, Pope's notorious "inconsistency" can be invoked to explain the aberration. The archetype of this approach is Bishop Warburton's explanation, after Pope's death, of why the pious Pope chose the notorious atheist Bolingbroke as his "guide, philosopher, and friend" in the *Essay* (IV:390): ignoring their close friendship, their mutual admiration, and the resemblances between the

Essay and Bolingbroke's writings, Warburton simply asserts that Pope misunderstood Bolingbroke's real meaning. Nuttall treats a recent counter-indication analogously. In the introduction to a facsimile of Pope's surviving manuscripts of the *Essay,* Maynard Mack notes repeated stylistic resemblances to William Wollaston's *Religion of Nature Delineated.*[50] "But Wollaston's thesis," Nuttall ventures, "that the evils and injustices of this world are gross and must be compensated in the next, is in unusually clear opposition to the views of both Bolingbroke and Pope!" Nuttall's exclamation point labels this observation as yet another example of Pope's "notably unsystematic" thought.[51] What has never been suggested is that Wollaston's dialect is that of Academic skepticism—a hypothesis that explains the resemblance between Pope's determination to "steer betwixt extremes" and Wollaston's quotation on his title page of Plutarch's warning against trampling "upon that piety which lies between either extreme."

A much more significant anomaly which criticism has not known what to do with and which it has consequently repressed is a gift given to the author of *An Essay on Man* by the aspiring young philosopher David Hume. In 1739, just as the Crousazian-Warburtonian bluster was at full gale and Pope was being castigated as "the Chief Cause of the present formidable Growth of Vice among Christians," Hume gave Pope an autographed copy of his *Treatise of Human Nature* with handwritten corrections of printer's errors. What is the philosopher who is going to awaken Kant from his dogmatic slumbers doing presenting this lesser Leibniz with his life's work? The answer is that Hume and Pope share the same Academic dialect—a discourse hostile to all dogmatic slumbers.

Although because of our academic pigeonholing it has not been suggested, Hume's *Treatise* is an ambitious if sometimes awkward working out in philosophic prose of the major assumptions of *An Essay on Man.* Hume's tripartite structure—"Of the Understanding," "Of the Passions," and "Of Morals"—parallels Pope's model of the psyche in Epistle II. Most relevant to their shared Academic dialect, however, is Hume's discussion "Of the Sceptical and other Systems of Philosophy." Dogmatic rationalism and total skepticism are mutually destructive extremes, Hume argues: "The sceptical and dogmatic reasons are of the same kind, tho' contrary in their operations and tendency." Although skeptical arguments are powerful weapons against dogmatizing, Pyrrhonian extremism can "subvert all conviction" and "totally destroy human reason." Fortunately, Hume says, "nature breaks the force of all sceptical arguments in time, and keeps them from having any considerable influence on the understanding." The conclusion of Book I of Hume's *Treatise* echoes Pope's admonition in the same position in his argument that "The Proper study of Mankind is Man" (II:2): Hume concludes that "Human Nature is the only science of man." In contrast to Pyrrhonian dogmatism, Hume asserts, a "true sceptic" is equally "diffident of his philosophical doubts, as well as of his philosophical conviction."[52]

Hume's "true" skepticism is the descendant of the "constructive or mitigated" skepticism that Richard H. Popkin sees as "a new way, possibly the closest to contemporary empirical and pragmatic methods, of dealing with the abyss of doubt that the crisis of the Reformation and the scientific revolution had opened up."[53] A confirming characterization of Hume's delineation of Academic skepticism occurs in James Balfour's *Philosophical Essays,* published in Edinburgh in 1768. "As Pyrrhonism represents the intellectual faculty as totally unsound and disordered," Balfour writes in "Of the Academical Philosophy," it is to be "rejected altogether." In contrast, "the solid foundation of the academical philosophy" modestly refuses "too easy an assent" to absolute skepticism and "makes way for the firmer and more perfect reception of truth" by "doubting in matters where there is something obscure or imperfectly apprehended." "Originally derived from the ever memorable Socrates," Academic skepticism is ideally suited to "check the presumption of those men, who, from a conceit of their own genius, boldly decide in matters above their spheres."[54]

The forgotten Balfour advocates a dialect alive from Socrates to his fellow Scotsman David Hume. An ambitious scholarly edition of Cicero's *Academica* was published in Cambridge and London in 1725 and reissued in a second edition shortly after *An Essay on Man* appeared.[55] In Cicero's *De Natura Deorum,* Cotta—an Academic skeptic—functions exactly as does Hume's "philosophical sceptic" Philo in *Dialogues Concerning Natural Religion.* Near the conclusion of the *Dialogues,* Philo says that true skeptics avoid metaphysics and "from a natural diffidence of their own capacity, suspend, or endeavour to suspend all judgement with regard to such sublime and such extraordinary subjects."[56] The ideal that recurs in Hume is that of the philosopher who takes his skepticism seriously but who defeats dogmatism by a return from his speculative chambers to the praxis of public life. Thus are rational excesses corrected by an "appeal to common sense, and the natural sentiments of the mind," and the philosopher "secures himself from any dangerous illusion." Cicero, Hume says, is the archetype. This Ciceronian world of Academic discourse is most effectively delineated in the concluding section of Hume's *Enquiry Concerning Human Understanding* on the "Academical or Sceptical Philosophy." To the "affirmative and dogmatical" on one side and the negative Pyrrhonists on the other, Hume advocates "a more *mitigated* skepticism or *academical* philosophy, which may be both durable and useful." Academic skeptics avoid metaphysics because "they consider the imperfections of those faculties they employ, their narrow reach, and their inaccurate operations," and confine themselves to the study of mankind, knowing that "philosophical decisions are nothing but the reflections of common life, methodized and corrected."[57]

Pope's *Essay* is never mentioned in discussions of Hume or Kant; by trivializing the poem, criticism has written it out of the histories of texts and philosophers it influenced. While some scholars acknowledge the broad debt of Hume and his contemporaries to Cicero, the assumptions of their shared world of Academic discourse are not the interpretive commonplaces they must be for us to read these authors as they read one another. The assumptions of Academic skepticism bind the discourses of Socrates to Cicero to Plutarch to Montaigne to Pope to Hume and to Kant. Nor are these vague, general associations: we can prove that Cicero read Socrates (in the texts of Plato and Xenophon); that Plutarch read Cicero and Socrates; that Montaigne read Plutarch, Cicero, and Socrates; that Bolingbroke and Pope read Montaigne, Plutarch, Cicero, Socrates, and each other; that Hume read Pope; and that Kant read Hume and Pope.

"It seems evident," Hume observes in a footnote to Philo's objection to both the "theist" and the "atheist," that "the dispute between the sceptics and the dogmatists is entirely verbal." In fact, they are equally "haughty dogmatists."[58] Academic discourse may be characterized by its contrast to both the Stoic and Skeptic extremes:

Dogmatic Discourse: Stoics and Pyrrhonians	*Academic Discourse: "Mitigated" Skepticism*
Rationalistic	Empirical
a priori	a posteriori
Supernaturalistic	Naturalistic
Metaphysical	Ethical
Comprehensive	Partial
Dogmatic	Doubting
Authoritarian	Commonsensical

Dogmatic Discourse: Stoics and Pyrrhonians	*Academic Discourse: "Mitigated" Skepticism*
Certain	Hypothetical
Definitive	Tentative
Exclusive	Eclectic
Univocal	Polysemous
Literal	Ironic
Monological	Dialogical
Tautological	Paradoxical
Propositional	Dialectical

The initial opposition between rationalism and empiricism conditions all others because, as Hume points out in the *Treatise,* both "sceptics" and "dogmatists" derive their absolutism from the authority of reason. In contrast, Hume says, a "true," "mitigated" skeptic acknowledges the "manifold contradictions and imperfections in human reason" and yields "to the currents of nature, in submitting to my senses and understanding; and in this blind submission I shew most perfectly my sceptical disposition and principles."[59] In the words of the poet to whom he presented his *Treatise,* "to reason right is to submit" (I:164).

In their use of "submission," Pope and Hume are writing at the interstices of philosophical, theological, and political discourse; and the submission of both to the acknowledged limits of human intellect contrasts strikingly with the theological and political implications of Bishop Butler's injunction that "we form our temper to an implicit submission to the Divine Majesty." Butler's submission is to a supernatural text, to the state church, and to King George as God's anointed; that of Pope and Hume is submission to the limits of human perception and its imperfect access to nature's empirical text. Butler's submission is the traditional theological cognate of rationalistic Christian apologists like Samuel Clarke who "soar with Plato to th' empyreal sphere" (II:23). Pope shares the low estimation of Platonism common in histories of philosophy at the time, conflating abstract rationalism and vacuous superstition.[60] "'Tis certain," Hume agrees, that such "superstition is much more bold in its systems and hypotheses" than true philosophy.[61]

All four characteristics of Academic discourse—skepticism, empiricism, eclecticism, and ethical naturalism—are, in various ways, rejections of the logocentric ideals of absolute clarity, consistency, coherence, and certainty. The "moderated" skepticism of Academic discourse is dialogical rather than dogmatic, attempting to find the probable by selecting the best from contending ideologies: (1) epistemologically the Academic steers between the rational certainty of the Stoic and the total suspension of judgment of the Pyrrhonian; (2) empirically the Academic steers between the emptiness of Stoic rational tautology (Locke's "What is, is"; Kant's "concepts without percepts") and the blindness of Pyrrhonian skepticism's incapacity to organize the sensory ("What is, isn't"; Kant's "percepts without concepts"); (3) eclectically the Academic steers between systems, ignoring their claims of definitiveness and exclusivity to fashion the wisest working hypothesis (Kant's "reflective" or "regulative" rather than "determinant" idea); and (4) ethically the Academic steers between the animalistic amorality of the Epicurean "Beast" (only the "Body" matters) and the "God"-imitating apathy of Stoic Reason (only the "Mind" matters), deriving morals from facts about human nature and the human condition (our "middle state").

Obviously, Academic skepticism threatens any logocentric dogmatism that proclaims it has the exclusive, entire, and absolute last word; and in retaliation logocentrists do a deconstructive critique of Academic discourse, indicting its eclecticism as unoriginal, unsystematic, and confused. The critique was customary long before Lord Hervey attempted to dismiss *An Essay on Man* as a plagiarized "Heap of poetical Contradictions." In characterizing the Academics a century earlier, Montaigne alludes to the criticisms of enemies threatened by their skepticism. Academics have, he asserts, "a way of writing, doubtful in Substance and Design, rather enquiring than teaching. Tho they mix their Style with some Dogmatical Periods. Is not the same thing seen in *Seneca* and *Plutarch*? How many contradictions are there to be found, if a Man pry narrowly into them?" Montaigne speculates that Plato "affected this method of *Philosophizing* in Dialogues . . . that he might with greater Decency, from several Mouths, deliver the Diversity and Variety of his own Fancies. To treat variously of things, is as well as to treat of them, as conformably, and better, that is to say, more copiously, and with greater Profit."[62] Montaigne's description of Academic discourse is quoted from the edition Pope owned. Donald Frame translates the last sentence: "To treat matters diversely is as good as to treat them uniformly, and better: to wit, more copiously and usefully."[63]

In defending the Academics Montaigne defends himself and from his perspective logocentric "uniformity" rids discourse of "contradictions" at the cost of richness and relevance. The world will not be limited to our intellectual categories, and logocentrism's absolutist canons impoverish reality, mandating a thin description in contrast to the eclectic *copia* of the Academics. Logocentrists have no taste for "the eclectic method of philosophizing, long approved by intelligent men and practiced by philosophers of the greatest ability," which Jakob Brucker enthusiastically chronicles in *Historia critica philosophiae* published only a decade after Pope's *Essay.* Pierluigi Donini reminds us that eclecticism has a long history as the ideal alternative to dogmatism. Representatively, Diderot propagandizes in his *Encyclopedie* article "Eclectisme": "The eclectic is a philosopher who, trampling underfoot prejudice, tradition, antiquity, general agreement, authority—in a word, everything that controls the minds of the common herd—dares to think for himself, returns to the clearest general principles, examines them, discusses them, admits nothing that is not based on the testimony of his experience and his reason." The Eclectics, Diderot exclaims, are the only philosophers "who have remained in the state of nature, where everything belonged to everyone."[64]

Cicero is, of course, a classical paradigm of the Eclectic; but Diderot, again following Brucker, praises Montaigne and especially Bayle. In a censored passage from his article on "Pyrrhonic or Skeptical Philosophy," Diderot's characterization of Bayle makes him the epitome of the rhetorically sophisticated Academic: "In order to mitigate his skeptical passages, he always introduced them under the pretext of confirming Revelation, while on the other hand, when the occasion presented itself, he knew full well how to undermine Revelation. He would alternately vindicate reason against authority and authority against reason. . . . He knew too much either to believe or to doubt everything."[65] A less august endorsement of eclecticism occurs in James Puckle's very popular advice book *The Club: Or, A Grey-Cap for a Green Head,* already in its seventh edition by 1743. Rather than adhere dogmatically to one school of thought, Puckle suggests, "Collect out of the Pythagorean—*the Stoick*—the Platonist—*the Academic*—the Peripatetick—the Epicurean—*the Pyrrhonian, or Sceptic*—and all other sects, whatever of method, principles, positions, maxims, examples, Ec. seem most consentaneous to verity; but refuse what will not endure the test of either right reason, or faithful experiment." Puckle designates Socrates as the first eclectic: "Socrates began to draw into some order the confused and obscure imaginations of those that went before him, and to adapt all parts of philosophy to the immediate service of the affairs of men, and the uses of life."[66]

In their admiration of *An Essay on Man,* Voltaire, Rousseau, and the

Encyclopedists acknowledged Pope as a powerful rhetor sharing their discourse world and their ideal of the philosopher as the ethically and intellectually honest man who, in contrast to the "impassive sage of the Stoics," does not cherish the "foolish desire . . . to destroy the passions" but instead "combines a reflective and precise mind with the manners and qualities of a social man."[67] For Voltaire Pope's epistles to his philosopher friend were the perfection of the Ciceronian ideal. On the inside of the back cover of the third volume of Montaigne's *Essays,* Pope wrote: "This is (in my Opinion) the very best Book, for Information of Manners, that has been writ. This Author says nothing but what every one feels att the Heart. Whoever deny it, are not more Wise than Montaigne, but less honest." In the margin of "A Consideration upon Cicero," an essay in which Montaigne quotes both Plutarch and Seneca, Pope puts an X beside Montaigne's observation that Cicero and his imitator Pliny the Younger were both philosophers who "promise Eternity, to the Letters they write to their Friends." Pope addressed four verse epistles to Bolingbroke, and Bolingbroke addressed four prose epistles to Pope. Thus, reading of Cicero, Plutarch, Pliny, and Seneca in Montaigne, Pope's notation links seven Academics.[68]

AGAINST ACADEMIC DISCOURSE

Even a succinct survey of hostile criticism of other Academics illustrates the pervasive preexistence of the "harmonious verse"/"discordant sense" objections made, and still being made, to the *Essay.* One English translator justifies his collection of Cicero's works despite "whatever Imperfections discover themselves in the Reasoning Part" (3rd edition, 1727); another apologizes for adding "distinguishing Terms" to *Tully's Three Books of Offices* by admitting that the "Method of the Discourse, and the Connection or Dependence of one part of it upon another" is "oftentimes very obscure" (5th edition, 1732).[69] As Montaigne before him, Conyers Middleton defends Cicero against objections that he is inconsistent and that his "glorious sentiments" are "flourishes rather of his eloquence, than the conclusions of his reason." Middleton's defense of Cicero's handling of the immortality of the soul and a future state of rewards and punishments is especially relevant to Pope: "We must remember always *that* CICERO *was an Academic*; and . . . he believed it as *probable* only, not as *certain:* and as probability implies some mixture of doubt, and admits the degrees of more and less, so it admits also some variety in the stability of our persuasion."[70]

Middleton merely continues a defense Cicero himself began. In *De Officiis,* from which Pope quotes in his correspondence, Cicero obviates the objection that his skepticism disqualifies him from making any positive ethical assertions. "Now some people raise an objection against me, and those who raise it are learned and studious men," Cicero writes. "Their objection concerns the apparent inconsistency of what I argue. Although I assert that absolute knowledge is impossible, I still cling to my practice of discussing numerous topics, and at this very moment I am reviewing instructions about responsibility." He is not "one of those people whose minds wander illogically, the kind who never understand the nature of their assumptions," he continues. "Just as other writers speak of things as being either certain or uncertain, I say some things are probable and others not probable. This is where we disagree. What prevents me from pursuing statements that seem probable to me or from rejecting improbable statements? By so doing I avoid the violence of flat assertion and escape the dogmatism that is the precise opposite of wisdom."[71] By another route we are back to the famous frontispiece of Pope's "sage Charron."

A dialect that regards "flat assertion" as "violence" bewilders univocal critics, and the tradition of logocentric interpretation that Cicero opposed two thousand years ago continues today in "the form of brief but severe criticism" of Cicero's mode of discourse.[72] The same is true of contemporary and modern criticism of Plutarch, Seneca, Erasmus, Montaigne, Bayle, Locke, Bolingbroke, Hume, and Voltaire—all writers whose assumptions are essentially Academic. Nero criticized Seneca's writings as a heap of sand without the cement necessary to unify the individual grains. A preface to *Plutarch's Morals* contemporary with Pope similarly characterized his eclecticism: "Take [Plutarch] altogether, he appears like a piece of *Mosaic Work,* which consists of several Parts, but all extreamly Beautiful."[73] In "Defence of *Seneca* and *Plutarch,*" Montaigne acknowledges his debt to both and defends them against charges that they are "false Pretender[s] to *Philosophy.*"[74] The very systematic Quintilian judged Seneca's denunciations of vice admirable but censured him for "a lack of critical powers" as a philosopher. Anticipatory of criticisms of Pope's style, Quintilian opines both that Seneca "impaired the solidity of his matter by striving after epigrammatic brevity" and that such a style on such matters is "exceedingly dangerous."[75] Pope's explanation in his "Design" of his choice of "verse, and even rhyme" for a subject that "might have been done in prose" anticipates exactly the criticism Crousaz and Johnson level at his "dangerous" and "bewitching" style. Pope defends his "*conciseness*" as Academic moderation: "I was unable to treat this part of my subject more in detail without becoming dry and tedious; or more *poetically*, without sacrificing perspicuity to ornament, without wandering from the precision, or breaking the chain of reasoning" (pp. 7–8).

Pope's prefatory apology anticipates logocentric trivializations of his philosophical poem, and contemporaneous discussions of Cicero and Seneca had alerted him what to expect. Thus Roger L'Estrange argues that Seneca's "excellency consists rather in a *Rhapsody* of Divine and Extraordinary *Hints* and *Notions*, than in any Regulated *Method* of Discourse." Citing earlier scholars to reinforce his contention that Seneca is "no profound *Philosopher*," L'Estrange retells the anecdote that his writings are "sand without lime," attributing the witticism to Caligula rather than Nero. Although "Divinely Sententious," Seneca would be a sounder philosopher "if his Judgment had been answerable to his Wit." L'Estrange offers his own apology for "Abstracting" Seneca's *Morals* by asserting that "it is not one jot Derogatory to *Seneca's* Character . . . that he made it his Profession, rather to give Lights, and Hints to the World, than to write *Corpus's* of Morality . . . in a set Course of Philosophy"; but the force of his logocentric assumptions is to demote Seneca's text from philosophy to poetry, from "profund[ity]" to "*Rhapsody.*" These are precisely the damning dichotomous terms used by the first enemies of the *Essay;* their characterizations of Pope's poem as a "hodge-podge," eclectic "mosaic" are indistinguishable from hostile eighteenth-century critiques of Plutarch, Seneca, and Cicero.[76]

Appropriately, the same issue of the *Present State of the Republic of Letters* that reviewed the first epistle of the anonymous *Essay on Man* contained a much longer critique of Seneca. The reviewer's criticisms are striking anticipations of the arguments very shortly to be deployed against Pope. "The Style of *Seneca* is abrupt, concise, unconnected, and moving by Leaps and Bounds, quite different from the coherent Style of the most approved Authors," the reviewer insists. Although his "Beauties" are many, he is sometimes "confused and immethodical." He "labours too much to be sententious and acute, and to give a witty turn to every thing," a style that "leads him to use Expressions that strike at first, and upon second Thoughts appear to have little in them." Moreover, the reviewer adds, "*Seneca* sometimes uses general Affirmations and Negations, which strictly speaking are not true."[77] Before *An Essay on Man* appeared, the hostile critiques of Hervey, Crousaz, and Johnson had already been written; they only needed to substitute Pope's name for Seneca's.

Unlike Pope's *Essay,* Seneca has modern defenders. Countering charges that Seneca "too much abounds in Stoic commonplaces" and is lacking in "depth of thought," Anna Motto suggests that "a careful reading . . . reveals eclecticism as the distinguishing mark of his philosophy. . . . By embracing the ethical precepts of all great thinkers, Seneca created his own moral philosophy." To search Seneca for "fixed and unalterable dogmatic principles" is a mistake, for what Quintilian ignored was that Seneca's "aims were practical and that he sought more to direct a conscience than expound a system." In describing the "humorous tactics" of Seneca's style with its enjoyment of "an unexpected turn, a jest, a pun," Motto characterizes a mode of discourse every way analogous to *An Essay on Man.*[78]

Contemporary Academics were liable to the same logocentrisms leveled against Cicero, Plutarch, and Seneca. The 1701 *Abstract Of the most Curious and Excellent Thoughts in Seigneur de Montaigne's Essays* justifies the editor's "Design, to cull out and put together many of the good Maxims in Montaigne's Works, where they are often spoil'd by a mixture of bad Things, or at least stifled under a confus'd heap of Rubbish."[79] The 1700 third edition of Cotton's three-volume *Essays of Michael Seigneur De Montaigne* added a fifteen-page "Vindication of *Montagne's* Essays" to counter the impertinence of "*Scribblers* who have taken pains to make little *Cavils* and *Exceptions,* to lessen the Reputation of this great *Man.*" The objections from which Montaigne is "vindicated" are the identical ones later ranged against Pope: impiety, plagiarism, ignorance of philosophy, and logical confusion and self-contradiction. Claiming that he wrote in a manner "unbecoming a Christian philosopher," his critics protest "that what is most admir'd in *Montagne* is stole from some ancient Author." He is criticized for relying on Seneca and Plutarch to the exclusion of "other Parts of Philosophy, as Physick, Metaphysick and Logick" and arraigned for "the confusion of his discourses." His *Essays,* one critic insists, are "a work wherein Judgment had no share, Because . . . every judicious man loves Order, and there is nothing but Confusion in that whole Book."[80] Like his fellow Frenchman, Pierre Bayle was also arraigned for lack of "system." While it was conceded that he could write intelligently on any position, Bayle was charged with not being able to "reconcile the points of view from which he felt compelled to write upon this author and that." In contrast to Leibniz, a modern philosopher observes, Bayle "was not a systematic mind. . . . It is hard to say what he was; his whole position as between faith and reason is hopelessly confused."[81]

Exactly the same criticisms were and are made of Locke. The frontispiece of Locke's *Essay* bears a relevant quotation from Cicero: "How fine it is to be willing to admit in respect of what you do know, that you do not know, instead of causing disgust with that chatter of yours which must leave you dissatisfied too!"[82] To the fourth edition he added a similarly skeptical verse from Ecclesiastes. Yet when "interpretations differ wildly"[83] on exactly what Locke meant at any point, the common response is to censure Locke as superficial or confused. Bolingbroke's tirade to Pope against those who laud Leibniz while disparaging Locke as unsystematic is an Academic's response to such criticisms.[84] John Passmore pronounces the modern consensus when he lumps Locke with Hume in their shared "insensitivity to consistency."[85] Paul Helm similarly censures Locke as confused and "contradictory."[86]

A few modern apologists defend Locke against allegations identical to the primary criticism still aimed at Pope's *Essay:* that his empiricism is contradicted by his rationalism. Acknowledging an "ironic balance of certainty and uncertainty" as Locke's primary rhetorical strategy, John Richetti contends that the "problem" chastised by earlier commentators as the self-contradiction of a "deferential empiricism" and a "bold rationalism" is resolved once we understand Locke's rhetorical stance.[87] Finding at least four different conceptions of ethics in Locke, John Herman Randall does not denigrate his inconsistency but interprets it as "typical of his extreme moderation and his desire to do justice to all views."[88] There is an increasing rhetorical sophistication evident in the questioning by some commentators on Locke "of the notion of the philosophical text as a peculiarly consistent, homogeneous one." Such a sensitivity to the "literary" dimension of Locke, William Walker suggests, "exerts some pressure against the various critical schematizations of the secondariness of literature to philosophical statement."[89] If so, the effect has not yet served to rehabilitate the status of Pope's text.

A plenitude of complaints analogous to those against both Locke's and Pope's *Essays* has been made against Bolingbroke, Shaftesbury, Voltaire, and Kant. Following the lead of Hugh Blair who objected to Shaftesbury's overuse of rhetorical embellishments, a recent historian objects that his writings are "at crucial points vague and imprecise, to say nothing of Shaftesbury's lack of concern with any consistency, so that it is almost impossible to define his position exactly at any point."[90] A. J. Ayer augments a long file of philosophers who indict Voltaire's philosophical writings for superficiality and lack of originality.[91] Even Kant is criticized as a "poor reasoner" who owes "his enormous influence on the development of moral thinking, in large part to the fact that his moral views are so obscurely expressed."[92]

However, the most suggestive Academic parallel with Pope may be David Hume. Unlike interpreters of Locke, critics of Hume are compelled to come to terms with a recalcitrant, nontransparent, often ironic and polysemous rhetoric. The wary tone of modern commentary was signaled in L. A. Selby-Bigge's influential introduction to the *Enquiries*. "Hume's philosophical writings are to be read with great caution. His pages, especially those of the *Treatise*, are so full of matter, he says so many different things in so many different ways and different connections, and with so much indifference to what he has said before, that it is," Selby-Bigge warns, "very hard to say positively that he taught, or did not teach, this or that particular doctrine. . . . This makes it easy to find all philosophies in Hume, or, by setting one statement against another, none at all."[93] No wonder the aspiring author of this Academic *copia* sent his *Treatise* to the author of an *Essay* ridiculed as an *"Olio, Hodge-Podge Mess of Philosophy,"* "a Heap of poetical Contradictions" distilled from "different Authors, writing upon different Principles."[94]

Donald Livingston adroitly defends Hume as a "dialectical thinker" who is not primarily concerned with organizing true propositions about the world into a system. Instead, Hume arranges propositions in dialectical relationships "to yield insights that may or may not be propositional." Quoting from the *Treatise* Hume sent Pope, Livingston contends that his philosophical method is "an attempt to come to terms with 'principles, which are contrary to each other, which are both at once embrac'd by the mind, and which are unable mutually to destroy each other.'"[95] Human intellect, Hume slyly says, seeks to elude the "contradiction betwixt these opinions" by constructing "a new fiction"; but "Nature is obstinate, and will not quit the field, however strongly attack'd by reason." Hume's "contradiction betwixt these opinions" echoes Pope's "betwixt the extremes of doctrines seemingly opposite"; as with Pope it became Hume's ideological stance. "From accusing me of believing nothing," Hume wrote of his critics, "they now charge me with believing every thing. I hope you will be persuaded, that the Truth lyes in the middle betwixt these Accusations." The "new fictions" produced by metaphysicians reduce the recalcitrant copia of reality into neat logocentric systems only, as Hume's Academical Philo says, by "the utmost license of fancy and hypothesis." The "religious hypothesis" is this kind of fiction, Hume explains in *An Enquiry Concerning Human Understanding*. Physico-theologists hypothesize that "the disposition of things proceeds from intelligence and design, But whatever it proceeds from, the disposition itself, on which depends our happiness and our misery, and consequently our conduct and disposition in life, is still the same." As Pope says, our "bliss depends on what we blame."

Pope concludes his skeptical first epistle with a turning away from metaphysics: "Whatever IS, is RIGHT." Tellingly, the final paragraphs of Hume's *Enquiry* reiterate exactly Pope's justification of the *Essay*'s empiricism as "destroying all school metaphysics" and the "church-writers" dependent on their "systems."[96] Opposing the logocentric canons of a priori rationalism as irrelevant to ethical inquiry, Hume asserts: "Whatever *is* may *not be*. No negation of a fact can involve a contradiction." Consequently, of "divinity or school metaphysics . . . let us ask, *Does it contain any abstract reasoning concerning quantity or number?* No. *Does it contain any experimental reasoning concerning matter of fact or existence?* No. Commit it then to the flames: for it can contain nothing but sophistry and illusion."[97] Hume thus concludes his advocacy for "a more *mitigated* skepticism or *academical* philosophy" that corrects "by common sense . . . the *excessive* skepticism" of Pyrrhonism.[98] In asserting that any metaphysics in which we "tacitly consider ourselves, as in the place of the Supreme Being" distracts us from "moral philosophy, or the science of human nature," Hume echoes exactly the words with which Pope informs us that his *Essay* is a theory of "Morality" founded on "the science of Human Nature."[99] Although criticism has yet to learn to read Pope with the energy and imagination it applies to Hume, philosopher Hume is speaking a dialect he learned from poet Pope.

Pope's frequent use of antithesis, John Wain notes, indicates "a deep emotional need to balance one consideration against another and play off one force against its equal and opposite."[100] Justin Broackes offers a similar summarizing characterization of Hume. His work "is immensely knotty and complex, and any general and sympathetic interpretation will have to take account of opposing tendencies that produce tensions between his views."[101] Although Wain never mentions Hume nor Broackes Pope, these complementary assessments by distinguished British academics in the respective fields of literature and philosophy were published in the same week in 1986. Only the continuing dichotomy and hostility of philosophic and literary discourse worlds are sufficient to explain the almost total absence of Pope in Hume scholarship and vice versa. Finding "striking anticipations of Hume" in Pascal and "since we know that Hume was familiar with Pascal's writing," Alasdair Macintyre suggests, "it is perhaps plausible to believe that here there is a direct influence."[102] How much more plausible, remembering Hume's gift of a hand-corrected copy of the *Treatise*, to see a direct influence from Pope?

There are rare, almost furtive exceptions to this dissociation of Pope and Hume scholarship. In characterizing the "academical philosophy" Hume advocates, Robert Fogelin borrows a phrase from Pope: "I call this *man's middle-state skepticism*, for it reflects the same sentiment as . . . 'An Essay on Man.'"[103] Occasionally a philosopher quotes the *Essay* to epitomize succinctly a Humean concept; one book on Hume goes so far as to use couplets from the *Essay* as epigraphs for each chapter without once mentioning Pope in the body of the text.[104] As far as I know, however, no philosopher attempts anything like a sustained comparison of the two. Alternatively, Hume is nonexistent in even the best scholarship on Pope. Mack's masterful Twickenham edition of the *Essay* mentions Hume once: to distinguish "Pope's work and the work of men like Hobbes or Hume."[105] Similarly contradistinguishing, David Morris's brilliantly suggestive study of the *Essay* warns readers that "Pope was incapable of the sustained conceptual thinking that distinguishes Locke and Berkeley and Hume."[106] More indicatively, Douglas White's survey of Pope's philosophical "Context" nowhere mentions Hume.[107]

A great truth is a statement
whose opposite is also a great truth.

—Niels Bohr

SIX

Paradox Against the Orthodox

HE "MIDDLE-STATE" or "mitigated" Academic skepticism that Pope eloquently exemplifies expresses itself methodologically as an eclectic dialectic "betwixt the extremes of doctrines." It is the energized opposite of the "stasis of optimistic theology" that modern criticism chisels on the *Essay*'s tombstone.[1] Remembering Livingston's characterization of Hume's "dialectical" method and the "ironic balance of certainty and uncertainty," which Richetti identifies as Locke's primary rhetorical strategy, we should not be surprised that Edward Young found that Pope's glorious poem ended without giving us "certain knowledge."[2] Wishing that Pope had "pursu'd the track, / Which opens out of darkness into day," Young supplements the *Essay* with his pious *Night Thoughts*, extrapolating from those "frequent Intimations of a more sublime Dispensation" that Warburton finds throughout the poem.[3] Crousaz objects to being "murdered with Questions" and "insinuations" only to be left guessing on the most important metaphysical matters.[4] Much criticism of the *Essay* has been extrapolation of surface hints and intimations with deforming disregard of Pope's mode of discourse.

Maurice Natanson argues that the specific arguments philosophers use are not necessarily synonymous with the "underlying structures" of their argumentation. Instead, concrete arguments "are rooted in a more primordial ground, the fundamental intent of the philosopher." Only when that intent is "shared and sympathetically taken up" can real dialogue between text and reader occur.[5] Natanson speaks exclusively of philosophers, but literary phenomenologists make the same point only slightly differently: the author's mind is the deep structure of the "intentional object" that is the text. If we force the text into our discourse categories rather than empathetically entering into those of the text, we misread. Pope's cast of mind animates the *Essay* just as God animates the great text of nature. Surface "hints" are "parts of one stupendous whole"; but Pope "fills, he bounds, connects, and equals all" (1:267, 280).

Modern criticism cannot sympathetically share Pope's "fundamental intent" because it does not acknowledge his Academic dialect; instead of respecting his "bounds," it erects interpretative borders of its own. The "fundamental intent" of most criticism, I argued earlier, is to put Pope in his place, to stop a disorienting dissemination of meanings, to pronounce the final word on the *Essay*. That proving impossible, Pope is pronounced out of bounds and stigmatized as a philosophical simpleton oblivious to incoherence and self-contradiction. That Pope could aphorize against scanning God "and then go on to construct a massive system of interdependencies between all things," Nicholas Hudson writes, "is one of the great curiosities of eighteenth-century literature."[6] Criticism has forgotten that Pope heard every such objection now made to the *Essay* and yet made only a few, insignificant changes during the many printings during his life and obliged his literary executor not to alter a word of the text after his death; but if it were remembered that would merely reinforce critics' assessment of Pope's incompetence.

Bolingbroke, Hume, Voltaire, Rousseau, Kant and most of Pope's contemporaries could read the *Essay* because they knew and often shared the dialect of middle-state skepticism. Middleton's *Cicero*, for example, was a best-seller, and Hume's *Enquiry* was scandalous rather than the dead-born flop his *Treatise* had been. All three were published while the *Essay* was phenomenally popular. Most of Pope's Crousazian contemporaries who damned the *Essay*'s impiety and most Warburtonians who praised its piety knew the Ciceronian dialect, and their coercive interpretations can be seen as deliberate actions in a holy war against the incursions of uncertainty. As Thomas Sloane recently documents, the antagonism of Christianity to Ciceronianism was habitual and acrimonious during the Renaissance.[7]

CICERONIAN *CONTROVERSIA*

Suggestively, a recurrent Christian criticism of the Ciceronian dialect was that it mixed the discourse modes of philosophy and poetry. In contrast to Christian dogma, Ciceronian *controversia* is a play of arguments avoiding "anarchy at one extreme and dogmatism at the other," a method of "controversial thinking" that "revels in contraries and ambiguities and delights in verbal irony." Early Christian theologians were frustrated with Cicero's facility at "capturing truth with an echoic and associative language" just as Crousaz is frustrated with Pope's "Homeric" style.[8] The Academics were "terrible" to their enemies, Bolingbroke writes Pope, because their avoidance of absolutes left their adversaries nothing to attack; and, as we saw earlier, he recommends the same ambiguous dialect to "screen" Pope's "freethinking" from direct charges of impiety.

Out of context, Bolingbroke's caution suggests rhetorical shiftiness; it seems to imply that Pope might have said what he meant unambiguously were it not for the consequences of candor. This, however, is the traditional hostile misreading of the Academic dialect as deliberate obfuscation, as a rhetoric disguising atheism. In fact, Cicero believed that he deserved a place among philosophers precisely because his dialect uniquely wedded wisdom *(sapientia)* with rhetorical power *(eloquentia).* Academics presume that univocal dialects deform reality because no language but "the fluid, paradoxical and ironic, language of the imagination, uniting as it does reason with emotion, can capture multiform truth."[9]

Irony, paradox, and metaphor are each simultaneously tensive and supplementary; they are the deep structures of Academic discourse because they are the discursive corollaries of our own human duality. In Academic discourse even the seemingly most straightforward constative proposition is problematic; in essence, Socrates' entire project was to expose the problems of univocal discourse. The destructive impulse of Socratic-Academic doubting has recently been rechristened deconstruction, and the parallels may help rehabilitate Pope's reputation as philosopher. One fundamental assumption of deconstruction, Vincent Leitch argues, is that "supplementarity names the condition of humanity."[10] We desire certitude but can only achieve it by coercive misreading because our dichotomies are not resolvable. In deconstructing Rousseau's primacy of nature over culture, Derrida is showing us something Rousseau and the Academics already know: as Pope says, conditioning human knowledge is always "an *If* instead of a *Since.*" In Pope, however, this qualification is no recipe for Pyrrhonian "disengagement" as many critics of deconstruction charge today. Rather, Pope embraces the "Ciceronian" tradition, recommended by Terry Eagleton and others, "in which the rhetorical arts are inseparable from the practice of a politics."[11] His ideological engagement is one reason Pope's philosophical attackers, like Lord Hervey, were also his political antagonists, and his philosophical friends, like Bolingbroke and Chesterfield, were his political allies.

Irony, paradox, and metaphor hold dichotomies in tension. Each element in each dichotomy supplements the other: presumption-despair, theism-atheism, optimism-pessimism, celebration-satire, rationalism-empiricism, freedom-fate, order-chaos. Each element is traced through with its counterconcept; each element is simultaneously written and erased, both asserted and doubted. Deconstruction argues that this is the condition of all discourse; Academic discourse presumes that it is. Pope deconstructs "Hope" by placing it in a rhetorical house of mirrors: the hope of "future bliss" is our "blessing now," an eternal spring of what "never Is, but always To be" (I:94–96). Modern criticism complains that Pope "never made up his mind" whether he said "Hope" as a prayer or a sneer. On such matters, Pope knows that minds are only made up by interpretive violence. Pope wrote "Hope" and traced it through with its supplement "Hopeless." It is that doubleness that creates the tone of "cosmic" irony—a resigned, wistfully comic melancholy at man's eternally disappointed optimism:

> Hope springs eternal in the human breast:
> Man never Is, but always To be blest.

Crousazians and Warburtonians want definitive pronouncement on whether there is or is not an afterlife. The interpretive furor over whether the soul is "at home" or "from home" perfectly illustrates the genius of Pope's supplementary irony. So balanced is this undecidable dichotomy that in a poem of 1,300 lines Pope's critics feel compelled to base their interpretation of whether Pope believed in an afterlife on one preposition.

Rousseau's letter to Voltaire praising the *Essay* stresses the hypothetical nature of human knowledge with its interrelated "IF" clauses. As his letter to Caryll makes clear, in Pope's Academic dialect every "IF" deliberately summons its supplementary "IF NOT":

> *If* to be perfect . . .
> (I:74)

> *If* the great end be human Happiness . . .
> (I:149)

> *If* plagues or earthquakes break not Heav'n's design . . .
> (I:155)

> Of Systems possible, *if* 'tis confest
> That Wisdom infinite must form the best. . . .
> (I:43–44)

> And *if* each system in gradation roll,
> Alike essential to th' amazing whole. . . .
> (I:247–48)

Although there is "an *If* instead of a *Since* that would overthrow his meaning," Pope writes Caryll, "his whole paragraph proves him quite Christian in his system."[12] Pope's play on belief "system" (metaphysics) and solar "system" (physics) reinforces his censure of the metaphysical presumption of "proud Science" in soaring "with Plato" (II:23).

Systems are suspect for the Academic skeptic; one thrust of the *Essay,* Pope said, was to destroy "school metaphysics" and the "systems" of "church-writers" dependent on them. Fifteen years earlier and five years before the *Essay* appeared, Pope had another conversation with Spence that has interesting implications for Epistle II. "As LEspirit, Rochefoucauld, and that sort of people prove that all virtues are disguised vices," Pope confided, "I would engage to prove all vices to be disguised virtues. Neither, indeed, is true, but this would be a more agreeable subject and would overturn their whole scheme."[13] Jacques Espirit's *Discourses on the Deceitfulness of Humane Virtues* (trans. 1706) systematizes a pessimistic, brutish Hobbesian-Mandevillean self-love just as Francis Hutcheson's *Inquiry into the Original of Our Ideas of Beauty and Virtue* (1725) systematizes an optimistic, Edenic Lockean-Shaftesburian social benevolence. The absolutist insistence on finding the true "Original of Our Ideas" correlates with Lord Hervey's indictment that Pope is not a "uniform Original." Pope distrusts such unitary "Origins" for the same reasons that Hume dismisses rational "fictions" that close the book of life by fiat or that Derrida dismantles the "myth" Rousseau makes to get back to a nature antecedent to culture.

Pope's performative rhetoric sets out to "destroy . . . systems" and "overturn . . . schemes" because "Neither, indeed, is true." His playful undercutting alternatively bewilders and badgers logocentrists. Thinking that Pope, at the end of Epistle II, is "proving" that "not a vanity is giv'n in vain" (II:290), Crousaz cannot conceive that Pope might have any aim more complex than explicating his own "system." Enraged at the impiety of making "the Virtues and Vices of Mankind equally Parts of the Divine Plan," Crousaz concludes, "The Verses that close this Epistle seem written wholly in favour of this System, nor can easily be taken in any other Sense."

Searching always for constative certainty, Crousazians are committed to "systematic" misreading of an Academic dialect. Confronted with disorienting irony and paradox, the philosopher's aversion to figurality becomes full-blown nightmare: meaning ("all virtues are disguised vices") is threatened by supplementary anti-meaning ("all vices . . . disguised virtues"). "Have Poets so extensive a Privilege," Crousaz complains, "that they may boldly assert the wildest Paradoxes, provided they utter them in sounding Language?" "Mere contradiction," "stark inconsistency," "intellectually inept," "thoroughly confused," "the very nadir of Augustan poetry," modern Crousazians concur, "notably unsystematic." "Not the style of Philosophy," Crousaz judges. "The sort of thing that gets poets a bad name with philosophers," modern Crousazians nod.[14]

"Irony" derives via the Greek *eirōneia* from *eirōn*, a dissembler in speech, and to logocentrists like Crousaz poets inevitably dissemble because "the language of *Homer*" is a dialect of paradox and metaphor deliberately devised to hold multiple meanings in tension. "Proud man, what a paradox you are to yourself," Pascal asserts. The "tangle" of the human condition cannot be resolved by any absolutist discourse, he says anticipating Pope and Hume, for "nature confutes the sceptics, and reason confutes the dogmatists." He characterizes his own rhetoric: "I always contradict [man], till he understands that he is . . . incomprehensible."[15] The closer we look at Pope's text the more resonant are those "enigmatic undecidables" that Academic discourse and deconstruction put *sous rature*.

A contentious epitome of Pope's Academic irony is his allusion to Matthew 10:29–31, the Biblical text that Aubrey Williams argues was the one most frequently cited in Pope's time "to expound God's providential control of worldly events."[16] There is no need to fear those who can kill the body for they cannot kill the soul, the gospel says: "Are not two sparrows sold for a farthing? and one of them shall not fall on the ground without your Father. But the very hairs of your head are all numbered. Fear ye not therefore, ye are of more value than many sparrows." "If [man] exalt himself," Pascal says in *Pensée* 418, "I humble him." Pope undercuts the comfortable anthropocentrism of the revelatory text by supplementing it with the cosmic perspective of one

> Who sees with equal eye, as God of all,
> A hero perish, or a sparrow fall,
> Atoms or systems into ruin hurl'd,
> And now a bubble burst, and now a world.
> (1:87–90)

The indignant author of *Common Sense* finds such indiscriminate "Order" indistinguishable from chaos, and calls for a God with "Pity . . . for the Miserable" rather than an emotionless cipher.[17]

Where Christians wish a Father, Pope hypothesizes a Force that "Warms in the sun, refreshes in the breeze / Glows in the stars, and blossoms in the trees." Where Christians require a Special Providence for "Miserable" man, Pope offers an "equal" Order devoid of special dispensations: "To him no high, no low, no great, no small; / He fills, he bounds, connects, and equals all." Elwin is still uncomprehendingly irate over a hundred years later. These lines "appear to be a false jingle of words which neutralize the whole of Pope's argument," he writes. "Pope's language throughout this epistle is unmeaning."[18] A hundred years later still, a modern Crousazian greatly admires the energy of such an unPopian pantheistic, "Romantic" image of "an organic universe" but assumes that the author did not understand what he was writing. The modern Crousazian's Pope is a philosophical dunce with intermittent surges of poetic power. When such a passage is effective, the modern Crousazian typically opines that "the energy of Pope's poetic genius perhaps works against the bias of his intellect" and his "style reflects, with great art, the deliberate anaesthesia of the argument."[19]

Crousazian fulminations against what Elwin calls Pope's "equivocal language" document the discomfiture of logocentric dialects by Pope's Academic skepticism as they see their "systems into ruin hurl'd." In *A Dialogue on One Thousand Seven Hundred and Thirty-eight,* one of the many attacks on Pope after the *Essay,* a speaker predicts that if Pope's enemies remain silent for fear they might be pilloried in one of his subsequent satires then both church and state face ruin:

> Adieu then Virtue! Sense and Truth, good-night!
> If fear of Scandal all your Friends can fright . . .
> Religion soon to Scepti[ci]sm shall yield,
> Which op'ning to wild Wits their wish'd-for Field,
> Our ancient Constitution, sacred Laws,
> And all that Wisdom's Approbation draws,
> Shall be wip'd out.[20]

The Heideggerian destructive impulse of Academic discourse that pits it against all Panglossian onto-theo-logocentrisms provocatively parallels the "Semiotic" undermining of traditional symbolic orders described by

Julia Kristeva.[21] Like Pope's perversion of Matthew, such semiotic play "threatens to split apart received social meanings" and wages a kind of guerrilla warfare against "all fixed, transcendental significations."[22] "Nothing is so plain," Pope wrote tongue-in-cheek about the anonymous author of the *Essay,* as that "he uses the words *God,* the *soul* of the *World,* which at first glance may be taken for heathenism, while his whole paragraph proves him quite Christian in his system."[23] This polysemous playing of "systems" off against one another is not some newfangled hypothesis but the self-acknowledged essence of Pope's Ciceronian *controversia.*

A dichotomous rhetoric that counterbalances Christian Father with "heathen" Force while knowing that "Neither, indeed is true" disconcerts dogmatism exactly as Pascal predicts. Pope's penchant for putting absolutes *sous rature* is done literally in the sixth line of Epistle I describing "all this *Scene of Man.*" The first edition reads:

> A mighty Maze! of walks *without* a Plan.
> A Wild . . .
> Or Garden . . .

All subsequent editions read:

> A mighty maze! but *not without* a plan.
> A Wild . . .
> Or Garden . . .[24]

Following the lead of a host of earlier Crousazians, Nuttall insists that "this plan is the subject of the poem and we must therefore explore it." Applying the template of rational optimism as what "Pope, perhaps confusedly, had in mind," the self-characterized "Crousazian" demonstrates Pope's "unsystematic" failure for 200 pages.[25] Yet just as Derrida argues that there is no unsupplemented original nature but only a human desire for it and so we must write "nature" and then cross it out, yet keep both "nature" and its erasure, so Pope both writes "without a Plan" and "not without a plan," thereby putting providential order *sous rature.* The simultaneity of world as a "Wild" "without a Plan" and as "Garden" "not without a plan" blinds Crousazians intent on doctrinal product and oblivious to rhetorical process. Perhaps Pope "had no other End than in being inconsistent," Crousazians complain, for that "seems to be his Rule of

Writing" (1751).[26] "An inner duplicity" haunts the *Essay*, they object; what begins "as a passing ironic paradox" becomes "at the major level of argument . . . mere contradiction" (1984).[27]

Something of the intertextual complexity of Pope's "Socratic" "Whatever IS, is RIGHT" has been discussed earlier. However, because by a distorting Crousazian interpretive focus on Pope's "metaphysics" of rational optimism it has become the most famous line in the poem, we should look closely at another "source" for the most notorious tautology/paradox in English literature. Pope annotated Dryden's version of *Oedipus*.[28] Anticipating the plague and earthquake with which Pope discomforts Presumptuous Man's arguments in Epistle I, Dryden has his Thebans debate whether their plague does not call into question the assumption that the gods have a plan "which can control the malice of man's fate." One Theban takes comfort from a rational fatalism:

> There's a Chain of Causes
> Link'd to Effects; invisible Necessity
> That what e're is, could not but so have been;
> That's my security.

This fatalistic "what e're is, must be" gives way to wiser words. Asked if the gods are deaf to the suffering of mortals, the blind seer Tiresias responds in phrases that read like an intertext between Milton's "justify" and Pope's "vindicate":

> The Gods are just.
> But how can Finite measure Infinite?
> Reason! alas, it does not know it self!
> Yet Man, vain Man, wou'd with his short-lin'd Plummet,
> Fathom the vast Abysse of Heav'nly justice.
> What ever is, is in it's causes just;
> Since all things are by Fate. But pur-blind Man
> Sees but a part o' th' Chain; the nearest links;
> His eyes not carrying to that equal Beam
> That poizes all above.[29]

Critics contest whether at this point or that Dryden is Pyrrhonian or fideist or Roman Catholic, but certainly there is scarcely a phrase of this passage that has not been drawn into Pope's powerful vortex.

Ironically and appropriately, as "What ever is, is just" becomes—in quotes—"'Whatever IS, is RIGHT,'" Pope's "optimism" is traced through with the Sophoclean tragic sense; just as the Leibnizian-Panglossian "all is for the best" is traced through with the Lockean-Bolingbrokean dismissal of the "what is, is" tautologies of "first philosophy"; just as Stoic rational certainty is traced through with the Pyrrhonism of "pur-blind Man." Pope's is the dialect of Academic doubt; whatever enriching supplements we seek out, Pope himself insisted that "Whatever is, is right" was "the saying of Socrates." And certainly the Socrates of Plato's *Apology* is the heroic archetype of Academic doubt. Eschewing interest in "natural philosophy," he is on trial for having used his doubting, deconstructing dialect against the "systems" of Athens. Characterizing his "wisdom" as not "supernatural" but such "as may be attained by man," Socrates is neither dogmatist nor atheist but skeptic: "I neither know nor think that I know." Condemned, he concludes his apologia with a resignation traced through with irony: "these things . . . are well."[30]

DARK WISDOM

Montaigne seeks to emulate Plutarch's "doubting and ambiguous manner" and Cicero's "Academic doubt": "I must speak in such a way as to affirm nothing; I shall search into all things, doubting most of them and mistrusting myself." The middle course of the Academics is appropriate, Montaigne stresses, because "the extremes of our investigations always fall finally into dazzlement."[31] Nothing is more dazzling in Pope's rhetoric than the tensions he establishes between the doctrines he "steers betwixt." After careful computation, Martin Kallich concludes that antithesis occurs about every four lines in the *Essay* and, consequently, "may rightfully be considered the dominating figure of the whole work."[32] David Morris insightfully reasserts this observation with special attention to paradox, which he sees as Pope's governing trope: "paradox is his way not of recommending or embellishing truth but of recognizing and expressing it."[33]

Logocentrism hates paradox for exactly the reason that William Spanos suggests: it unsettles the reified beliefs that are the hallmark of the "spatial/metaphysical imagination." The "metaphysical" critics Spanos attacks repress the anxiety of their human "temporality" by ordering texts according to the "disinterested" categories of logic and mathematics.[34] Crousazian theologians and "first philosophers" are, of course, the unrecognized antecedents of Spanos's modern metaphysical critics; their fulminations against Pope's "wildest Paradoxes" (Crousaz 1739) and their consequent coercive interpretation of "ironic paradox" into "mere inconsistency" (Nuttall 1984) are evasions of a threatened symbolic order from what Johnson designates as "unprofitable and dangerous enquiries, from difficulties vainly curious, and doubts impossible to be solved."[35]

Contradiction as rhetorical device has been fundamental to skeptical discourse from the beginning. The paradoxical "modes" of classical skepticism are techniques for inducing rational humility, Pope's intellectual "Modesty" (II:43). The statements of the Pyrrhonists, Diogenes Laertius generalizes, are "a record in which everything is set alongside everything else and is found in the comparison to contain a great deal of anomaly and disturbance." Like modern deconstructors, "to arrive at the oppositions inherent in inquiries [skeptics] would first demonstrate the modes in which things convince us, and then use the same modes to destroy our conviction about them." Sextus Empiricus catalogs the modes. The seventh he cites uses empirical evidence from "existing objects" to force us to acknowledge the relativity of our perceptual powers and, thereby, to induce us "to suspend judgment."[36] This tradition of skeptical *paradoxa* accords with the Academic Cotta's summary near the end of Cicero's *De Natura Deorum:* "Now all this that I have said about the nature of the gods was not said in denial of their existence, but to make you realize how difficult a question this is and how dubious is every theory which has been evolved to answer it." Cotta's disturbing juxtapositions convince Velleuis that "even dreams have more substance than a Stoic discourse on the nature of the gods."[37]

The performative play of Pope's text, which disquiets the dogmatic, sustains the wise, as Hume, Voltaire, Rousseau, and Kant testify. For an Academic, paradox is not irresponsible irrationality but a trope that epitomizes all that middle-state humanity knows. Paradox cannot be deconstructed into mere contradiction because, as Pascal says, "Contradiction is not a sign of falsity, nor want of contradiction a sign of truth." Giving the reverse formulation of Pope's "neither, indeed, is true," Pascal writes: "All the principles of sceptics, stoics, atheists, etc., are true. But their conclusions are false, because the opposite principles are also true."[38] A later scientist, Niels Bohr, called this the principle of complementarity, insisting that profound truths had as their opposites profound truths.

Humans "hang between" such antinomies, which, as Hume says, their discomforted reason wishes to resolve with a new "fiction"; Pope's Academic rhetoric, in contrast, utilizes paradox both to refute and reveal. One precedent for Pope's dual use of paradox is Cicero. In a 1727 third edition of *His Stoical Paradoxes*, Cicero contrasts himself to the "rigid *Stoick*" Cato but undertakes to defend some of their paradoxes as profound truths. "I look upon those *Paradoxes*, as they call them," Cicero writes, "as *Socratic* Doctrines, and very certain Truths." Significantly, the first two paradoxes anticipate Pope's *Essay:* Cicero's "I. VIRTUE *is our only Good*" forecasts Pope's penultimate line "VIRTUE only makes our Bliss below" (IV:397), and Cicero's "II. *The full Happiness of Life is compriz'd in* VIRTUE" forecasts Pope's "'Virtue alone is Happiness below'" (IV:310). As with his "Socratic" paradox "Whatever IS, is RIGHT," Pope puts "Virtue alone is Happiness" in quotation marks, perhaps suggesting it as another Ciceronian "*Socratic* Doctrine."[39]

Both the critical-discomforting and the creative-comforting uses of paradox can be traced to a common source before Socrates and Cicero, one from whom both the Stoics and the Skeptics traced their heritage: Heraclitus.[40] Pope's edition of Stanley's *History of Philosophy* devotes its tenth part to "the HERACLITIAN Sect" and is prefaced with an engraving of Heraclitus thinking.[41] To have the "real" knowledge that lies between Stoic and Pyrrhonian extremes, Academics adopt the binocular vision of paradox. Anticipating Bohr's principle of complementarity, Heraclitus offered his principle of the unity of opposites as an alternative to the rationalist Principle of Excluded Middle according to which "either p is true or not-p is true, with no third possibility."[42] The dialect Heraclitus offered was so appealing to skeptics that Stanley's *History* quotes Sextus's explanation "Wherein *Scepticism* differs from those Philosophical Sects, which are most like it; and first wherein it differs from the Philosophy of *Heraclitus*." He differs from the Pyrrhonians because "*Heraclitus* asserted dogmatically, concerning many things not-manifest." Those err who say "the *Skeptick* Institution is the way to the *Heraclitian* Philosophy, Because that *Contraries appear in the same Thing*, is precedent to *Contraries are in the same Thing*" for true "*Skepticks* say, *Contraries appear in the same Thing*, and the *Heraclitians* go on farther, affirming *Contraries are in the same Thing*." Two pages later Sextus proceeds to distinguish the "*Academicks*" from true skeptics on the same grounds of positive affirmation.[43]

The ringing paradoxes that conclude Pope's first epistle are the modes of the Heraclitian's and the Academic skeptic's mind. They are explicit polarities, inscriptions traced with their supplementary erasures:

All Nature is Art.
All Chance is Direction.
All Discord is Harmony.

The last paradox of *discordia concors* takes us most directly to Heraclitus, and it is also the paradox that animates the deep structure of the *Essay*, an inherently conflictual energy equally opposed to Stoic "apathy" and Pyrrhonian "indisturbance" and, consequently, allowing no "calm resolution" of the kind Crousaz complains the *Essay* frustrates. Pope's pervasive analogy between physics (our "objective" perspective) and psychology (our "subjective" perspective) is based on the paradox that all stability is strife:

ALL subsists by elemental strife;
And Passions are the elements of Life.
(I:167–70)

The "balance of the mind," Pope says, is achieved by "well accorded strife" (II:121). "Such is the World's great harmony" that the same balance works at the social level, as

jarring int'rests of themselves create
Th' according music of a well-mix'd State.
(III:293–95)

Images for this harmonic discord vary from the organic pantheism of God as the soul of the world to a mechanistic, Newtonian gravitational "attraction":

Look round our World; behold the chain of Love
Combining all below and all above.
See plastic Nature working to this end,
The single atoms each to other tend,
Attract, attracted to, the next in place
Form'd and impell'd its neighbour to embrace.
(III:7–12)

From microcosmic atoms to the macrocosmic movement of "worlds unnumbered," the same paradox reigns.

Discordia concors has a rich history in Western thought, both with pagans and Christians.[44] At the root of that history is Heraclitus. Characterized by Aristotle as frequently ambiguous and by Theophrastus as sometimes blatantly self-contradictory, Heraclitus begins the line of poet-philosophers that leads through Cicero and Seneca to Pascal and Pope. Author of "terse and intentionally memorable prose sentences composed with great attention to rhythm," Heraclitus is ambiguous and paradoxical not to be obscure but because he "believed his style of utterance to be uniquely suitable to his subject-matter."[45] Epistemologically, he is skeptical: "There is no man that has seen, nor any that will ever know, the exact truth concerning the gods and all the other subjects of which I speak." In pursuing knowledge, a cautious empiricism is best. "I value highest," he says, that which "can be learnt of by seeing and hearing." Convinced by observation that the universe is a unity, he says "it is wise to concur that all is one."[46] Almost every Heraclitian fragment prefigures an idea or an image in Pope's *Essay:* "All are but parts of one" (I:267).

Many of the fragments that survive describe paradoxes drawn from human experience. Rhetorically intent upon demonstrating the unity of the universe while acknowledging the diversity we perceive, Heraclitus insists that "certain opposites [are] not merely coexistent or mutually interdependent, but identical with each other." He seeks to show, as he says himself, "how what is at variance is in agreement with itself: *a back-turning structure* [*palintropos harmonie*] like that of the bow and the lyre." He succinctly illustrates this *discordia concors:* "But one must know that war is universal . . . and that justice *is* strife." Similarly anticipatory of Pope is another fragment: "The same thing is in us as the living and the dead, the awake and the sleeping, the young and the old; these change to become those, and those change back again to become these." Immediately following his gravitational metaphor, Pope gives an organic embodiment of the same idea:

> See Matter next, with various life endu'd,
> Press to one centre still, the gen'ral Good.
> See dying vegetables life sustain,
> See life dissolving vegetate again,
> All forms that perish other forms supply,
> (By turns we catch the vital breath, and die)
> Like bubbles on the sea of Matter born,
> They rise, they break, and to that sea return.
> Nothing is foreign: Parts relate to whole;
> One all-extending, all-preserving Soul.
> (III:13–22)

"It is all one to be living and dead," Heraclitus says in Pope's copy of Stanley's *History of Philosophy,* "waking and sleeping, young and old; for each of these alternately changeth into the other."[47] Stanley reprints several variations of Heraclitus's description of the universe as a sea of matter ceaselessly in motion. "All things are made by Contrariety," Stanley quotes, "and the whole flows like a River." Pope's depiction of the universe as a Heraclitian "back-turning structure" immediately follows his mesmerizing close of Epistle II where the stages of life (Heraclitus's "the young and the old") are conflated to prove that "Tho' Man's a fool, yet GOD IS WISE" (II:294). As Heraclitus says, "It is characteristic of God, but not of man, to have discernment. . . . A Man is considered silly by God."[48]

The characterization of Heraclitus in Stanley's *History of Philosophy* would have impressed Pope as analogous both to Socrates and to himself as satirist and skeptic. "Whil'st he was yet young," Stanley quotes, Heraclitus was "the wisest of men, because he knew that he knew nothing." Immediately after the closing Heraclitian paradoxes of Epistle I, which culminate with the "Socratic" "Whatever IS, is RIGHT," Pope begins Epistle II with "Know then thyself." Stanley introduces Plutarch's commendation of the "memorable saying" of Heraclitus that "*I have been seeking out my self*" by noting the "strict enquiry, which he used to make into himself, according to the *Delphian* Motto, *Know thy self.*" The Socratic parallels continue with the trial of Heraclitus for impiety. Exiled and physically ill, an unrepentant Heraclitus rails at the ignorant venality of those presuming to judge him, predicting that could they "return to life 500 years hence" they "would find *Heraclitus* still alive, but not the least of [their] names."[49]

Paradox is the dominant trope for both Heraclitus and Pope because it embodies the duality of human perception. It is not superficial rhetorical flourish, Edward Hursey asserts in defending Heraclitus, but the trope that most adequately embodies his realization that "the perpetual struggle of opposites and the justice that balances them are indistinguishable and both equally present in every event."[50] Heraclitus's "justice that balances" appropriately recalls Dryden's Tiresias asserting "What ever is, is in its causes just" due to "that equal Beam / That poizes all." Heraclitian man lacks "discernment" just as Dryden's "pur-blind Man / Sees but a part o' th' Chain." The first two paragraphs of Epistle III render Dryden's "Chain" in terms of Heraclitus's *palintropos harmonie:*

"The Universal Cause
"Acts to one end, but acts by various laws."

. . . .

Look round our World; behold the chain of Love
Combining all below and all above.

. . . .

All serv'd, all serving! nothing stands alone;
The chain holds on, and where it ends, unknown.
(III: 1–2, 7–8, 25–26)

The Ovidian, Boethian, Chaucerian analogues to Pope's self-described "cant" metaphor of the chain of being are many, amounting as Maynard Mack says to a sort of "traditional 'poetic' metaphysics."[51] Dryden's modernization of Chaucer's *Knightes Tale* supplements his translation of Sophocles:

The Cause and Spring of motion, from above,
Hung down on earth a golden chain of love.
Great was th' effect, and high was his intent,
When peace among the jarring seeds he sent. . . .
The chain still holds; for tho' the forms decay,
Eternal matter never wears away.

Pope reanimates this traditional "peaceful" image with Heraclitian "strife."

To relax this tension from paradox into constative proposition is not wisdom but myth. Cicero says that for utilizing paradox and metaphor, Heraclitus was denounced for "speaking obscurely on purpose" and for not wishing "his meaning to be understood."[52] Stanley quotes King Darius inviting Heraclitus to come to Persia to explicate his "Book Concerning Nature, hard to be understood and interpreted," a work that has led Darius's most able scholars "to doubt what is the true meaning of what you have written." Heraclitus "delivers nothing plainly" and "affected to write obscurely," Stanley records, whence he was called "*Dark* Heraclitus, he *that doth despise / The Multitude.*" Stanley retells the story that "Euripides brought this Book of *Heraclitus* to *Socrates* to be read; and asking his opinion of it: 'The things, said *Socrates*, which I understand in it, are excellent, and so, I suppose, are those which I understand not; But they require a *Delian Diver*,'" glossed by Stanley as "one that is able to explain Oracles."[53] Using the loaded dichotomy of poetic to philosophic discourse, Lucretius attacks Heraclitus in the first book of *De Rerum Natura*. Heraclitus is "famed for his cloudy speech more among fools than among earnest Greeks who seek the truth," Lucretius charges. "For fools, you see, admire and love all things that they spy lurking under twisted words, and they call true all that can deftly touch the ear and is distempered with sweet sound." This matter/music dichotomy was turned against Heraclitus two thousand years before Lord Hervey and Johnson used it to discredit the *Essay*, and classical criticisms of "cloudy" Heraclitus are precursors of Crousazian irritation that Pope's style leaves readers in a "smoak" or in "a kind of mist."[54]

Yet the dialect of "*Dark* Heraclitus" is exactly the dialect for beings "short-sighted" (Glanvill), "pur-blind" (Dryden), in "intellectual twilight" (Bolingbroke), only "darkly wise" (Pope), for beings who know "there are not *many certain truths* in the world" (Pope), who know "there is no man that has seen, nor any that will ever know, the exact truth" (Heraclitus): a paradoxical dialect for a "paradox" (Pascal), "an incomprehensible . . . tangle" (Pascal), a "riddle" (Pope). Pope uses the dialect of the Academics to deconstruct rationalist dogma, but simultaneously he uses paradox with an Heraclitian oracular flair to speak the tentative insights of our limited and dual vision.

To read "Whatever IS, is RIGHT"—one of the intertextually richest aphorisms in literature—as a jingoistic rendering of Leibnizian theodicy is to translate the resonant profundities of a "dark" Heraclitus into static Stoic logocentrisms. It is to resolve the paradox by normalizing it into a straightforward logical proposition. To make it our interpretative focus is ultimately to misread Pope's entire poem as metaphysics rather than as the "*temperate* yet not *inconsistent* . . . system of Ethics" he wrote. The mixture of Academic skepticism and rhetorical genius that Heraclitus and Pope share speaks both our human insight and our ignorance. Their paradoxical *discordia concors* perfectly expresses our duality as subject and object, our simultaneous sense of alienation from (*discordia*) and our oneness with (*concors*) the strange and "unknown" seas on either side of our "isthmus."

"*DELIAN DIVING*"

Like Heraclitus, Pope vivifies *discordia concors* in various metaphors, and therein lies the deepest logocentric discomfort of all. Academic discourse embraces metaphor, and the ontological status of metaphor is a crucial question in the interpretation of all philosophical poetry. However, the abiding mutual hostility between logocentric transparency and aesthetic figurality makes the question difficult to formulate in a manner acceptable to both discourse worlds.[55] Although metaphor "has always been one of the central problems of philosophy," Douglas Berggren contends, philosophers usually dismiss it as "nothing more than a stylistic ornament, superimposed on cognitive discourse for emotive purposes, or else a mere illustrative comparison whose possible meaning and truth could emerge only when the metaphor was reduced to literal statements."[56] Consequently, the routine methodology of modern philosophers is to "separate the chaff of persuasive tone and matter from the logical kernel."[57] Logocentric discourse has an abiding fear of this "disfiguring power of figuration." For philosophy, Paul de Man argues, "metaphors, tropes, and figural language in general have been a perennial problem." To the philosopher figurality is superfluous and distracting: a marginal otherness that propositional rigor strives to eliminate. When unable to eliminate figurality outright, philosophy seeks to keep its malign influence within boundaries, an explanation for the recurrent efforts to "map out the distinctions between philosophical, scientific, theological, and poetic discourse."[58]

The British tradition of translating metaphor into literal statement antedates *An Essay on Man*, of course. Repeating Bacon, in *Leviathan* Hobbes cautions against the infection of philosophical discourse by "the use of metaphors, tropes, and other rhetorical figures, instead of words proper." Similarly, in *An Essay Concerning Human Understanding*, Locke advises that "if we would speak of things as they are, we must allow that all the arts of rhetoric . . . all the artificial and figurative application of words eloquence hath invented, are for nothing but to insinuate wrong *ideas*, move the passions, and thereby mislead the judgment." As stressed in the first chapter, this characterization of figurality as disfigurement or disease lay ready-to-hand for Crousaz to use in dismissing Pope's philosophy as "infected" by his poetry. Even though deconstructors have exposed the inability of philosophers to do without figurality—Hobbes's *Leviathan* is, after all, "very like a whale"—logocentric distrust of figurality is undiminished.[59] Even as he offers a justification for metaphor, philosopher Max Black warns that "metaphors are dangerous—and perhaps especially so in philosophy. . . . To call attention to a philosopher's metaphors is to belittle him."[60] Since language by its very nature seethes with disturbing figurality, Richard Rorty maintains that philosophers would rather dispense with writing altogether and just *show,* like physics.[61] Philosophers long for a logocentric *Principia* to do for their discourse what Newton did for physics. Only such a literal "steno-language," with univocation and an unambiguous distinction between symbol and referent, Philip Wheelwright complains, seems acceptable for philosophic discourse.[62]

Metaphor is endemic in religious and literary texts and is self-consciously active in the critical vocabularies of most theologians and literary critics, but most enthusiastically embrace the notion that they are playing language "games" that distinguish them from scientists and philosophers.[63] Some distinguish with a vengeance, condemning "mixed modes of writing which enlist the reader's feeling as well as his thinking" and calling instead for "a spell of purer science and purer poetry."[64] To such purists philosophical poetry, as the genre constituted by the union of this diverse pair, is the most impure. Like paradox, metaphor is binocular. Lockean wit synthesizes similarities while judgment discriminates differences. Wit and judgment, Pope argues in *An Essay on Criticism,* are meant to be "each other's aid, like man and wife." Both logocentric and aesthetic critics want them divorced.

As the quintessence of binocularity and the opposite of univocality metaphor is where hostile critics first insert the thin end of their deconstructing wedge. Those most eager to discredit the multiform truth of Academic discourse as disfigurement are those who feel their own system being threatened or disassembled. Thus, for Pope's first Christian critics—including theologian Crousaz—the metaphor of God as the soul of the world, which precedes the final string of paradoxes concluding Epistle I, becomes *the* interpretive crux. Pope's "God" must fit the Christian system or Pope must be discredited as a "fatalist," a "pantheist," a "Spinozist," an "atheist." To put Pope in his place, critics cut metaphor into its constituent halves and make the text yield a univocal meaning. Yet Pope, the "knowing" deconstructor, has already anticipated them when he playfully writes to Caryll that the *Essay* has a few "inaccuracies in the expressions" that may, he fears, "cause the author's sense to be turned, contrary to what I think his intention a little unorthodoxically." Specifically, "he uses the words *God,* the *soul* of the *World,* which at first glance may be taken for heathenism."[65] Pope was right; but despite such misinterpretations of his "intention," he never corrected his "inaccuracies." The reason he did not is also a key to characterizing the role of metaphor in the

Essay, in Academic discourse, and—perhaps—in philosophical poetry generally.

The use of metaphor in Academic discourse may best be conceived as the solution to a problem.[66] Pope was faced with both a logical and an empirical impasse. Few things were clearer to Pope's age than the inadequacy of finite reason to reach infinity: a fundamental axiom of Academic skepticism and of Christian dogma alike, an axiom inscribed in pulpit sermon and epistemological tome. The "Modes" of classical skepticism that Kant systematizes as the irreconcilable antinomies of the human mind are the age's assumptions about the limits of intellect. The "high priori road" was closed. Analogously, there was no way to the noumenal through the phenomenal. Whatever our private hopes, Tennyson's phenomenal stairs slope upward into darkness; where the chain ends is "unknown," say Bacon and Pope alike. And in spite of Warburton's invocation of the hocus-pocus of Analogy as the key to Pope's "Art of Converting Poetical Ornaments into Philosophical Reasoning,"[67] Pope's "freethinking" contemporaries ridiculed the reverse-revelation recommended by Bishop Peter Browne whereby *Things Divine and Supernatural* [*are*] *Conceived by Analogy with Things Natural and Human* (1733). Our ideas extend no further than our impressions, Hume says, and that's that: we can only reason, Pope asserts, "from what we know."

The discrepancy between "what we know" (1:18) and the "unknown" (1:27) leads us into the dazzlement that Montaigne mentions and that Pope's marvelous metaphors approximate. Certain matters, as Nagel argues, are beyond the nature of minds like ours. On the other hand, questions about those dazzling matters are neither confusions we can clear up with greater scientific sophistication nor non-questions we have tricked ourselves into believing real. The problem of consciousness, as Colin McGill admits, presents a real question that Wittgensteinian sleights-of-hand cannot make disappear, but our intellect is impotent before it. The relation of our mind to all bodies, including our own, remains an intractable mystery. "Optimism remarks," Jerry Fodor notes, "that problems that seem utterly intractable have been known to turn inside out when somebody has a good idea." Nevertheless, he concludes, the question of consciousness "seems academic even by academic standards; what's clear is that nobody has had any good ideas about consciousness yet."[68]

In *The Nature of Metaphysical Thinking,* Dorothy Emmet suggests that while the transcendent may be beyond our intellectual categories that does not mean that it is entirely beyond our experience.[69] Academic skepticism would formulate the same insight differently, I believe: Montaigne's "dazzlement" is not a mistake. We are surrounded by things "too wonderful" for our limited Jobian intellects. The fact that our uncomprehending awe has, in metaphysical-religious matters, "less sharpened the *wits* than the *hearts* of men against each other" (Pope's "Design") does not mean that our awe is an error. The error, for the Academic skeptic, is to solve the mystery through either rationalistic or revelatory dogma. Nature, as Hume repeatedly insists, is wiser than the "fictions" we fashion to make it tractable. Kant read Pope's *Essay* to his classes because he felt that he as a philosopher and Pope as a poet shared a freethinking temperament: philosophical and religious dogmas were superstitious cessations of thought precisely because there *are* more things in heaven and earth than our philosophy *can* dream of. Kant adroitly exposes the intellectual inadequacies of the physico-theological argument but, paradoxically, insists that it deserves respect. It is a "paradox," Bolingbroke writes to Pope; but because of the kind of mind we have, our knowledge "must be superficial to be real." The thing-in-itself reaches us only as "superfluities" flung our way by a world always out of reach. Kant knew the intellectual impossibility of "philosophical theology," but it fascinated him. Responsive to the immensity and awesome order of the world without and the beauty of the moral law within, Kant found the "Transcendental Aesthetic Ideas" of both in Pope's sublime poem without the dogmatic closure that falsifies experience.

Pope's problem—a problem common to poets and philosophers—was to synthesize realms of human experience without distortion of their constituent elements: to see real similarities while respecting real differences. "We live in a Critical Age," William Sherlock writes in 1694, "which will not allow us to speak intelligibly of God because we lack Words sufficiently to distinguish between the Motions and Actings of the Divine Mind and the Passions of Creatures."[70] Pope's consequent challenge was at least threefold: (1) to create a dialect that synthesized Sherlock's latent Stoic, Neoplatonic, and Christian dichotomy of Passionate Creatures and Divine Mind into our "doubtful" dual perspective of a "Chaos of Thought and Passion, all confus'd"; (2) to use that dialect to acknowledge a reality beyond our rational and empirical impasses without lapsing into mere "pseudo-statement," the purely emotive alternative to the ethical and affective barrenness of mathematical description; and (3) to animate that "darkly wise" dialect so that it can simultaneously clarify and dazzle with a Jobian intensity.

Faced with our subjective and objective perspectives that, like Kant's phenomenal and noumenal realms, resist any satisfactory logical unification, Pope's used metaphor regulatively rather than as either mere ornament or revelatory analogical argument. Again, Kant's distinction between reflective and determinant ideas is a useful analogue. Our epistemological limitations make any teleological model suspect; however, Kant argues, we are—for pragmatic purposes—justified in viewing reality *as if* it were purposive as long as we do not confuse our useful "fiction" with reality apart from our perceptions. All science, in fact, depends upon what Hume would quite rightly call just such a convenient fiction. Reflective Ideas order and synthesize our experience *to be used.* They are pragmatic hypotheses with which to regulate practice rather than determinations authorizing dogma. The Aristotelian First Cause or "God" is, thus, not a fact deduced a priori or discovered a posteriori but is a working hypothesis of reason functioning regulatively. Kant even argues that some Reflective Ideas, including teleology, are intellectually inevitable for human beings.

Such provisional metaphorical models have always been the alternatives to dogmatic closure. Heraclitus's *discordia concors* is such a reflective or regulative metaphor. Although "no man can ever know," he says, we are "wise to conclude that all is one." The modern pervasiveness of such regulative ideas is evident in such phrases as "root metaphor," "scientific paradigm," "hermeneutic circle," "episteme," "model," and "hypothesis." To attribute an analogous regulative use of metaphor to Pope is justified not only by its inevitability in Academic discourse but also by the consensus of Pope's contemporaries. Although scientists like Newton and philosophers like Hume denounced groundless speculation, they assumed the necessity of working hypotheses.[71]

Pope's major metaphors—including the chain of being, *discordia concors,* and God as World-Soul—are hypothetical and regulative. Figurative language synthesizes disparate but significantly similar realms of experience by constituting a unifying "strife." When Johnson disparages the "Metaphysicals," he objects to the arbitrariness of their *discordia concors* whereby things fundamentally unlike are "yoked by violence together." In *Biographia Literaria,* Coleridge characterizes the poetic function as a *discordia concors* that "reveals itself in the balance or reconciliation of opposite or discordant qualities."[72] Johnson negatively and Coleridge positively are reinscribing the same consensus expectation for the "harmonizing" power of great poetry that Mark Akenside characterizes in *Pleasures of the Imagination* (1744): the poet speaks, as Emerson would phrase it, among partial beings for the whole being. This synthesizing is foregrounded in the genre of philosophical poetry. In contrast to logocentric philosophy that strives to eradicate all figurality (mathematics as paradigm) and purely emotive lyric poetry (music as paradigm), philosophical poetry undertakes to unite the two discourse worlds without subordinating one to the other.

We may broadly characterize Pope's challenge by distinguishing the three primary realms of experience he is obligated to make complementary in his "Anatomy of the Mind" ("Design"). Extrapolating from the parallel between Epistle II (1733) and the tripartite organization of Hume's *Treatise* (1739), we may identify them as (1) the rational (Hume's "Of the Understanding"/Pope's "Reason"), (2) the emotional (Hume's "Of the Passions"/Pope's "Passion"), and (3) the ethical (Hume's "Of Morals"/ Pope's "Virtue"). Both Pope and Hume reverse the Stoic hierarchy that defines virtue as the subordination of passion to reason. Reason is and ought to be the slave of the passions, Hume asserts. Pope's more eclectic dialect retains the characterization of conscience as the "God within the mind" that divides "This light and darkness in our chaos join'd" (II:203–04), but "Virtue" consists not in the subordination of our emotions to reason but in rational implementation of our passions for our good as both autonomous individuals and members of the human community ("true SELF-LOVE and SOCIAL are the same"). By stressing the interdependence of our personal and public selves, Pope shares with Aristotle and with Joseph Butler a resistance to both Mandevillean and Shaftesburian reductionism of human nature into the dichotomy of selfishness or benevolence.[73]

Pope's challenge is threefold: to argue and give evidence (Reason), to inspire or depress (Passion), and to sanction ethical action (Virtue). To the Horatian admonition simultaneously to move the emotions and improve the morals, philosophical poetry adds the obligation to characterize reality as accurately and as fully as human faculties allow. Regulative metaphor is the means by which Pope does justice to these different experiential claims. Successful regulative metaphor holds differences in complementary tension at the same time it mandates appropriate attitudes and actions. The sensuous analogy of the noumenal that Kant finds in the Aesthetic Ideas of great poetic and religious figurative language—including Pope's—prefigures Philip Wheelwright's insistence on the "ontological status of radical metaphor." Wheelwright argues that metaphor achieves a transcendence of either-or distinctions, "an ontological overlapping by which emotionally congruent things, qualities, and events blend into oneness."

To any faculty in isolation this "oneness" appears paradoxical, a *discordia concors* violently yoked. Yet if we conceive of reality, as distinguished from our perceptions of reality, as "coalescent"—to use Wheelwright's term—then envisioning sharp lines between human faculties and kinds of experiences may be merely the contentious attempt of each faculty to claim priority. All is passion, says the Epicurean; all is reason, says the Stoic. All is selfishness says the Hobbesian; all is benevolence says the Lockean. No, say Heraclitus and Pope, "All is One." Limitation of reality to our human subcategories is distortion; while all our categories may refer to reality, to the extent that each makes a univocal pronouncement from its unique point of view that particular utterance is inadequate. As physicist Niels Bohr might paraphrase Pope, "Neither the particle nor the field theory, indeed, is true." Metaphor overcomes this desiccation of reality by holding such potentially complementary descriptions in a fructifying tension.

As Douglas Berggren argues, metaphor is indispensable for integrating diverse phenomena without sacrificing their diversity. However, in Academic discourse the faculties united are limited faculties still. While as poet-philosopher the author creates the richest description of reality available to human perception, as an Academic the author makes no unbracketed claims. Metaphors are regulative rather than "ontological" in Wheelwright's revelatory sense. They coordinate human perceptions; they do not "transcend" them. The theory of incarnative language, which Walker Percy admires in the Scholastics whereby "symbols come to contain within themselves the thing symbolized *in alio esse,* in another mode of existence," is the ideology of those metaphysical "church-writers" Pope opposes.[74] The "Romantic" extreme is to read Kant's "Aesthetic" sensuous analogies of the noumenal as transcendental visions, thereby turning the poet into a seer. The "Rational" extreme is to deconstruct the "ontological overlapping" into an arbitrary conjunction of tenor and vehicle, thereby reducing the poet to a rhetor vivifying a preexisting reality.

Right reading of regulative metaphor moves between the two extremes. Most readings of Pope's metaphors, predictably, have been either Aesthetic or Logocentric deformations. Everyone agrees that Pope's poetry is ravishing; almost everyone also agrees that its rhetorical effectiveness is irrelevant to its failed philosophy. Logocentric deconstructors translate Pope's metaphors into literal, determinant statements, and by so doing they relax the tension between competing perspectives and ascribe reality to the rational alone. The metaphor now reduced to constative statement, the critic places it in its "context" according to the procedures described in chapter two: either placing it in the context of other assertions alleged to be its logical presuppositions or implications, or placing it in the history of outdated ideas.

Indicative of the first procedure is Crousaz's fatalistic reading of Pope's metaphor "of a Universe, formed with a mutual Dependence of one Part upon another, in the manner of a Machine." This "grand and magnificent" figure, the theologian-logician objects, vivifies an "Idea" with "very destructive Consequences."[75] As a recent Crousazian writes, "the asserted transcendence of the system as a whole over the isolated functioning of any parts" runs the risk of "turning God into a sadistic mechanic." Critics have similarly extrapolated dangerous consequences from Pope's use of the metaphor of a chain of beings. Acknowledging to Spence that "chain of beings" was a "cant" phrase of his contemporaries,[76] Pope reanimates a familiar formula to create the "responsive awe" that Wheelwright says great metaphors can make us feel in the presence of the irreducible mystery of reality—that awe Bacon calls "broken knowledge" and Montaigne "dazzlement." "Cosmic Toryism" is the static nugget of paraphrasable dogma critics have extrapolated from Pope's metaphor. The chain of being becomes the "metaphysical sanction," an influential critic asserts, for keeping people within their social class. The metaphor, another critic argues, sanctions a necessitarian doctrine of social submission.[77] Even the hostile Samuel Johnson objected, in his translation of Crousaz, that it was an interpretive error to have "too great an Inclination to draw Consequences";[78] yet from that day to this critics regularly simplify his metaphor into a justification for classist submission to social superiors, which is precisely that "enormous faith of many made for one" that Pope attacks throughout the *Essay*.

Interpretation of the chain of being also illustrates the second procedure for contextualizing metaphor. Arthur O. Lovejoy's placement of Pope in the "history of ideas" is a definitive example. For Lovejoy, Pope's *Essay* is a marginal, nonphilosophical chapter in the transmission of an exploded idea.[79] The metaphor was never more popular than in the eighteenth century, Lovejoy admits, an image expatiated upon by such authors as Addison, King, Bolingbroke, Haller, Thomson, Akenside, Buffon, Bonnet, Goldsmith, Diderot, Kant, Lambert, Herder, and Schiller.[80] So congenial and adaptable was the metaphor, another scholar asserts, that it could be deployed by people of "varied philosophical opinions."[81] This assessment should give critics pause. When writers of differing ideologies use the same metaphor, caution is essential in interpreting each occurrence of the figure if we are to avoid an undiscriminating conflation. Metaphors have distinctive meaning only in the context of individual works because the "same metaphor may acquire various, even contrasting, meanings in different writers."[82]

Unfortunately, Lovejoy's summary of *An Essay on Man* is an unsubtle conflation where Pope is reduced to an amalgam of Soame Jenyns and Professor Pangloss. He solely attends to the generic formula of Pope's admittedly "cant" metaphor and entirely ignores his uniqueness. In Lovejoy's ambitious survey, where Pope is treated as a literary popularizer of ideas better expressed in philosophic prose, this distortion is understandable. However, because of Lovejoy's deserved eminence, this misreading has been received as gospel. Assuming Lovejoy's mantle as a historian of ideas putting each antiquated idea in its place, a recent Pope scholar writes of the chain of being metaphor: "Once we have recognized this way of thinking as natural to its time, limited as that time was by certain habits of religious thought, political institutions, social customs, and a restricted knowledge of the world outside Europe, we can see how the social divisions that keep every man in his place were seen at the time as sacred."[83] That social distinctions are sacred is not what Pope says or ever believed, but such misrepresentation is typical of the "patronizingly supercilious" dismissal of Pope that F. E. L. Priestly finds endemic in criticism of the *Essay.*[84]

READING REGULATIVE METAPHOR

Both kinds of misreadings are also endemic in interpretations of Pope's metaphor of God as soul of the world:

> All are but parts of one stupendous whole,
> Whose body Nature is, and God the soul;
> That, chang'd thro' all, and yet in all the same,
> Great in the earth, as in th' aethereal frame,
> Warms in the sun, refreshes in the breeze,
> Glows in the stars, and blossoms in the trees,
> Lives thro' all life, extends thro' all extent,
> Spreads undivided, operates unspent,
> Breathes in our soul, informs our mortal part,
> As full, as perfect, in a hair as heart;

As full, as perfect, in vile Man that mourns,
As the rapt Seraph that adores and burns;
To him no high, no low, no great, no small;
He fills, he bounds, connects, and equals all.
(1:267–80)

Interpreting in the narrow context of the debate over God's immanence or transcendence, an early critic deconstructed the metaphor into a univocal denial of God's transcendence and drew the atheistic and fatalistic "consequences."[85] The argument extracted from Pope's metaphor places him in the history of ideas among those godless writers who "pretending to philosophy . . . talk much indeed of God, but mean such a one, as is not really distinct from the animated and intelligent universe."[86] The either-or deconstruction of tensive metaphor refuses to let Pope "steer betwixt" immanence and transcendence because its logocentric canons insist that the question be determined one way or the other in a constative proposition without the ambiguity and evasion of figurative language. For logocentric critics, in the beginning was the Word and the word was God; consequently, to speak the first and final Word we must be able to say what Pope means by "God." This is also the key to discrediting Pope as a "circular" rather than linear reasoner. "To the present-day reader, though not to him alone," a recent critic writes, "the major, most beggarly question assumed by Pope, the big *donum,* has to do with the existence and nature of the God whose ways the poet sets out to vindicate."[87]

Right reading of Pope's metaphors begins where he tells us it does in *An Essay on Criticism:* with acknowledgment of the writer's intention. Writing at the conjunction of poetic and philosophic discourse, the philosophical poet undertakes to steer eclectically betwixt discourse worlds. To the obvious opposition of the logical and the emotive, Pope adds the ethical. Additionally, and especially with regulative metaphor, the text has a performative aspect. The writer must hold the constative, the emotive, and the directive discourse worlds in a satisfying tension that makes them complementary rather than contradictory. "All [is] contrariety," Heraclitus says in Pope's edition of Stanley's *Philosophy,* adding: "It is all one." Thus, to read Pope's metaphors we must ask: (1) What is asserted as fact? (2) What emotion is urged? (3) What action is mandated? and (4) What is the tension among these speech acts that makes them complementary?

The interpretive categories suggest evaluative criteria. (1) The constative component constitutes a covenant between writer and reader not to retreat into the subjectivism of purely evocative metaphor. The metaphor must square with "what we know." The suggestiveness characteristic of figurative language should not contradict empirical evidence, and some specifiable degree of factual similarity must warrant the metaphor. It should not lose sight of what Dorothy Emmet calls the world's "matter-of-factness." (2) Emotively, the metaphor should be subjectively significant; it should feel important and appropriate. (3) Directively, it should sanction moral action. (4) Performatively, the metaphor simultaneously should activate the constative, emotive, and directive functions of language to give a "thicker" description of reality than any single discourse function in isolation. The metaphor should hold varied perspectives in tension, as "coalescent"; the richness and justness of the juxtaposition determines its value.

Pope's metaphor of God as World-Soul deliberately bridges the discourse worlds of science and theology. Scientists and theologians alike tried to fashion a discourse that could acknowledge the world's matter-of-factness without the death of God. Robert Boyle endowed lectures to do exactly what Bacon warned against: to use science to prove the existence and attributes of God. In fact, all of Natural Theology attempts to link "our ordinary everyday discourse about the world or even our scientific discourse on the one side, and theological discourse on the other."[88] In this regard, few analogies linking the natural to the supernatural were more frequent in sermon and song than the comparison of God's relation to the world to that of the soul's animation of the body. Remembering Pope's alternate "heathen" and Christian readings in his letter to Caryll, it is suggestive that he adopts a metaphor that Ralph Cudworth argued in *The True Intellectual System of the Universe* (1678) was warranted by the consensus of pagan and Christian alike. The metaphor was a commonplace in contemporary works of morality or theology like J. F. Senault's *Uses of Passion*, Robert Bellarmine's *The Soul's Ascension to God*, and John Toland's *Clito;* and it was similarly a classical commonplace, as in Anchises's revelation to his son in the *Aeneid*, translated by Sir Walter Ralegh:

> The heavens, the earth, and all the liquid mayne,
> The Moones bright Globe, and Starres Titanian,
> A Spirit in this maintains: and their whole Masse,
> A Minde, which through each part infus'd doth passe,
> Fashions, and workes, and wholly doth transpierce
> All this great body of the Universe;

and retranslated by Dryden:

> Know, first that heaven and earth's compacted frame,
> And flowing waters, and the starry flame,
> And both the radiant lights, one common soul
> Inspires and feeds, and animates the whole.
> This active mind, infused through all the space,
> Unites and mingles with the mighty mass.
> Hence men and beasts the breath of life obtain,
> And birds of air, and monsters of the main.
> The ethereal vigor is in all the same;
> And every soul is filled with equal flame.[89]

Because the metaphor might be interpreted as "heathenism," most authors were sensitive to the pantheistic implications that antagonists could draw from the immanent metaphor. Representatively, in the "General Scholium" to the *Principia,* Newton pointedly disassociates himself from the pantheistic implications of his "system" by affirming God's transcendence as a being who "governs all things, not as the soul of the world, but as Lord over all." Pope acknowledged that his use of "the Words *God,* the *soul* of the *World*" might be taken for "heathenism"; but unlike Newton, Pope's "God-talk" audaciously synthesizes the pagan-pious disjunction of Newton's discourse. Richard Westfall argues that Newton was, in fact, "one of the more advanced heretics of his day" but that his fear of ostracism led him constantly to conceal his real opinions, a hypocrisy he finds endemic in Newton's contemporaries: "The constant references to God and to Christianity in the writings of scientists, like those of Newton, are usually taken as testimonies to the piety of the age. They derived rather from the fact that traditional piety had been called into question."[90] Pope's letter to John Caryll acknowledges the semantic tyranny of "God-talk" and the danger, explained by Thomas Merrill, "when utterances of one language-game are interpreted according to the rules appropriate to another."[91] Thus Pope is eager to know what his friend makes of his World-Soul metaphor "after twice or thrice reading" because Pope's figural effectiveness consists in steering betwixt a "heathen" and a "Christian" description of reality.

Pope's metaphor is unmistakably regulative rather than determinant for two contextual reasons. First, Pope has unequivocally and repeatedly stressed the impossibility of comprehensive metaphysical understanding. Second, elsewhere he metaphorically characterizes the universe in Newtonian mechanistic terms that, if taken as an ontologically adequate description, would "contradict" his organic metaphor. However, as Douglas White alertly notes, Pope was "not satisfied with the mechanical description alone."[92] His organic complement reinscribes a metaphor that powerfully organizes our experience without presuming to be a determinant description, and it may be assessed by the criteria proposed for regulative metaphor.

First, what is asserted as fact? Pope's metaphor asserts that an awesome energy animates and orders the universe into one organic, interdependent unity. All parts participate in this energy but none is uniquely privileged. Beyond these assertions, the propositional implications of the metaphor are deliberately problematic and provocative. What was Caryll to make of "the Words *God*" and "the *soul* of the *World*" when their tendency to semantic control is undercut by the impersonality of a World-Soul that does not distinguish between a hair or a heart? The comforting father-figure of *Matthew* allusively combines with an impersonal pantheistic force that "sees with equal eye . . . now a bubble burst, and now a world."

Second, what emotions does the metaphor acknowledge or urge? Pope's image of the unity of creation reinforces a feeling of connectedness in the individual with the force that "Glows in the stars, and blossoms in the trees." Our sense of being part of a universal order is acknowledged. However, this exhilarating identification of the individual with the universal life-force involves an appropriate depersonalization. In contrast to an anthropocentric Stoicism or Christianity, Pope's metaphor asserts that involvement in the godhead is common to all creation. Consequently, our exhilaration coexists with our recognition that we are not accorded special treatment by "God." Pope's placement of the providentially comforting hair and sparrow from the gospel of Matthew in a pantheistic context acknowledges the undecidability of the cosmic significance of human life. Pope's "tensive" metaphor mortifies and exhilarates us simultaneously. Above all, we are encouraged to contemplative wonder at the immensity and variety of a reality that is mysteriously united by a common energy. The sublimity of the metaphor, as even the hostile Joseph Warton acknowledged, demands our awe.[93]

Third, what ethical action does the metaphor mandate? Like the earlier parts-whole metaphor and the later chain of love metaphor, the World-Soul metaphor emphasizes the connectedness of the microcosm to the macrocosm at the same time that it warns against the blind presumption of a mind that is categorically phenomenological ("What can we reason, but from what we know?") attempting the metaphysical ("Why Heav'n has made us as we are"). In the ecology of a universe that privileges "no high, no low, no great, no small," the greatest sin is the "enormous faith of many made for one," a social and economic politicizing of anthropocentric metaphysics. By stressing that "All are but parts of one stupendous whole," Pope's metaphor denounces hierarchical valuation and encourages a sense of solidarity with all creation as a "union of the rising Whole" (IV:337). Our sharing of a common soul is both ethical ground and an admonition to respect and relish diversity rather than insensitively to "destroy all creatures for our sport or gust." As John Sisk acknowledges, humans begin to move toward inhumanity when they doubt that "they have a vital connection with the force that moves the heaven and all the stars, when they begin to doubt that their sense of justice has some ground in the order of things."[94] Pope's *discordia concors* establishes that universal consanguinity. Charity for "all above and all below" is, paradoxically, self-love cognizant of our complicity in "one close system of Benevolence" (IV:358).

Fourth, what makes the constative, emotive, and directive aspects of the metaphor "coalescent" rather than contradictory? The generative tension among these uses of language grows out of the dual heathen and pious derivation of the metaphor Pope alludes to in his letter to Caryll. As theological God-talk, the metaphor of God as the soul of the world is redolent with revelatory power. As scientific description, the metaphor is heuristically suggestive in acknowledging at once the objectivity of universal gravitation and our subjective sense of connectedness. The tension between "God" as theological language and "God" as scientific cipher alters both terms. "God" is neither the solicitous father-figure in Matthew nor an alien cosmic energy. Instead, "God" functions as a regulative metaphor correlating nature's order, animation, and interrelatedness with our human rational, passionate, and ethical experiences.

In Pope's copy of Stanley's *Philosophy* Heraclitus is quoted defending himself against charges of impiety identical to those Newton dreaded and Bolingbroke warned Pope to "screen" himself against in writing the *Essay*. "Where is God?" Heraclitus demands sarcastically of his orthodox accusers, "Shut up in Temples? . . . You ignorant people! You know not, that God is not made with Hands, neither hath he any Basis from the beginning, nor hath one Circumference; but the whole World, adorned with living Creatures, Plants and Stars is his Mansion." In a separate epistle in Stanley, with precisely the World-Soul metaphor Pope uses, Heraclitus explains how "God cures the great bodies in the World, reducing their inequality to an even temper": "he makes whole those that are broken, stops such as are falling, gathers the dispersed together into one body, polisheth the deform'd, those which are taken he puts into Custody, those which flye he pursues, illuminates the dark with his light, terminates the infinite with certain bounds, gives form to those which have none, gives sight to things void of sense, permeates through all substance, Striking, Composing, Dissolving, Condensing, Diffusing."[95]

Heraclitus's unorthodox "God"—master harmonizer of the world's great text—is identical to Pope's "great directing MIND of ALL" (I:266). The Heraclitian "God" who "permeates through all substance" is the same "Order" (I:281) that in Pope "extends thro' all extent / Spreads undivided, operates unspent." Pope's "*All* are but *parts* of *one* stupendous *whole,* / Whose body Nature is, and God the soul" operates at exactly the suspect intersection of scientific, ethical, and religious discourse occupied by Charron's analogous image: "The Divine Wisdom so ordering the Matter, that the several *Parts* of the Creation should be so nicely interwoven, so closely connected, that Each should have some Pre-eminence peculiar to it self; and from *All* together, shou'd result the perfect Harmony, and uninterrupted Order, of *One* most compact and beautiful *Whole*."[96]

Steering betwixt theological and scientific discourse, Pope's "stereoscopic" metaphor straddles the gap between Kant's empirical and transcendental perspectives, between Nagel's subjective and objective perspectives. Pope's middle-state skepticism generates a vision appropriate to a creature who, as Addison says in *Spectator* No. 519, "fills up the middle space between the Animal and Intellectual Nature, the visible and invisible world." Pope's "synoptic" vision fuses realms of experience. Like the "fables of identity" celebrated by Northrop Frye, Pope's metaphor captures that rich sense "of lost rapport with nature which logic, reason, and the dualistic differentiation of consciousness have destroyed."[97] Viewing Pope's regulative metaphor as either reifiable or as an alogical "supreme fiction" is equally disintegrative. If philosophical poetry is merely a construct of fictive "pseudo-statements" telling the anthropoid ear only what it wishes to hear, then it is trivial. If, on the other hand, regulative metaphor is read as a metaphysically accurate and adequate description of reality, then the poet becomes a megalomaniacal mythmaker whose utterances are revelations.

Pope has deconstructed the argument from design in a way that at once refutes and reveals, that chastises and consoles simultaneously. Order, Pope ringingly asserts, is the primary law of nature; and certainly order is that part of the design argument that increasingly commands our awe from the regular-irregularity of fractals to the astonishing three-dimensional analogue of Penrose tiles in the atomic structure of crystals. We are compelled by the image of the black megalith found by astronauts in *2001*. In contrast, the anthropocentric egotisms and anthropomorphic projections of the argument from design increasingly seem to us mythic anachronisms, as they already did to Pope, Hume, and Kant. Yet, Pope stresses, although we are not all being's end and aim, not that Hegelian and Tennysonian "one far-off divine event, / To which the whole creation moves," we are standing miracles to an order that modern science reads inscribed in the double helix structure of an unpronounceable acid.

In a way that must always seem both undeniable and strange we are consanguine with the cosmos, "our mortal part" part of an "Order" that "Glows in the stars, and blossoms in the trees." His Academic dialect makes Pope our contemporary by distinguishing him from what William James characterizes as the now "quite grotesque . . . books of natural theology which satisfied the intellects of our grandfathers." In contrast to natural theology's God "who conformed the largest things of nature to the paltriest of our private wants," James writes, "The God whom science recognizes must be a God of universal laws exclusively. . . . He cannot accommodate his processes to the convenience of individuals. The bubbles on the foam which coats a stormy sea are floating episodes, made and unmade by forces of the wind and water. Our private selves are like those bubbles,—epiphenomena."[98] In knowingly bridging the discourse worlds of natural theology and science, Pope said it more compellingly and succinctly: we are "bubbles on the sea of Matter born."

Thus, perhaps Pope's greatest genius is to have solved the task Richard Rorty says was Heidegger's: "How to work within a final vocabulary while somehow simultaneously 'bracketing' that vocabulary—to keep the seriousness of its finality while letting it itself express its own contingency. . . . to construct a vocabulary which would constantly dismantle itself and constantly take itself seriously."[99] Pope's Heraclitian oracular energy operates always within the brackets of Academic skepticism. Warburton objected that Bayle "strikes frequently into the province of paradox."[100] Perhaps Pope liked Bayle for the same reason that Bayle found Pascal and the Manichees intriguing: in analogous ways they provided paradoxical discourse worlds congenial to our human chaos of light and darkness.[101]

Resolving Pope's paradoxical discourse into singular allegiance to Pyrrhonian Skepticism or to Stoic Rationalism is misreading. Asserting that Pope's "basic point" in the *Essay* is that "all metaphysics are inadequate" and that, therefore, "the danger for Pope's readers is that we concentrate too steadily on the articulation of the poem's philosophies" errs toward Pyrrhonian relativism.[102] In contrast, asserting that "Pope proposes to begin with doubts so that he may end in certainties" disparages his skepticism as a mere rhetorical flourish preliminary to Stoic proclamation.[103] Both misreadings relax the tension of irony, paradox, and metaphor into the opposed univocal, dogmatic dialects Pope explicitly disavows.

The regulative metaphor of Academic discourse that Pope adopts aspires, as Bacon says, "to give some shadow of satisfaction to the mind of man in those points wherein the nature of things doth deny it." Bacon's shadow metaphor is inappropriately disparaging, for as Joseph Glanvill argues in *Scepsis Scientifica* even the laws of physics are "hypotheses" or "convenient supposals for the use of life. Nor can any further account be expected from humanity, but how things possibly may have been made consonantly to sensible nature: but infallibly to determine how they truly were effected, is proper to him only that saw them in the chaos, and fashioned them out of that confused mass."[104] That regulative metaphor is hypothetical rather than determinant—a "convenient supposal" like Kant's reflective ideas—does not diminish its value "for the use of life."

The biblical metaphor that we see through a glass darkly (*per speculum in enigmate*) corresponds perfectly with the epistemological modesty of Academic Skepticism; as a recent theologian acknowledges, it is no discredit "but something every hearer of poetry should understand, that all the statements theologians make about God are similitudes, as it is written, *per speculum in enigmate*."[105] Writing nearly three hundred years earlier, William King similarly cautioned theologians "to remember, that the Descriptions which we frame to our selves of God . . . are not taken from any direct or immediate Perceptions that we have made of him" but are only analogies seen "thro a Glass darkly."[106] Addison concurs in *Spectator* No. 237: "We are not at present in a proper situation to judge of the counsels by which Providence acts, since but little arrives at our knowledge, and even that little we discern imperfectly; or, according to the elegant Figure in Holy Writ, *we see but in part, and as in a Glass darkly.*"

Extrapolating an enigmatic figure from *enigmate,* Pope characterizes our human perspective as "darkly wise" (II:4), ambitious for but estranged from apodictic certainty regarding our "being's end and aim." Pope and Addison, however, differ fundamentally. Addison's epistemological modesty is the defensive antechamber to Christian faith; Pope's Academic Skepticism forbids such revelatory closure and distinguishes him from Pascal, Milton, King, Sherlock, Butler, and Addison and allies him with Heraclitus, Socrates, Cicero, Montaigne, Charron, Bayle, Bolingbroke, Hume, Voltaire, and Kant. This dichotomy partly explains the contrast of Pope and Addison in Edward Young's sermonic *Conjectures on Original Composition.* There Pope appears as the epitome of the poet who sinned against his genius; Addison, in contrast, is Young's Christian saint inviting his friends to see with what equanimity a Christian could die. The missing connective is his earlier *Night Thoughts,* which Young says he wrote as a pious supernatural supplement to Pope's naturalistic *Essay on Man.* In the mind of the author of *A Vindication of Providence,* Pope had reneged on his promise to vindicate the ways of God to man.

Regulative metaphor is hypothesis, "an *If* instead of a *Since*"; and Pope knows that the philosophical poet can organize humanity's multiple perspectives only provisionally. This limitation frustrates the rationalist—Christian or Stoic—who reasons in defense of an absolutist, logocentric ideology. For Young, Pope's poem does not say enough. In contrast, empiricism is hostile to hypothesis because it says too much; but, as Emmet observes, any description of reality "which attempts an estimate of the significance of events, whether philosophical or theological, cannot be merely empirical."[107] As Douglas Berggren concludes, "truly creative and non-mythic thought, whether in the arts, the sciences, religion, or metaphysics, must be invariably and irreducibly metaphorical."[108]

For a synoptic rendering of reality, the philosopher—knowingly or not—depends as fully as the poet on metaphor to harmonize diverse perspectives; and both, finally, are judged by the success of their metaphorical world views. The reduction of metaphor to constative proposition is the reverse of right reading because it destroys what Berggren calls the "stereoscopic vision" of metaphor and thereby deconstructs the author's "world hypothesis." Unlike most philosophers, poets are at home with metaphor, and that may make them, at their best, the best philosophers. This possibility helps explain why Kant judged Pope, as a philosopher, superior to Leibniz: his vision was less dogmatic and more comprehensive and compelling. Pope's Academic Skepticism admits the recalcitrance of reality to our human categories; but, within the limits of that regulative proviso, Pope creates a compelling metaphorical world of great density and comprehensiveness. As master harmonizer of the constative, emotive, directive, and performative uses of language, Pope creates the most powerful and profound synoptic description of reality in English.

Axioms in philosophy are not axioms until they are proved upon our pluses.

—*John Keats (3 May 1818)*

CONCLUSION

Naturalizing Philosophical Poetry

TWO HUNDRED AND FIFTY YEARS of coercive misreading of *An Essay on Man* has implications for the interpretation of philosophical poetry generally. My initial chapter argues that the history of interpretation of *An Essay on Man* has been a story of continuous deformation of the work into one of two opposed modes of discourse: the Logocentric or the Aesthetic. Pope's *Essay* was read as either philosophy or poetry but not as the kind of text it was and is: a philosophical poem. Effective commentary on the *Essay* must identify a mode of discourse appropriate to the genre of philosophical poetry, and that has been the burden of subsequent chapters. Clearly, neither the logocentric discourse of traditional philosophy and history of ideas nor the aesthetic discourse of traditional literary history and literary criticism suffices. Those dialects deconstruct the genre into "mere" philosophy or "mere" poetry. Michel Foucault's argument that a culture's episteme mandates who may speak authoritatively on which matters and what may "reasonably" be said has implications for interpretation of philosophical poetry. Succinctly stated, the logocentric episteme authorizes the philosopher while the aesthetic episteme authorizes the literary critic. Not surprisingly, the philosopher marginalizes Pope's poetry and the literary critic marginalizes Pope's philosophy.

Effective commentary must recognize philosophical poetry as an autonomous genre. As suggested earlier, Tzvetan Todorov's discussion of the fantastic as a literary genre is suggestive. In reading fantasy, Todorov says, we hesitate between a natural and a supernatural explanation of events; and to choose between them is to destroy the genre of fantasy and enter a neighboring genre: either the strange or the supernatural.[1] In a distinct sense common to eclectic, middle-state Academic Skepticism, I have argued that Pope's *Essay* deliberately "steers betwixt" or "hangs between" opposed epistemes, but certainly all philosophical poems occupy Todorov's "space of uncertainty" between the constative claims of propositional prose and the affective assumptions of emotive poetry.

In structuralist terms, commentary must "naturalize" philosophical poetry; it must create a mode of discourse in which it is "natural" to discuss the genre. To interpret a text, as Jonathan Culler explains, is to bring it "within the modes of order which culture makes available, and this is usually done by talking about it in a mode of discourse which a culture takes as natural."[2] As we saw in the initial chapter, as soon as the *Essay* appeared critics asserted that "Poetry and Metaphysics . . . are generally considered as two Kinds of Writing inconsistent with each other." This generic dichotomy authorized logician Crousaz to sneer that Pope's "Physics smelled of the Poet," and it authorized theologian Elwin to pronounce in the most influential scholarly edition of the *Essay* that "the false scheme of embodying scientific philosophy in verse determined in advance the failure of the Essay." *An Essay on Man* was, he concludes, "altogether a mistake." The identical dismissal continues today in critics' confident assertion that the *Essay* undertakes a subject "not suited to the muse" and is, consequently, a "poetic disaster." Clearly, in our interpretative community, as Maynard Mack says, "Poems in the genre of the *Essay* are not, as the saying goes, our thing." Until our interpretive community changes, philosophical poetry will continue to be trivialized as "unnatural"; poems like *An Essay on Man* will remain unreadable; and the admiration of Voltaire, Rousseau, and Kant will strike us as incomprehensible and, in a recent critic's characterization, "notorious."

The logocentric canons of the Crousazian critique that dismisses the *Essay* as "incoherent," "inconsistent," and intellectually "infantile" authorize the trivialization of "mixed modes" of writing. However, philosophical poetry is the marriage rather than the divorce of wit with judgment; it is a *discordia concors*. To help revalue *An Essay on Man,* I have attempted to delineate an Academic world of discourse that Pope indisputably shared with many of his contemporaries and that stands opposed to the norms of Crousazian logocentrism. Academic Skepticism is an episteme characterized by (1) skeptical opposition to philosophical dogmatism, (2) eschewal of the abstract or otherworldly for the pursuit of practical knowledge through doubt and empirical observation, (3) deliberate eclecticism, and (4) ethical naturalism. Resisting definitive closure, Academic Skepticism affirms the generative energy of contending opposites. Sharing the epistemological modesty and rhetorical audacity of Heraclitus, Socrates, and Cicero, Pope realizes regarding contending ideologies that "neither indeed, is true"; but he steers between dogmatic extremes with an eclectic richness and an intertextual resonance characteristic of the greatest philosophical poetry.

Thus the discourse world of the *Essay* is fundamentally different from the assumptions of Pope's logocentric critics from Crousaz to "Crousazian" Nuttall.[3] G. S. Rousseau contends that no modern critic "has succeeded in raising Pope's *Essay on Man* to a position of eminence" or in "telling us why it is so important as philosophy that we today should change our minds about it."[4] We should change our minds, I believe, because as philosophy Pope's *Essay* offers a manifestly "thicker" and more "modern" description of reality than the logocentrisms that denigrate it:

	An Essay on Man	*Crousazian Criticism*
MODE:	philosophical poetry	philosophy
METHOD:	eclecticism	"uniform Originals"
PURPOSE:	"ethics"	theodicy [metaphysics]
VOICE:	polysemous	univocal
TONE:	skeptical and ironic	dogmatic and literal
FIGURE:	metaphor	afigurality [transparency]
TROPE:	paradox: "Whatever IS, is RIGHT."	logical tautology: "Whatever is, is."

Crousazian criticism translates the dangerous doubleness of irony into static univocality. Analogously, figurality is banished. All mists of metaphor must be dispelled to arrive at a Cartesian clarity and distinctness, poetic words yielding to the philosophic Word. Paradox is stigmatized as "mere contradiction," as rhetorical obfuscation, as an irresponsible Heraclitian darkness evading the logocentric ideal of perfect coherence and clarity, of exact equivalence. Pope's "Socratic" paradox ("Whatever IS, is RIGHT") is interpreted as the rationalistic tautology that Locke, Bolingbroke, and Hume ridicule as the vacuous paradigm of "first philosophy" ("What is, is"/"Whatsoever is, is"/"Whatever is, is"/"Whatever *is* may *not be*"). *Discordia concors* is deconstructed to Leibnizian rational optimism.[5] The misreading is complete when interpretation transforms Pope's "system of Ethics" into a metaphysics. Pope's sixteenth line—"vindicate the ways of God to Man"—is, Mark Pattison representatively asserts, "a better description of the Subject of the Essay than that of the title, Essay on Man."[6]

With a bias that is pervasive but largely unconscious, logocentric criticism treats art as deception, bewitchment, seduction, as the triumph of lower affective drives over higher ratiocinative powers; and the misreading of *An Essay on Man* is simply an extreme example of this endemic strategy of misinterpretation. The logocentric tradition does most damage to philosophical poetry because it has authority to speak on philosophical matters; however, the aesthetic tradition capitulates both by deferring to the logocentric on "philosophical" matters and by devaluing all that is not art. If Crousaz's "Mr. Pope's Physics smell of the Poet" is the archetypal utterance of Logocentrism, Aestheticism's archetype is "Mr. Pope's Poetry stinks of the Philosopher." Argument is trivialized and art extolled. For a philosophical poem to be successful, the aesthetic critic writes, the poet must be "in complete control over the philosopher."[7] Usually, however, this "Romantic" tradition of denigration has asserted consistently from Joseph Warton through Thomas De Quincey to Harold Bloom that philosophical poetry is an inconceivable oxymoron, a "false scheme" that "determined in advance the failure of the Essay on its poetic side" (Elwin, 1871), an "aesthetic impossibility" that doomed in advance Pope's "absurd theodicy" (Bloom, 1986).[8]

Neither tradition can read the mixed mode of discourse that is philosophical poetry because both logocentric and aesthetic critics write in defense of epistemes analogous to the "ontotheological" or "metaphysical" traditions that Heidegger and, more recently, William Spanos, attempt to destroy. "That meaning, like form, is infinitely open," Vincent Leitch writes, eludes these metaphysical interpretative systems. In their demands for and expectation of totality, in their will-to-power over texts, in their repressed anxiety in the face of continuous uncertainty, these spacial methods turn "disorder into Order, differences into Identities and words into the Word."[9] Such "metaphysical" interpretation, Derrida argues, dreams "of deciphering a truth or an origin" beyond short-sighted mortality. In contrast, effective interpretation "affirms freeplay" in its effort to get beyond our logocentric illusion "of metaphysics or of ontotheology . . . of full presence, the reassuring foundation, the origin and the end of game."[10] To Presumptuous Man's demand for such totality, Pope answers with a geometric axiom: "Can a part contain the whole?" The best readers of the *Essay* have been responsive to Pope's play. As David Morris astutely writes, "The language of *An Essay on Man* is far more rich, distinctive, and problematic than most modern expositors of Pope's doctrines believe."[11]

Any interpretive system that has no place for doubts and differences cannot read *An Essay on Man* or any philosophical poem that refuses to subordinate our multiple perspectives to one. *Discordia concors* is Pope's metaphor for our human condition, and his eclectic "steering betwixt" doctrines is his methodology for coming to terms with, in Hume's words, "principles, which are contrary to each other, which are both at once embrac'd by the mind, and which are unable mutually to destroy each other." Unable to reconcile our contradictions, Hume argues in discussing skepticism, "we endeavor to set ourselves at ease as much as possible, by successively granting to each whatever it demands."[12] What Crousaz demands of Pope's *Essay* but cannot get is relief from the "Oppositions which disturb" him, and "from the clearing up of which" he hopes "for the most satisfactory Calm." Crousazian "Calm"—the "ease" of "a new fiction" that Hume denigrates—is logocentric stasis: paradox resolved into true proposition. Neither the logocentric nor the aesthetic critic accepts Thomas Nagel's challenge: "The task of accepting the polarity of our subjective and objective perspectives without allowing either of its terms to swallow the other should be a creative one. It is the aim of eventual unification that I think is misplaced, both in our thoughts about how to live and in our conception of what there is. The coexistence of conflicting points of view, varying in detachment from the contingent self, is not just a practically necessary illusion but an irreducible fact of life."[13]

Philosophical poetry constitutes itself as a genre by accepting this irreducible polarity. Pope's *Essay* is greater than its posttexts because it is more true to the great text that is our experience of life and the world. "While we are in this life," Pope told Spence, "we can only speak from the volume that is laid open before us."[14] To close the volume by metaphysical fiat is bad faith, but this is exactly what Crousaz and Johnson did when they subordinated one of their perspectives to another. Never was he so moved by a piece of writing, Crousaz admits, as by Pope's intellectually worthless poem. "Never," Johnson admits, was philosophy "enchained" by such "dazzling splendour." Recounting in his *Autobiography* how poetry saved his life, John Stuart Mill recalls "how powerfully"

Pope's *Essay* affected him "though every opinion in it was contrary to mine." Not all philosophical poems adopt Pope's dialect of Academic Skepticism, but all do acknowledge "the coexistence of conflicting points of view." This constitutive coexistence of the "philosophical" and the "poetic" promises a thicker description of reality than either the desiccated "steno-language" of logocentric discourse or the emotive pseudo-statements of aesthetic discourse.

"Any position, whether scientific or religious, that claims to be absolute," Hans Kung asserts, "puts itself into question, because reality is multidimensional."[15] Similarly, Gerald Graff argues that in the greatest literature "we get both the tragic and the comic"; he agrees with Northrop Frye concerning the desirability of presenting "the up and down views, often at the same times, as different aspects of the same event."[16] David Vieth believes that the most rewarding Restoration texts express a "many-sided awareness," usually employing "multiple ironies to reflect all possible views of a situation, no matter how contradictory"; and Henry Fielding's best work, J. Paul Hunter writes, "derives much of its power from his tendency to wrestle central contradictions . . . only to a standoff."[17] Opposing any dialect that has as its norm "experience-as-systematized in referential and propositional discourse," Murray Krieger argues "against any cosmic resolution" of the richness of experience "to the single-mindedness of 'philosophy.'"[18]

The "mixed" genre of philosophical poetry aspires to do justice to the Manichaean complexity of what Krieger calls the "raging existential world," and I suspect the dualism of Manichaeism attracted Bayle and Pope's contemporaries for the same reason it seems paradigmatic to Krieger of the greatest literature: no monocularism can accommodate our various visions. "Something is always happening to the way we think," Stanley Fish hypothesizes, and "it is always the same thing, a tug-of-war between two views of human life and its possibilities, no one of which can ever gain complete and lasting ascendancy because in the very moment of its triumphant articulation each turns back in the direction of the other."[19] With binocular irony, metaphor, and paradox, with a "darkly wise" epistemology, and with an eclectic methodology of middle-state Academic Skepticism, Pope brilliantly articulates the constituting dichotomy of all philosophical poetry.

As long as philosophical poetry remains unnaturalized we are as blind as Homer's lumbering Cyclops, for we cannot read the richest philosophy or literature either. "Philosophy seems so singular a crossbreed of art and science," Arthur Danto notes, "that it is somewhat surprising that only lately has it seemed imperative to some that philosophy be viewed as literature." Danto argues that being sensitive to the literariness of philosophical writing is an alternative to misreading that need not deconstruct philosophy into poetry.[20] Yet whatever distinction we continue to wish to make "between literature and philosophy," Paul de Man categorically asserts, "cannot be made in terms of a distinction between aesthetic and epistemological categories." All philosophy is "condemned," he continues, to be literary.[21]

"But can philosophy become literature and still know itself?" Stanley Cavell asks. "Certainly not as long as philosophy continues, as it has from the first, to demand the banishment of poetry from its republic."[22] Presently, Robert Nozick complains, philosophy lives an impoverished existence "in which the rational mind speaks (only) to the rational mind." Plato argued but he also wrote "evocative myths that linger in memory—about people in a cave, about separated half-souls. Descartes rooted his most powerful writing in what was then Catholic meditative practice; Kant expressed his awe of two things, 'the starry heavens above and the moral law within.' Nietzsche and Kierkegaard, Pascal and Plotinus: the list could continue. . . . What happens in philosophy now is that the same part speaks and listens, the rational mind speaks to the rational mind."[23]

There are signs that the ancient quarrel between philosophy and poetry, which Socrates mentions in Book X of the *Republic*, may be on the mend. In *The Examined Life* Nozick consciously attempts to speak to more than one human "part." Similarly sensitive to the competing conceptions of the "hard 'philosophical' style" and a style "that lies closer to poetry and makes its appeal to more than one 'part' of the person," Martha Nussbaum chooses in *The Fragility of Goodness* to use both and betray neither.[24] I have tried to do the same in this book.

Recently, invoking Kant, Roger Scruton made a plea for the remarriage of philosophy and aesthetics as essential to a richer, human description of reality.[25] "That is not the Style of Philosophy," Crousaz grumbled, "but the language of Homer."[26] Kant, in contrast, relished the *Essay*, and the greatest minds of his age spoke a common language with Pope. Each knew, unlike stolid theologians like Crousaz, that, as Pope says of Virgil in *An Essay on Criticism:*

> when t'examine ev'ry Part he came,
> Nature and Homer were, he found, the same.

Our only hope of recovering communion with such minds in reading the *Essay* is to take philosophical poetry seriously as a genre. To do so may allow us to read for the first time Pope's glorious poem, still "the most beautiful, most useful, most sublime didactic poem" in English, and perhaps, as Voltaire insisted, the most sublime in any language.

NOTES

Introduction

1. François Marie de Voltaire, *Philosophical Letters,* trans. Ernest Dilworth (Indianapolis: Bobbs-Merrill, 1961), p. 147.

2. *The Indispensable Rousseau,* ed. John Hope Mason (London: Quartet Books, 1979), p. 112.

3. *Kant's Gesammelte Schriften* (Berlin: Walter de Grunter, 1926), 17:233–34.

4. Wallace Jackson, *Vision and Re-vision in Alexander Pope* (Detroit: Wayne State University Press, 1983), p. 67.

5. Maynard Mack, ed., *Essential Articles for the Study of Alexander Pope* (Hamden, CT: Archon, 1964), p. 20.

6. Harold Bloom, *Alexander Pope: Modern Critical Views* (New York: Chelsea House, 1986), pp. 3–4.

7. Robert M. Adams, "Putting Pope in His Place," *The New York Review of Books* (13 March 1986): 29.

8. G. S. Rousseau, *The Eighteenth Century: A Current Bibliography,* n.s. 3 (1981): 259.

9. A. D. Nuttall, *Pope's "Essay on Man"* (London: George Allen & Unwin, 1984), preface and pp. 190, 192.

10. David Nokes, "A Bout of Commentary," *Times Literary Supplement* 4246 (17 August 1984): 925.

11. Maynard Mack, *Alexander Pope: A Life* (New York: Norton, 1985), p. 541.

12. William John Courthope, *The Life of Alexander Pope* (London: John Mur-

ray, 1889), p. 244 (volume 5 of *The Works of Alexander Pope,* ed. Rev. Whitwell Elwin and W. J. Courthope, 10 vols. [London: John Murray, 1871–89]).

13. G. S. Rousseau, *The Eighteenth Century,* 258–59.

14. Lawrence Lipking, "Wise Guy," *American Scholar* 56:3 (Summer 1987): 439.

15. Cf. J. A. Cuddon, *A Dictionary of Literary Terms and Literary Theory,* 3rd ed. (Oxford: Blackwell, 1991), pp. 12–14 (for "Aestheticism") and 510–11 (for "Logocentrism").

16. John J. Richetti, *Philosophical Writing: Locke, Berkeley, Hume* (Cambridge: Harvard University Press, 1983), p. 17.

17. Gerald Graff, *Poetic Statement and Critical Dogma* (Chicago: University of Chicago Press, 1970); Phillip Harth, "The New Criticism and Eighteenth-Century Poetry," *Critical Inquiry* 7 (1981): 521–37.

18. Paul de Man, *Blindness and Insight: Essays in the Rhetoric of Contemporary Criticism,* 2nd ed. (Minneapolis: University of Minnesota Press, 1983), p. 139. In *Quests of Difference: Reading Pope's Poems* (Lexington: University Press of Kentucky, 1986), G. Douglas Atkins has suggestively used deconstruction to discuss *An Essay on Man* (pp. 39–65); however, our interests, approaches, and conclusions are very different.

19. *Essay on Man,* ed. Mark Pattison (Oxford: Clarendon Press, 1904), pp. 6, 14 (first published in 1869 and frequently reprinted).

20. Michael Ayers, *Locke* (London: Routledge, 1992).

21. Paul de Man, "The Epistemology of Metaphor," *Critical Inquiry* 5 (1978): 16.

22. de Man, *Blindness and Insight,* p. 139.

23. Vincent B. Leitch, *Deconstructive Criticism* (New York: Columbia University Press, 1983), p. 58.

24. *Martin Heidegger: Basic Writings,* ed. David Farrell Knell (New York: Harper, 1977), pp. 64–73.

25. James Wood, "Derrida in Oxford," *Times Literary Supplement* 4644 (3 April 1992): 13.

1. Trivializing *An Essay on Man*

1. *The Collected Writings of Thomas De Quincey,* ed. David Masson, 14 vols. (London: A. and C. Black, 1897), 11:86.

2. Geoffrey Tillotson, Paul Fussell, Jr., and Marshall Waingrow, eds., *Eighteenth-Century English Literature* (New York: Harcourt, 1969), p. 635.

3. Leopold Damrosch, Jr., *The Imaginative World of Alexander Pope* (Berkeley: University of California Press, 1987), p. 191.

4. David Foxon, *Pope and the Early Eighteenth-Century Book Trade,* revised and edited by James McLaverty (Oxford: Clarendon Press, 1991), p. 121.

5. Alexander Pope, *Imitations of Horace,* ed. John Butt, 2nd edition revised (New Haven: Yale University Press, 1961), p. 17.

6. Alexander Pope, *An Essay on Man,* ed. Maynard Mack (New Haven: Yale University Press, 1950), p. 11. Unless otherwise noted all quotations from the *Essay* are from this volume of the Twickenham Edition of the *Poems of Alexander Pope* and will be identified by page or line number.

7. On this and many other matters I am indebted to Maynard Mack's learned introduction to the Twickenham Edition of the *Essay,* pp. xi–lxxx.

8. "Occasion'd by reading the Essay on Man, first Part," *The London Evening-Post* 826 (15–17 March 1733): 2; *The Weekly Miscellany* 22 (12 May 1733): 2.

9. *The Gentleman's Magazine* 4 (February 1734): 97, 98.

10. Robert Dodsley, *An Epistle to Mr. Pope, Occasion'd by his Essay on Man* (London: L. Gilliver, 1734), p. 3.

11. *The Correspondence of Alexander Pope,* ed. George Sherburn, 5 vols. (Oxford: Clarendon Press, 1956), 3:400.

12. Lady Mary Pierrepont Wortley Montagu, *Essays and Poems and Simplicity: A Comedy,* ed. Robert Halsband (Oxford: Clarendon Press, 1977), p. 274.

13. *The False Patriot. An Epistle to Mr. Pope* (London: James Roberts, 1734), p. 11.

14. *The Present State of the Republic of Letters* 14 (October 1734): 254–55, 257.

15. *The Prompter* 111 (2 December 1735): 1–2.

16. Thomas Bentley, *A Letter to Mr. Pope, Occasion'd by Sober Advice From Horace* (London: T. Cooper, 1735), pp. 9–10.

17. *Correspondence of Alexander Pope,* 3:433.

18. *The Weekly Miscellany* 94 (28 September 1734): 1–2.

19. Mr. Bridges, *Divine Wisdom and Providence: An Essay Occasion'd by The Essay on Man* (London: J. Roberts, 1736), pp. ii–iii.

20. Edward Young, *Night Thoughts,* ed. Stephen Cornford (Cambridge: Cambridge University Press, 1989), p. 48. It is interesting that most of the "Nights" were initially published by the poet-bookseller Robert Dodsley, Pope's young friend and an early panegyrist of the *Essay on Man*: *The Complaint: or, Night-Thoughts on Life, Death, & Immortality* (London: for R. Dodsley, at Tully's Head in *Pall-Mall,* 1742).

21. *An Essay on Man,* ed. Mack, p. xviii. The fullest surveys of the French reception of the *Essay* are Robert W. Rogers, "Critiques of the *Essay on Man* in France and Germany 1736–1755," *ELH* 15:3 (1948): 176–93; and Richard Gilbert Knapp, *The Fortunes of Pope's "Essay on man" in 18th century France,* vol. 82 of *Studies on Voltaire and the Eighteenth Century,* ed. Theodore Besterman (Geneva: Institut et Musée Voltaire, 1971). Vincent Giroud describes a 750-page unpublished manuscript reaction to Pope's "principes des Pyrrhoniens et des Materialistes" in "An Early French Commentary on Pope's *Essay on Man,*" *Yale University Library Gazette* 57:1 (October 1982): 10–17. The anonymous author

predictably praises Pope as a master poet while censuring him as an obscure and inconsistent philosopher, a "Spinosiste" out of ignorance.

22. J. P. de Crousaz, *A Commentary on Mr. Pope's Principles of Morality, or Essay on Man,* trans. Samuel Johnson (London: A. Dodd, 1739), p. 302. Jean-François du Bellay du Resnel's preface and poetic translation are included in Johnson's edition of Crousaz, hereafter cited as "Johnson's *Crousaz.*"

23. *An Essay on Man,* ed. Mack, p. xix.

24. Reissued as *A Critical and Philosophical Commentary on Mr. Pope's Essay on Man* (London: John and Paul Knapton, 1742).

25. Nuttall, *Pope's "Essay on Man,"* p. 184.

26. Ibid., p. 182.

27. William Warburton, *The Works of the Right Reverend William Warburton,* 12 vols. (London: Printed by L. Hansard for T. Cadell and W. Davies, 1811), 12:335. Cf. *The Works of . . . Henry St. John, Lord Viscount Bolingbroke,* ed. David Mallet, 5 vols. (London: D. Mallet, 1754), 3:239.

28. William Warburton, *A View of Lord Bolingbroke's Philosophy* (London: J. and P. Knapton, 1754–55), 1:80–81.

29. *The Works of Alexander Pope,* ed. Joseph Warton et al., 9 vols. (London: B. Law, 1797), 3:14, 10. This view was earlier perpetuated in the second volume of Warton's *Essay on the Genius and Writings of Pope*, 2 vols. (London: J. Dodsley, 1782).

30. *The Works of Alexander Pope,* ed. William Roscoe, 10 vols. (London: Longman, 1824), 5:9.

31. *The Works of Alexander Pope,* ed. Rev. Whitwell Elwin and W. J. Courthope, 10 vols. (London: John Murray, 1871–89), 2:276, 313, 326.

32. Leslie Stephen, *Alexander Pope* (London: Macmillan, 1880), pp. 159–60, 166.

33. John Hervey, *A Letter To Mr. C——b-r, On his Letter to Mr. P——* (London: J. Roberts, 1742), pp. 14–15.

34. De Quincey, *Writings,* 11:92, 94.

35. *Works,* ed. Elwin, 2:319, 326.

36. *Essays by the Late Mark Pattison,* ed. Henry Nettleship, 2 vols. (Oxford: Clarendon Press, 1889), 2:130.

37. *Works,* ed. Elwin, 2:312, 332; Samuel Johnson, *Lives of the English Poets*, 2 vols. (London: Dent, 1925), 2:226; Stephen, *Pope,* p. 162.

38. Cecil A. Moore, "Did Leibniz Influence Pope's *Essay*?" *Journal of English and German Philology* 16 (1917): 84.

39. Donald J. Greene, "'Logical Structure' in Eighteenth-Century Poetry," *Philological Quarterly* 31 (1952): 330.

40. R. L. Brett, *Reason and Imagination* (London: Published for the University of Hull by Oxford University Press, 1960), p. 55.

41. Frederick S. Troy, "Pope's Images of Man," *Massachusetts Review* 1 (1960): 374.

42. James Reeves, *The Reputation and Writings of Alexander Pope* (London: Heinemann, 1976), p. 217.

43. David B. Morris, *Alexander Pope: The Genius of Sense* (Cambridge: Harvard University Press, 1984), p. 156.

44. de Man, *Blindness and Insight,* p. 111.

45. Johnson's *Crousaz,* p. 302.

46. John Clarke, *An Enquiry into the Causes and Origin of Moral Evil* (London: J. Knapton, 1721), p. 31. Clarke's Boyle lectures were aimed at advocates of the "Manichaean scheme, particularly Mr. Bayle."

47. Bolingbroke, *Works,* 3:317–18.

48. David Hume, *Enquiries Concerning the Human Understanding and Concerning the Principles of Morals,* ed. L. A. Selby-Bigge, 2nd ed. (Oxford: Clarendon Press, 1902), p. 17.

49. John Locke, *An Essay Concerning Human Understanding,* ed. Alexander Campbell Fraser, 2 vols. (New York: Dover, 1959), 2:146.

50. These phrases are taken from the section describing "Their manner of Discourse" in Thomas Sprat's 1667 *The History of the Royal Society.* Written just a few years after the chartering of the Royal Society, Sprat's *History* was really a manifesto for the future.

51. J. P. de Crousaz, *A Commentary on Mr. Pope's Four Ethic Epistles, Intituled, An Essay on Man. Wherein His System is fully Examin'd,* trans. Charles Forman (London: E. Curll, 1738), p. 20 (hereafter cited as "Curll's *Crousaz*"); Johnson's *Crousaz,* p. 26.

52. William Ayre, *Truth. A Counterpart to Mr. Pope's Esay* [*sic*] *on Man, Epistle the First* (London: R. Minors, 1739), contents.

53. William Ayre, *Memoirs of the Life and Writings of Alexander Pope* (London: For the Author, 1745), 2:329, 374, hereafter cited as Ayre, *Life of Pope.*

54. Johnson's *Crousaz,* p. 59; Johnson, *Lives of the English Poets,* 2:226.

55. Warton, *Essay,* 2:58, 1:x–xi, 2:143.

56. *The Correspondence of Edward Young, 1683–1765,* ed. Henry Pettit (Oxford: Clarendon Press, 1971), p. 448.

57. Warton, *Essay,* 1: x.

58. De Quincey, *Writings,* 11:89.

59. *Works,* ed. Elwin, 2:337.

60. Bloom, *Alexander Pope,* pp. 3–4.

61. Johnson, *Lives of the English Poets,* 2:226.

62. Bentley, *Letter To Mr. Pope,* p. 9.

63. Bezaleel Morrice, *To the Falsely Celebrated British Homer. An Epistle* (London: Printed for the Author, 1742), p. 8.

64. James Boswell, *Life of Johnson,* ed. R. W. Chapman (London: Oxford University Press, 1953), p. 1032.

65. Joseph Spence, *Observations, Anecdotes, and Characters of Books and Men,* ed. James Osborn, 2 vols. (Oxford: Clarendon Press, 1966), p. 311.

66. Brean S. Hammond, *Pope and Bolingbroke: A Study of Friendship and Influence* (Columbia: University of Missouri Press, 1984), p. 87.

67. *Common Sense: Or, The Englishman's Journal* 14 (10 December 1737): 1.

68. Stephen, *Pope,* p. 159.

69. Spence, *Observations,* p. 258.

70. Johnson, *Lives of the English Poets,* 2:226.

71. Pattison, *Essays,* 2:130.

72. John Sparrow, *Independent Essays* (London: Faber and Faber, 1963), p. 75.

73. George S. Fraser, *Alexander Pope* (London: Routledge, 1978), p. 74.

74. Johnson's *Crousaz,* pp. 150, 207; Curll's *Crousaz,* pp. 36, 64.

75. Ayre, *Truth,* p. 6; Ayre, *Life of Pope,* 2:252, 374.

76. *Common Sense a Common Delusion. Or, The generally-received Notions of Natural Causes, Deity, Religion, Virtue, &c. As exhibited in Mr. Pope's Essay on Man, Proved Ridiculous, Impious and the Effect of Infatuation; and the chief Cause of the present formidable Growth of Vice among Christians, and the great Stumbling-block in the Way of Infidels . . . By Almonides, a believing Heathen* (London: T. Reynolds, 1751), pp. 7, 27.

77. Johnson, *Lives of the English Poets,* 2:226–27.

78. Pattison, *Essays,* 2:386; Stephen, *Pope,* p. 164.

79. *Essay on Man,* ed. Pattison, pp. 16, 13; Stephen, *Pope,* p. 169.

80. Courthope, *Life of Alexander Pope,* pp. 245, 251.

81. H. A. Taine, *History of English Literature,* trans. H. Van Laun, 4 vols. (Edinburgh: Edmonston and Douglas, 1873), 3:359.

82. John Dennis, *The Age of Pope* (London: G. Bell, 1894), p. 112.

83. Warburton, *Critical and Philosophical Commentary,* p. 2. Following the focus of his title, *A Critical and Philosophical Commentary on Mr. Pope's Essay on Man,* Warburton makes clear that his defense will be limited to nonaesthetic matters.

84. *An Essay on Man,* ed. Mack, pp. xli–xlii.

85. Cf. Rogers, "Critiques of the *Essay on Man* in France and Germany," pp. 188–90.

86. Martin Kallich, *Heav'n's First Law: Rhetoric and Order in Pope's Essay on Man* (De Kalb: Northern Illinois University Press, 1967), p. 136.

87. *Essay on Man,* ed. Pattison, pp. 16–17.

88. *An Essay on Man,* ed. Mack, pp. xxiii, xlvii–xlviii.

89. Kallich, *Heav'n's First Law,* p. vii.

90. Douglas H. White, *Pope and the Context of Controversy: The Manipulation of Ideas in An Essay on Man* (Chicago: University of Chicago Press, 1970).

91. Nuttall, *Pope's "Essay on Man,"* pp. 195–219, 188.

92. Nicholas Hudson, *Samuel Johnson and Eighteenth-Century Thought* (Oxford: Clarendon Press, 1988), p. 99.

93. Donald J. Greene characterizes Bolingbroke as Johnson's *bête noire* in *The*

Politics of Samuel Johnson, 2nd ed. (Athens: University of Georgia Press, 1990), p. 262.

94. Martin Maner, *The Philosophical Biographer: Doubt and Dialectic in Johnson's "Lives of the Poets"* (Athens: University of Georgia Press, 1988), p. 127.

95. Samuel Johnson, *Diaries, Prayers, and Annals*, ed. E. L. McAdam, Jr., with Donald and Mary Hyde (New Haven: Yale University Press, 1958), pp. 46, 63, 77, 73, 268, 266, 303, 305, 289, 364–65, 271, 273, 265, 297, 300, 363, 368, 393, 414. Three chapter titles in Charles E. Pierce's *Religious Life of Samuel Johnson* (Hamden, CT: Archon Books, 1983) are indicative of Johnson's state of mind: "The Anvil of Anxiety," "The Character of Fearing," and "A Crisis of Faith."

96. Johnson, *Diaries,* pp. 294, 383.

97. Harry M. Solomon, *Sir Richard Blackmore* (Boston: Twayne, 1980), p. 140.

98. Johnson, *Lives of the English Poets,* 2:25.

99. Solomon, *Sir Richard Blackmore,* p. 128.

100. Johnson, *Diaries,* pp. 383–84.

101. Joseph Addison, et al., *The Spectator,* ed. Gregory Smith, 4 vols. (London: Dent, 1945), 3:278.

102. *Works,* ed. Elwin, 2:338–39.

103. Geoffrey Tillotson, *Pope and Human Nature* (Oxford: Clarendon Press, 1958), p. 42.

104. *An Essay on Man,* ed. Mack, p. xlvii.

105. Damrosch, *Imaginative World of Alexander Pope,* pp. 164, 183, 190.

106. *An Essay on Man,* ed. Mack, p. xxi.

107. The attitude of Richard Rorty's logocentric Kantians to physics and to writing provides a suggestive parallel to Crousaz's reaction to Pope's *Essay.* Cf. "Philosophy as a Kind of Writing: An Essay on Derrida," *New Literary History* 10 (1978), 156; Jonathan Culler, *On Deconstruction* (Ithaca: Cornell University Press, 1982), pp. 91, 147.

108. Yasmine Gooneratne, *Alexander Pope* (Cambridge: Cambridge University Press, 1976), p. 105.

109. Nuttall, *Pope's "Essay on Man,"* pp. 189, 43, 48, 61–62, 94, 98, 73, 75, 86, 84, 188, 182, 68, 54, 202, 219, 208.

110. Ibid., pp. 219, 213, 176.

111. William V. Spanos, "Heidegger, Kierkegaard, and the Hermeneutic Circle: Toward a Postmodern Theory of Interpretation," in *Martin Heidegger and the Question of Literature: Toward a Postmodern Literary Hermeneutics,* ed. William V. Spanos (Bloomington: Indiana University Press, 1976), p. 116.

112. Nuttall, *Pope's "Essay on Man,"* pp. 203, 194, 202.

113. J. Douglas Canfield, "A. D. Nuttall. *Pope's 'Essay on Man,'" Eighteenth-Century Studies* 19:2 (1985–86): 291.

114. Mack calls Nuttall's book "brilliant" if "sometimes rather off-the-cuff" (*Alexander Pope*, p. 899).

2. Disseminating Theodicy

1. *Princeton Encyclopedia of Poetry and Poetics*, ed. Alex Preminger, Enlarged Edition (Princeton: Princeton University Press, 1974), p. 615.

2. Jonathan Culler, *Structuralist Poetics* (Ithaca: Cornell University Press, 1975), p. 137.

3. Tzvetan Todorov, *Introduction à la littérature fantastique* (Paris: Seuil, 1970), p. 29.

4. Jacques Derrida, *Of Grammatology*, trans. G. C. Spivak (Baltimore: Johns Hopkins University Press, 1976), p. lxxxix.

5. Cf. Jacques Derrida, "Living On: Border Lines," *Deconstruction and Criticism*, ed. Harold Bloom, et al. (New York: Seabury Press, 1979), pp. 75–175.

6. *Essay on Man*, ed. Pattison, p. 9.

7. John Herman Randall, Jr., *The Career of Philosophy*, 2 vols. (New York: Columbia University Press, 1976), 1:749–50; William E. Alderman, "Pope's *Essay on Man* and Shaftesbury's *The Moralists*," *Publications of the Bibliographical Society of America* 67 (1973): 131–40. The earliest attacks on Pope's *Essay* accused him of plagiarizing Shaftesbury.

8. Bernhard Fabian, "On the Literary Background of the *Essay on Man:* A Note on Pope and Lucretius," in *Pope: Recent Essays by Several Hands,* ed. Maynard Mack and James A. Winn (Hamden, CT: Archon, 1980), pp. 417, 422.

9. Hammond, *Pope and Bolingbroke*, pp. 69–91.

10. Morris, *Alexander Pope*, p. 156. William Bowman Piper similarly sees *De Rerum Natura* as "an implicit ground" for Pope, "especially of Epistle I." Cf. "Pope's Vindication," *Philological Quarterly* 67:3 (Summer 1988): 320.

11. Nuttall, *Pope's "Essay on Man,"* pp. 43, 45, 51.

12. Damrosch, *Imaginative World of Alexander Pope*, p. 162.

13. Basil Willey, *The Eighteenth-Century Background* (London: Chatto and Windus, 1940), pp. 43–56.

14. A. O. Lovejoy, *The Great Chain of Being* (Cambridge: Harvard University Press, 1936), pp. 183–226.

15. Nuttall, *Pope's "Essay on Man,"* pp. 195–219.

16. An interesting variant on placing Pope occurs in an article by Douglas H. White and Thomas P. Tierney, "*An Essay on Man* and the Tradition of *Satires on Mankind*," *Modern Philology* 85:1 (1987): 27–41. They attempt to rehabilitate the *Essay* by stressing "the wit of the poem since, in truth, Pope's primary credentials are not philosophical" (p. 27).

17. Typical is I. R. F. Gordon's recommendation of both in *A Preface to Pope* (London: Longman, 1976), p. 192.

18. Leitch, *Deconstructive Criticism,* p. 124.

19. Shoshana Felman, *Jacques Lacan and the Adventure of Insight: Psychoanalysis in Contemporary Culture* (Cambridge: Harvard University Press, 1987).

20. Dodsley, *Epistle to Mr. Pope,* p. 4.

21. Nokes, "A Bout of Commentary," p. 925.

22. Leitch, *Deconstructive Criticism,* pp. 59, 68, 99, 110.

23. Maynard Mack provides facsimiles and printed transcriptions of the manuscripts of *An Essay on Man* in *"The Last and Greatest Art": Some Unpublished Poetical Manuscripts of Alexander Pope* (Newark: Delaware University Press, 1984), pp. 190–418.

24. Warburton, *Critical and Philosophical Commentary,* p. 2.

25. John Milton, *Complete Poems and Major Prose,* ed. Merritt Y. Hughes (New York: Odyssey, 1957), p. 212 (1:22–26). Subsequent citations from *Paradise Lost* are from this edition.

26. Warton, *Essay,* 2:61–63.

27. Nuttall, *Pope's "Essay on Man,"* pp. 56–58, 51. Cf. J. Douglas Canfield, "The Fate of the Fall in Pope's *Essay on Man,*" *The Eighteenth Century: Theory and Interpretation* 23 (1982): 134–50.

28. *Oxford Companion to English Literature,* ed. Margaret Drabble, 5th ed. (Oxford: Oxford University Press, 1985), p. 326.

29. Nuttall, *Pope's "Essay on Man,"* pp. 57–58, 98, 86, 51.

30. Warton, *Essay,* 2:410.

31. Leitch, *Deconstructive Criticism,* pp. 245–46.

32. William Sherlock, *A Discourse Concerning the Divine Providence* (London: William Rogers, 1694), p. 147. In demonstrating the interest in theodicy, Douglas White notes that Sherlock's *Discourse* had gone through six editions by 1725 and was a "classic" (p. 16); however, he never mentions Sherlock again. Neither Mack nor Nuttall mentions Sherlock at all.

33. Sherlock, *Discourse,* pp. 86–87.

34. Manuscript of Epistle II now at the Morgan Library in New York City (facsimile in Mack's *"Last and Greatest Art"*).

35. Arthur Ashley Sykes, *The True Foundations of Natural and Reveal'd Religion Asserted* (London: James and John Knapton, 1730), p. 94.

36. White, *Pope and the Context of Controversy,* p. 125.

37. *The Philosophical Works of Mr. William Dudgeon* (Edinburgh: privately printed, 1765), p. viii.

38. William Dudgeon, *A View of the Necessitarian or Best Scheme: Freed From The Objections of M. Crousaz, in his Examination of Mr. Pope's "Essay on Man"* (London: T. Cooper, 1739).

39. Daniel W. Odell, "Young's *Night Thoughts* as an Answer to Pope's *Essay on Man,*" *Studies in English Literature* 12 (1972): 481–501.

40. Harold Bloom, *The Anxiety of Influence* (New York: Oxford University Press, 1973), p. 141.

41. *The Correspondence of Edward Young,* ed. Henry Pettit (Oxford: Clarendon Press, 1971), p. 59.

42. Edward Young, *The Complete Works, Poetry and Prose,* ed. James Nichols, 2 vols. (London: William Tegg, 1854), 2:323; *An Essay on Man,* ed. Mack, p. 8.

43. Sir Richard Blackmore, *Creation: A Philosophical Poem. In Seven Books,* reprinted in *Works of the English Poets,* ed. Alexander Chalmers, 21 vols. (London: C. Whittingham, 1810), 10:328, 331. Hereafter cited with page but without volume number.

44. Sherlock, *Discourse,* p. 10.

45. Solomon, *Sir Richard Blackmore,* pp. 122–27.

46. *The Critical Works of John Dennis,* ed. Edward Niles Hooker, 2 vols. (Baltimore: Johns Hopkins University Press, 1939), 2:120.

47. Johnson's *Crousaz,* p. 302.

48. Fabian, "On the Literary Background of the *Essay on Man,*" pp. 416–27.

49. Hammond, *Pope and Bolingbroke,* pp. 69–91.

50. Clifford Geertz, "Thick Description: Toward an Interpretive Theory of Culture," *The Interpretation of Cultures* (New York: Basic Books, 1973), pp. 3–30.

51. Johnson, *Lives of the English Poets,* 2:230.

52. *The Poems and Fables of John Dryden,* ed. James Kinsley (London: Oxford University Press, 1962), p. 283.

53. Italics added.

54. As fellow Kit-Cats Addison probably read Blackmore's *Creation* in manuscript; and he certainly praised it in the *Spectator* when published. Blackmore solicited corrections while his works were in manuscript so Addison's "borrowings" from Blackmore may be simply taking a bit of his own back.

55. Sykes, *Foundations,* p. 94.

56. Derrida, "Living On: Border Lines," p. 81.

57. Roland Barthes, "The Death of The Author," *Image, Music, Text,* trans. Stephen Heath (New York: Hill and Wang, 1977), p. 146.

3. The Self as Aporia

1. David Hume, *Enquiries,* p. 165.

2. *Present State of the Republic of Letters* 14 (1734): 254–55.

3. Philip Dormer Stanhope, Fourth Earl of Chesterfield, *Characters by Lord Chesterfield Contrasted with Characters of the Same Great Personages by other respectable Writers* (London: Edward and Charles Dilly, 1778), pp. 20, 14. As G. Douglas Atkins notes, the question of Pope's own beliefs—particularly whether or not he was a deist—has obsessed scholars since the publication of *An*

Essay on Man. Cf. Atkins, "Pope and Deism: A New Analysis," in *Pope: Recent Essays*, ed. Mack, pp. 392–415.

4. Nuttall's objection is representative (pp. 76–77) and reinscribes Crousaz's made 250 years earlier.

5. Charles Williams, *Reason and Beauty in the Poetic Mind* (Oxford: Clarendon Press, 1933), p. 50.

6. William Bowman Piper, "Leopold Damrosch, Jr., *The Imaginative World of Alexander Pope*," *The Scriblerian* 24:1 (Autumn 1991): 46.

7. Johnson's *Crousaz*, p. 25.

8. Johnson, *Lives of the English Poets*, 2:226.

9. *Present State of the Republic of Letters* 14 (1734): 255.

10. Warton, *Essay*, 2:115–16; see also *Works*, ed. Elwin, p. 267.

11. Reuben Brower, *Alexander Pope: The Poetry of Allusion* (Oxford: Oxford University Press, 1959), p. 239.

12. Simon Varey, "Rhetoric and *An Essay on Man*," in *The Art of Alexander Pope*, ed. Howard Erskine-Hill and Anne Smith (New York: Barnes and Noble, 1979), pp. 132, 144.

13. Dustin Griffin, *Alexander Pope: The Poet in the Poems* (Princeton: Princeton University Press, 1978), p. 153.

14. Martin Price, *To the Palace of Wisdom: Studies in Order and Energy from Dryden to Blake* (Garden City, NY: Anchor, 1964), p. 133.

15. Richard Striner, "Felicity Rosslyn. *Alexander Pope: A Literary Life*," *The Scriblerian* 24:1 (Autumn 1991): 50.

16. S. L. Goldberg, "Integrity and Life in Pope's Poetry," in *Studies in the Eighteenth Century: III*, ed. R. F. Brissenden and J. C. Eade (Toronto: University of Toronto Press, 1976), pp. 191–92.

17. Richard Rorty, *Contingency, Irony, and Solidarity* (Cambridge: Cambridge University Press, 1989), pp. 198, 61; Richard Rorty, *Philosophy and the Mirror of Nature* (Princeton: Princeton University Press, 1979).

18. Curll's *Crousaz*, p. 25.

19. Ayre, *Life of Pope*, 2:309.

20. *Common Sense*, p. 16.

21. Stanley L. Jaki, *The Road of Science and the Ways to God* (Chicago: University of Chicago Press, 1978), p. 87.

22. Henry Pemberton, *A View of Sir Isaac Newton's Philosophy*, ed. I. B. Cohen (New York: Johnson Reprint, 1972), p. 23. Originally published shortly before *An Essay on Man* (London: S. Palmer, 1728).

23. Sherlock, *Discourse*, p. 355.

24. *The Ethics of Aristotle: The Nicomachean Ethics*, trans. J. A. K. Thompson (New York: Penguin, 1976), p. 101.

25. Conyers Middleton, *The History of the Life of Marcus Tullius Cicero*, 2 vols. (Dublin: John Smith, 1741), 2:601.

26. William Wollaston, *The Religion of Nature Delineated,* 7th ed. (London: J. and P. Knapton, 1750). The first edition has the quotation only in Greek.

27. John Wilkins, *The Principles and Duties of Natural Religion* (London: T. Basset, 1678).

28. John Tillotson, "Sermon I," in *Eighteenth-Century English Literature,* ed. Tillotson et al., p. 209.

29. Anthony Ashley Cooper, Third Earl of Shaftesbury, *Characteristics of Men, Manners, Opinions, Times,* ed. John M. Robertson (Indianapolis: Bobbs-Merrill, 1964), p. 75.

30. *The Works of the Reverend and Learned Isaac Watts* (London: J. Barfield, 1810), 2:315–425. Advertized as "lately printed" opposite the title page of *Thoughts on Religion, and other Curious Subjects . . . By Monsieur Pascal,* trans. Basil Kennet, 3rd edition (London: John Pemberton, 1731). Pope owned Kennet's translation, hereafter cited as "Kennet's *Pascal.*"

31. Michael B. Prince provides useful summary notes on relevant scholarship in "Hume and the End of Religious Dialogue," *Eighteenth-Century Studies* 25:3 (Spring 1992): 283–308.

32. Reinhold Niebuhr, *The Nature and Destiny of Man, A Christian Interpretation,* 2 vols. (New York: Scribner, 1941–43).

33. Thomas Nagel, *Mortal Questions* (Cambridge: Cambridge University Press, 1979), pp. 196, 14, 213.

34. J. Hillis Miller, "Ariachne's Broken Woof," *Georgia Review* 31 (1977): 56.

35. J. Hillis Miller, "Stevens' Rock and Criticism as Cure," *Georgia Review* 30 (1976): 341.

36. Culler, *On Deconstruction,* p. 155. *Larouse* defines "aporia" as a logical difficulty without resolution. J. A. Cuddon derives the word from the Greek meaning "impassable path": *Aporia* indicates "a kind of impasse or insoluble conflict between rhetoric and thought. *Aporia* suggests the 'gap' or lacuna between what a text means to say and what it is constrained to mean" (*Dictionary of Literary Terms,* p. 55).

37. Hayden White, *Metahistory: The Historical Imagination in Nineteenth-Century Europe* (Baltimore: Johns Hopkins University Press, 1973), p. 37.

38. Rorty, *Contingency, Irony, and Solidarity,* p. 73.

39. *Correspondence of Alexander Pope,* 1:202–3.

40. Leitch, *Deconstructive Criticism,* p. 250.

41. David Hume, *A Treatise of Human Nature,* ed. L. A. Selby-Bigge, 2nd ed. (Oxford: Clarendon Press, 1978), p. 273.

42. As Maynard Mack notes (*Essay on Man,* pp. xli–xlii), Kant frequently quotes Pope with respect. A. O. Lovejoy judges Kant's *Allgemeine Naturgeschichte und Theorie des Himmels* (1755) as an "amplification" of Epistle I of *An Essay on Man* (*The Great Chain of Being,* p. 357).

43. Cf. Ernest Tuveson, "*An Essay on Man* and 'The Way of Ideas,'" *ELH* 26 (1959): 368–86.

44. Norman Hampson, *The Enlightenment* (Baltimore: Penguin, 1968), pp. 75–76.

45. Bolingbroke, *Works,* 3:361, 383.

46. Ibid., 4:229.

47. Robert Jenkins, *The Reasonableness and Certainty of the Christian Religion* (London: Richard Sare, 1715), 2:1, 5–6.

48. *The Works of Joseph Butler,* ed. W. E. Gladstone, 2 vols. (Oxford: Clarendon Press, 1897), 2:219, 221, 223–25.

49. Ibid., 2:218, 229, 231.

50. Another line pursued by the telescopes and microscopes of the physico-theologists. Cf. Solomon, *Sir Richard Blackmore,* pp. 122–27.

51. "Although it was not Pope's intention to undermine the basic doctrines of Christianity," Richard Gilbert Knapp concludes, "he was, nonetheless, viewed as a fellow deist by Voltaire" (*The Fortunes of Pope's "Essay on man" in 18th century France,* p. 122).

52. *Oxford Companion to English Literature,* p. 326.

53. Thomas Hobbes, *Thomas White's De Mundo Examined,* trans. Harold Whitmore Jones (London: Bradford University Press, 1976), p. 391.

54. Bolingbroke, *Works,* 3:328–29.

55. *The Dialogues of Plato,* trans. Benjamin Jowett, 2 vols. (New York: Random House, 1937), 1:421.

56. *Works of Joseph Butler,* 2:229.

57. Thomas Stanley, *The History of Philosophy: Containing the Lives, Opinions, Actions and Discourses of the Philosophers of Every Sect. Illustrated with the Effigies of divers of Them.* 2nd ed. (London: Thomas Bassett, Dorman Newman, and Thomas Cockerill, 1687), pp. 71–72. Maynard Mack notes Pope's autograph inscription in a copy now privately owned (*Collected in Himself: Essays Critical, Biographical, and Bibliographical on Pope and Some of His Contemporaries* [Newark: University of Delaware Press, 1982], p. 442).

58. White, *Pope and the Context of Controversy,* p. 82.

59. Warburton, *Critical and Philosophical Commentary,* p. 137.

60. White effectively provides the context of this debate (pp. 77–81 of *Pope and the Context of Controversy*).

61. Peter Browne, *The Procedure, Extent and Limits of Human Understanding* (London: William Innys, 1728), p. 86.

62. John Balguy, *The Law of Truth: Or, the Obligations of Reason Essential to All Religion* (London: John Pemberton, 1733), p. xii.

63. Peter Browne, *Things Divine and Supernatural Conceived by Analogy with Things Natural and Human* (London: William Innys, 1733), p. 1.

64. Cf. White, *Pope and the Context of Controversy,* pp. 81–82, and Nuttall, *Pope's "Essay on Man,"* p. 61.

65. Bolingbroke, *Works,* 4:229.

66. Patricia Meyer Spacks, *An Argument of Images: The Poetry of Alexander Pope* (Cambridge: Harvard University Press, 1971), p. 78.

67. John Barker, *Strange Contrarieties: Pascal in England during the Age of Reason* (Montreal: McGill-Queens University Press, 1975), p. 128.

68. Kennet's *Pascal,* p. 151.

69. Ibid., p. 162.

70. Ibid., pp. 151, 40–41, 44.

71. Alasdair Macintyre, *After Virtue: A Study in Moral Theory,* 2nd ed. (Notre Dame: University of Notre Dame Press, 1984), p. 40.

72. Hampson, *The Enlightenment,* p. 35.

73. Nagel, *Mortal Questions,* p. 197.

74. Richard Willis, *The Occasional Paper: Number III. Being Reflections on Mr. Toland's Book, call'd Christianity Not Mysterious: With Some Considerations about the Use of Reason in Matters of Religion* (London: M. Wotton, 1697), p. 10.

75. Bolingbroke, *Works,* 3:312–13, 327, 561.

76. Spence, *Observations,* p. 135.

77. Phillips Gretton, *A Review of the Argument A Priori, In Relation to the Being and Attributes of God* (London, 1726), p. iii.

78. Blackmore, *Creation,* p. 352. The parallels between Blackmore and Pope on this matter extend beyond style and semantics to use of larger literary devices, including dialogue, cf. *Creation,* pp. 340ff.

79. *Common Sense,* p. 15.

80. Jeffrey Barnouw, "The Separation of Reason and Faith in Bacon and Hobbes, and Leibniz's *Theodicy,*" *Journal of the History of Ideas* 42:4 (October–December 1981): 610.

81. James E. Force, "Hume and the Relation of Science to Religion among Certain Members of the Royal Society," *Journal of the History of Ideas* 45:4 (October–December 1984): 517–36.

82. Immanuel Kant, *Lectures on Philosophical Theology,* trans. Allen W. Wood and Gertrude M. Clark (Ithaca: Cornell University Press, 1978), pp. 79, 118.

83. Sherlock, *Discourse,* pp. 135–36.

84. Browne, *The Procedure, Extent and Limits of Human Understanding,* p. 447.

85. Blackmore, *Creation,* p. 359.

86. Matthew Prior, *Poems on Several Occasions,* ed. A. R. Waller (Cambridge: Cambridge University Press, 1905), pp. 262, 283. The resemblances to Pope's first verse paragraph ("be *wild*er'd"/"*fruit*less") correctly suggest a significant, direct relationship between *An Essay on Man* and *Solomon.*

87. *An Essay on Man,* ed. Mack, p. lxix; Maynard Mack, "Pope's Books: A Biographical Survey with a Finding List," in *English Literature in the Age of Disguise,* ed. Maximillian Novak (Berkeley: University of California Press, 1977), pp. 225–26.

88. *The Complete Essays of Montaigne,* trans. Donald M. Frame (Stanford: Stanford University Press, 1958), pp. 368, 328, 401.

89. *The Oxford Dictionary of the Christian Church*, ed. F. L. Cross and E. A. Livingstone, 2nd ed. (Oxford: Oxford University Press, 1978), p. 666.

90. Jurgen Moltmann, *Theology of Hope* (New York: Harper and Row, 1967), p. 23.

91. Jeremy Collier, *Essays upon Several Moral Subjects*, 6th ed., 2 vols. (London: D. Brown, 1722), 1:233, 2:125.

92. *Rousseau*, p. 112; Warburton, *Critical and Philosophical Commentary*, p. 117.

93. Spence, *Observations*, p. 76.

94. Nagel, *Mortal Questions*, p. 21.

95. *Complete Essays of Montaigne*, p. 371.

96. Marjorie Hope Nicolson, *Newton Demands the Muse: Newton's Opticks and the Eighteenth-Century Poets* (Princeton: Princeton University Press, 1946), p. 134.

97. Bentley, *A Letter to Mr. Pope*, p. 9.

98. Warburton, *Critical and Philosophical Commentary*, p. 73.

99. *Essay on Man*, ed. Pattison, p. 92.

100. Nuttall, *Pope's "Essay on Man,"* p. 86.

101. *Works of Joseph Butler*, 2:219.

102. Blackmore, *Creation*, p. 349.

103. *Newton's Philosophy of Nature: Selections from His Writings*, ed. H. S. Thayer (New York: Hafner, 1953), p. 53.

104. Joseph Glanvill, *Essays on Several Important Subjects in Philosophy and Religion* (London: J. D. for John Baker and Henry Mortlock, 1676), p. 32.

4. Optimism and Pessimism

1. Frances Bacon, *Essays, Advancement of Learning, New Atlantis, and Other Pieces*, ed. Richard Foster Jones (New York: Odyssey, 1937), pp. 177–79. Cf. Barnouw, "The Separation of Reason and Faith in Bacon and Hobbes, and Leibniz's *Theodicy*," pp. 610–11.

2. *Works of Joseph Butler*, 2:229–30.

3. Ibid., 2:228.

4. Nuttall, *Pope's "Essay on Man,"* p. 68.

5. Spence, *Observations*, p. 136.

6. Ibid., p. 226.

7. *Correspondence of Alexander Pope*, 3:354.

8. Douglas Lane Patey, *Probability and literary form: Philosophical theory and literary practice in the Augustan age* (Cambridge: Cambridge University Press, 1984), p. 128.

9. White, *Pope and the Context of Controversy*, p. 13.

10. Damrosch, *Imaginative World of Alexander Pope*, p. 174.

11. White, *Pope and the Context of Controversy*, p. 82.

12. Johnson's *Crousaz,* p. 89.

13. Warton, *Essay,* 2:67.

14. Nuttall, *Pope's "Essay on Man,"* p. 69.

15. *Common Sense,* pp. 16, 30–31.

16. Williams, *Reason and Beauty in the Poetic Mind,* pp. 46–47.

17. R. D. Stock, *The Holy and the Demonic from Sir Thomas Browne to William Blake* (Princeton: Princeton University Press, 1982), pp. 123, 130.

18. Nuttall, *Pope's "Essay on Man,"* pp. 54, 70.

19. Spence, *Observations,* p. 240.

20. *Complete Essays of Montaigne,* pp. 431–33; the "poor Indian" in *The Works of . . . Isaac Watts,* 2:333.

21. *An Essay on Man,* ed. Mack, p. 228.

22. *Works of Joseph Butler,* 2:224; *An Essay on Man,* ed. Mack, p. 7.

23. J. L. Austin, *How to do Things with Words* (Cambridge: Harvard University Press, 1975), p. 1.

24. Stanley Fish, "Rhetoric," in *Critical Terms for Literary Study,* ed. Frank Lentricchia and Thomas McLaughlin (Chicago: University of Chicago Press, 1990), p. 213.

25. Spence, *Observations,* p. 134.

26. Italics added.

27. Randall, *The Career of Philosophy,* 1:685.

28. Nuttall, *Pope's "Essay on Man,"* p. 54.

29. Curll's *Crousaz,* p. 25.

30. Nuttall, *Pope's "Essay on Man,"* pp. 73, 75, 84, 61, 105–106.

31. *Works of Joseph Butler,* 2:229.

32. Browne, *The Procedure, Extent and Limits of Human Understanding,* pp. 87, 468.

33. Albion Roy King, *The Problem of Evil: Christian Concepts and the Book of Job* (New York: Ronald Press, 1952), p. 99; Solomon, *Sir Richard Blackmore,* pp. 83–93.

34. Pierre Bayle, *The Dictionary, Historical and Critical of Mr. Peter Bayle,* 2nd ed., 5 vols. (London: J. J. and P. Knapton et al., 1734–38), 4:513, 527.

35. Bacon, *Essays,* pp. 177–79.

36. Nuttall, *Pope's "Essay on Man,"* pp. 62–63.

37. Robert Uphaus, *The Impossible Observer: Reason and the Reader in 18th-Century Prose* (Lexington: University Press of Kentucky, 1979), p. 30.

38. Griffin, *Alexander Pope,* p. 130.

39. Spacks, *An Argument of Images,* pp. 45–46.

40. Thomas R. Edwards, Jr., "Visible Poetry: Pope and Modern Criticism," *Twentieth-Century Literature in Retrospect,* ed. Reuben A. Brower. Harvard English Studies 2 (Cambridge: Harvard University Press, 1971), p. 315.

41. Jackson, *Vision and Re-vision in Alexander Pope,* p. 72.

42. Edwards, "Visible Poetry," pp. 312–15.

43. Simon Varey, "Rhetoric and *An Essay on Man*," in *The Art of Alexander Pope*, ed. Howard Erskine-Hill and Anne Smith (New York: Barnes and Noble, 1979), pp. 132–43.

44. Fredric V. Bogel, *Acts of Knowledge: Pope's Later Poems* (Lewisburg, PA: Bucknell University Press, 1981), p. 30.

45. Rebecca Ferguson, *The Unbalanced Mind: Pope and the Rule of Passion* (Philadelphia: University of Pennsylvania Press, 1986), p. 90.

46. Howard D. Weinbrot, *Alexander Pope and the Tradition of Formal Verse Satire* (Princeton: Princeton University Press, 1982), p. 364.

47. Nagel, *Mortal Questions*, pp. 13–21.

48. *The Philosophy of Kant: Immanuel Kant's Moral and Political Writings*, ed. Carl J. Friedrich (New York: Random House, 1949), p. 327.

49. Barnouw, "The Separation of Reason and Faith in Bacon and Hobbes, and Leibniz's *Theodicy*," p. 628.

50. *Rousseau*, pp. 112, 116–17.

51. Kant, *Lectures on Philosophical Theology*, pp. 138–39. Cf. Allen Wood, *Kant's Rational Theology* (Ithaca: Cornell University Press, 1978).

52. *Complete Essays of Montaigne*, pp. 389, 384.

53. Nagel, *Mortal Questions*, pp. 19–20, 13.

54. Johnson's *Crousaz*, p. 154.

55. Warburton, *Critical and Philosophical Commentary*, p. 100.

56. Nuttall, *Pope's "Essay on Man,"* pp. 100, 48, 101, 84, 155.

5. Academic Discourse

1. Locke, *Essay*, 1:202–203.

2. Johnson's *Crousaz*, p. 1; Warburton, *Critical and Philosophical Commentary*, pp. 2, 5.

3. Leitch, *Deconstructive Criticism*, pp. 77–78.

4. *Works*, ed. Elwin, p. 375; *An Essay on Man*, ed. Mack, pp. 54, xl.

5. In his subsequent biography of Pope, Maynard Mack assumes but does not develop the epistemological contrast between "the Pyrrhonist's total mistrust of reason and the Stoic's excess of confidence in it" (*Alexander Pope*, p. 531).

6. Middleton, *Cicero*, 2:601–602.

7. Peter Gay, *The Enlightenment: An Interpretation*, 2 vols. (New York: Norton, 1977), 1:109.

8. Bolingbroke, *Works*, 3:312–13, 317–18.

9. Cf. Mack's index, *An Essay on Man*, pp. 171–86.

10. Bolingbroke, *Works*, 3:319, 333, 335, 329.

11. Stanley, *History of Philosophy*, p. 155.

12. Scholars continue to debate whether Montaigne was an Academic or a

Pyrrhonist at any particular time in his life. Zachary Schiffman says Montaigne "did not fully accept his own radical skepticism until reading Sextus's *Outlines of Pyrrhonism,* probably around 1576, when he composed the Pyrrhonistic core of the 'Apology.' Sextus provided Montaigne with a detailed, forceful account of Pyrrhonism and its challenge to Academic skepticism" ("Montaigne and the Rise of Skepticism," p. 512). I would argue that both were dialects alternately congenial to Montaigne.

13. Stanley, *History of Philosophy,* p. 776.

14. Bayle, *Dictionary, Historical and Critical,* 4:653. Maynard Mack mentions Pope's fondness for Bayle (*Alexander Pope,* p. 841).

15. Frank Thilly and Ledger Wood, *A History of Philosophy,* 3rd ed. (New York: Holt, Rinehart, 1963), p. 143; I. G. Kidd, "Greek Academy," in *The Encyclopedia of Philosophy,* ed. Paul Edwards, 8 vols. (New York: Macmillan, 1967), 3:382–85.

16. Stanley, *History of Philosophy,* p. 225. Both Stanley (pp. 222–26) and Bayle (2:325–35) treat Carneades as a major figure, Stanley even including an engraving (p. 222).

17. Stanley, *History of Philosophy,* pp. 777, 791.

18. Kidd, "Greek Academy," 3:384.

19. Gay, *The Enlightenment,* 1:107–108.

20. Jaroslav Pelikan, *The Melody of Theology: A Philosophical Dictionary* (Cambridge: Harvard University Press, 1988), p. 73.

21. Maynard Mack says that Erasmus was Pope's "lifelong hero" (*Alexander Pope,* p. 81); *Correspondence of Alexander Pope,* 1:118–19. Cf. also 1:128 where Pope uses "vindicate" again to refer to his identification with Erasmus.

22. Pope, *Imitations of Horace,* 4:11.

23. *Twenty Two Select Colloquies out of Erasmus Roterdamus, Pleasantly representing several Superstitious Levities That were Crept into the Church of Rome In His Days. By Sir Roger L'Estrange, Kt. To which are added, Seven More Dialogues, with the Life of the Author. By Mr. Tho. Brown* (London: B. Motte et al., 1725), pp. 115, 98, 102.

24. *Wit against Wisdom: Or The Praise of Folly. Made English from the Latin of Erasmus. By an Eminent Hand,* 3rd ed. (London: John Wilford, 1722), pp. xiii, 60, 79. Robert M. Adams concludes that "Folly's judgment of [the Academics] (as 'least insolent') was probably in large part that of Erasmus as well" (Desiderius Erasmus, *The Praise of Folly and Other Writings,* trans. Robert M. Adams [New York: Norton, 1989], p. 46). Pope's admiration of Erasmus is discussed by Bruce Mansfield in *Phoenix of His Age: Interpretations of Erasmus c 1550–1750* (Toronto: University of Toronto Press, 1979), pp. 256–58.

25. *Correspondence of Alexander Pope,* 4:479.

26. Mack, *Alexander Pope,* p. 835.

27. Cotton's *Montaigne* (1700), 2:379.

28. Bayle, *Dictionary, Historical and Critical,* 2:326.

29. Ibid., 5:798, 5:831, 2:487.

30. Ibid., 2:454. The objections to the impiety of Charron's *De la Sagesse* prefigure the same objections to *An Essay on Man*, and some of Bayle's strategies for defending Charron bear comparison with Warburton's defense of Pope.

31. Pierre Charron, *Of Wisdom. In Three Books. Written Originally in French, By the Sieur de CHARRON*, trans. George Stanhope, 2nd ed., 2 vols. (London: J. Tonson et al., 1707), 1:324.

32. Ibid., 1:1, 9, and "An Explanation of the Figure in the Frontispiece of this Book."

33. Ibid., 1:360, 365, 370, and "Explanation."

34. Few critics make even perfunctory use of the parallels between Pope and Charron. In *Alexander Pope*, Maynard Mack stresses Montaigne's influence on Pope but nowhere mentions Charron. Nuttall mentions Charron once to show "the Stoic credentials" of Pope's concept of "self-love" (*Pope's "Essay on Man,"* pp. 88–89).

35. Charron, *Of Wisdom*, 1:13.

36. Alexander Pope, *Epistles To Several Persons*, ed. F. W. Bateson, 2nd ed. (New Haven: Yale University Press, 1961), p. 27. Rebecca Ferguson offers a surprising interpretation of Pope's praise of Charron: "The word 'sage' is surely to be taken ironically ('knowing') in view of what might be termed Charron's 'extravagant rationalism'" (*The Unbalanced Mind*, p. 111).

37. Bolingbroke, *Works*, 3:313.

38. Ibid., 4:358ff.

39. *An Essay on Man*, ed. Mack, p. xxx.

40. *Correspondence of Alexander Pope*, 2:220.

41. Marcus Tullius Cicero, *Tusculan Disputations*, trans. J. E. King (London: William Heinemann, 1927), pp. 62–63; Mack (*An Essay on Man*, p. 53) quotes Xenophon.

42. Lisa Jardine, "Lorenzo Valla: Academic Skepticism and the New Humanist Dialectic," in *The Skeptical Tradition*, ed. Myles Burnyeat (Berkeley: University of California Press, 1983), p. 260.

43. Cicero, *The Nature of the Gods*, p. 74.

44. Bolingbroke, *Works*, 4:121 and 3:312–13.

45. Mack, *Collected in Himself*, p. 401.

46. Hammond, *Pope and Bolingbroke*, pp. 143–46.

47. Douglas White's learned *Pope and the Context of Controversy* pays primary attention to Pope's immediate contemporaries.

48. Nuttall, *Pope's "Essay on Man,"* pp. 44–52.

49. Cf. *An Essay on Man*, ed. Mack, pp. xxix–xxxi; Nuttall, *Pope's "Essay on Man,"* p. 48. On page 48 Nuttall says that "Maynard Mack has exposed the weakness of the case for regarding Bolingbroke as an exclusive or overriding influence"; on page 45 he says that Bolingbroke was "Pope's philosophical mentor."

50. *An Essay on Man: Reproductions of the Manuscripts in the Pierpont Morgan*

Library and the Houghton Library with the Printed Text of the Original Edition, intro. Maynard Mack (Oxford: Roxburghe Club, 1962).

51. Nuttall, *Pope's "Essay on Man,"* pp. 48–49.

52. Hume, *Treatise,* pp. 181, 273.

53. Richard H. Popkin, *The History of Scepticism from Erasmus to Descartes,* rev. ed. (New York: Harper, 1964), p. 151.

54. James Balfour, *Philosophical Essays* (Edinburgh: For John Balfour, 1768), pp. 46, 28, 59.

55. M. Tullii Ciceronis, *Academica* (Londinenses: Jacobum Knapton, 1725); "editio secunda" 1736.

56. David Hume, *Dialogues Concerning Natural Religion,* ed. Norman Kemp Smith (New York: Macmillan, 1947), p. 227. Among a "host of recent commentators" stressing the "rhetorical, dramatic, or literary qualities of the *Dialogues,*" Michael B. Prince first cites W. B. Carnochan's contention that the overriding theme of Hume's *Dialogues* is the "Ciceronian virtue of friendship" ("Hume and the End of Religious Dialogue," *Eighteenth-Century Studies* 25:3 [Spring 1992]: 283).

57. Hume, *Enquiries,* pp. 7, 161–62.

58. Hume, *Dialogues,* p. 227.

59. Hume, *Treatise,* pp. 186–87, 269.

60. *An Essay on Man,* ed. Mack, pp. 57–58.

61. Hume, *Treatise,* p. 271.

62. Cotton's *Montaigne,* 2:226.

63. *Complete Essays of Montaigne,* p. 377.

64. Pierluigi Donini, "The History of the Concept of Eclecticism," *The Question of "Eclecticism": Studies in Later Greek Philosophy*, ed. John M. Dillon and A. A. Long (Berkeley: University of California Press, 1988), pp. 18–19.

65. *Encyclopedia,* trans. Nelly S. Hoyt and Thomas Cassirer (Indianapolis: Bobbs-Merrill, 1965), pp. 294–95.

66. James Puckle, *The Club: Or, A Grey-Cap for a Green Head. Containing Maxims, Advice, and Cautions,* 7th ed. (Dublin: Peter Wilson, 1743). Italics added.

67. *Encyclopedia,* pp. 288–89.

68. Cotton's *Montaigne,* 1:396; Mack, *Collected in Himself,* pp. 431, 427.

69. Marcus Tullius Cicero, *Tully's Two Essay* [*sic*] *of Old Age, and of Friendship with His Stoical Paradoxes, and Scipio's Dream,* trans. Mr. [S.] Parker, 3rd ed. (London: H. P. for J. Wilford, 1727), preface; *Tully's Three Books of Offices, In English. With Notes explaining the* METHOD and *MEANING* of the *AUTHOR*, trans. Thomas Cockman, 5th ed. (London: A. Bettesworth et al., 1732).

70. Middleton, *Cicero,* 2:624.

71. Cicero, *De Officiis,* trans. Harry G. Edinger (New York: Bobbs-Merrill, 1974), pp. 78–79.

72. Richard McKeon in the introduction to Cicero's *Brutus, On the Nature of the Gods, On Divination, On Duties,* trans. Hubert M. Poteat (Chicago: University of Chicago Press, 1950), p. 56.

73. *Plutarch's Morals: Translated from the Greek by Several Hands,* 3rd ed. (London: Tho. Braddy II, 1694), preface.

74. Cotton's *Montaigne* (1700), 2:625.

75. *The Instituto Oratoria of Quintilian,* trans. H. E. Butler, 4 vols. (Cambridge: Loeb Classical Library by Harvard University Press, 1922), 4:73.

76. *Seneca's Morals by Way of Abstract,* trans. Sir Roger L'Estrange, 12th ed. (London: W. Meadows, 1722), "To the Reader" and p. 516.

77. *Present State of the Republic of Letters* 14 (August 1734): 96–98, 102.

78. Anna Lydia Motto, *Seneca Sourcebook: Guide to the Thought of Lucius Annaeus Seneca* (Amsterdam: Adolf M. Hakkert, 1970), pp. ix–xi, xv.

79. *An Abstract Of the most Curious and Excellent Thoughts in Seigneur de Montaigne's Essays: Very Useful for Improving the Mind, and Forming the Manners of Men* (London: R. Smith, 1701), "Advertisement."

80. Cotton's *Montaigne* (1700), 1:1–3.

81. Austin Farrer in his introduction to Leibniz's *Theodicy* (New Haven: Yale University Press, 1952), pp. 34–35.

82. John Locke, *An Essay Concerning Human Understanding,* ed. Peter H. Nidditch (Oxford: Clarendon Press, 1975), p. 823.

83. David C. Snyder, "Faith and Reason in Locke's *Essay,*" *Journal of the History of Ideas* 47:2 (April–June 1986): 197.

84. Bolingbroke, *Works,* 3:329.

85. John Passmore, *Hume's Intentions* (Cambridge: Cambridge University Press, 1952), p. 93.

86. Paul Helm, "Locke on Faith and Knowledge," *Philosophical Quarterly* 23 (1973): 52–66.

87. Richetti, *Philosophical Writing,* pp. 99, 91.

88. Randall, *Career of Philosophy,* 1:718.

89. William Walker, "Locke Minding Women: Literary History, Gender, and the *Essay,*" *Eighteenth-Century Studies* 23:3 (Spring 1990): 268.

90. Randall, *Career of Philosophy,* 1:742.

91. A. J. Ayer, *Voltaire* (New York: Random House, 1986).

92. R. C. S. Walker, *Times Literary Supplement* 4023 (2 May 1980): 506; Jaki, *The Road of Science and the Ways to God,* p. 112.

93. Hume, *Enquiries,* p. vii.

94. Hervey, *A Letter to Mr. C——b-r,* pp. 14–15.

95. Donald W. Livingston, *Hume's Philosophy of Common Life* (Chicago: University of Chicago Press, 1984), pp. 34–36.

96. Spence, *Observations,* p. 134.

97. Hume, *Enquiries,* pp. 164–65.

98. Ibid., pp. 164, 161.

99. Hume, *Dialogues,* pp. 219, 169; *Enquiries,* pp. 140, 5, 145; *New Letters of David Hume,* ed. Raymond Klibansky and Ernest L. Mossner (Oxford: Clarendon Press, 1954), p. 231.

100. John Wain, "A Proper Study of the Man," *The New York Times Book Review* (2 March 1986): 11.

101. Justin Broackes, "Hume and Scepticism," *London Review of Books* 8:4 (6 March 1986): 22.

102. Macintyre, *After Virtue,* p. 54.

103. Robert J. Fogelin, "The Tendency of Hume's Skepticism," in *The Skeptical Tradition,* ed. Myles Burnyeat (Berkeley: University of California Press, 1983), pp. 409–10.

104. Barry Stroud, *Hume* (London: Routledge & Kegan Paul, 1977).

105. *An Essay on Man,* ed. Mack, p. viii.

106. Morris, *Alexander Pope,* p. 156.

107. White, *Pope and the Context of Controversy.*, p. 197.

6. Paradox Against the Orthodox

1. Nuttall, *Pope's "Essay on Man,"* p. 219.

2. Odell, "Young's *Night Thoughts* as an Answer to Pope's *Essay on Man,*" p. 500.

3. Warburton, *Critical and Philosophical Commentary,* p. 136.

4. Curll's *Crousaz,* p. 7.

5. Maurice Natanson, "Rhetoric and Philosophical Argumentation," in *Philosophical Style,* ed. Berel Lang (Chicago: Nelson-Hall, 1980), p. 232.

6. Nicholas Hudson, *Samuel Johnson and Eighteenth-Century Thought* (Oxford: Clarendon Press, 1988), p. 119.

7. Thomas O. Sloane, *Donne, Milton, and the End of Humanist Rhetoric* (Berkeley: University of California Press, 1985).

8. Ibid., pp. 86, 93, 112.

9. Ibid., pp. 113, 164.

10. Leitch, *Deconstructive Criticism,* pp. 169–73. Cf. Gregory Vlastos, *Socrates, Ironist and Moral Philosopher* (Ithaca, NY: Cornell University Press, 1991), p. 41.

11. Fish, "Rhetoric," p. 216.

12. *Correspondence of Alexander Pope,* 3:354.

13. Spence, *Observations,* pp. 134, 219.

14. Johnson's *Crousaz,* pp. 155, 28, 23; Nuttall, *Pope's "Essay on Man,"* pp. 54, 98, 86, 156, 100, 48, 84.

15. *Pascal's Pensées,* trans. W. F. Trotter, intro. T. S. Eliot (New York: Dut-

ton, 1958), pp. 111, 121. On irony and paradox in Socrates see Vlastos, *Socrates*, pp. 21–44.

16. Aubrey L. Williams, *An Approach to Congreve* (New Haven: Yale University Press, 1979), p. 31.

17. *Common Sense*, p. 39.

18. *Works*, ed. Elwin, 2:370.

19. Nuttall, *Pope's "Essay on Man,"* pp. 76, 75, 106.

20. *A Dialogue on One Thousand Seven Hundred and Thirty-eight: Together with a Prophetic Postscript as to One Thousand Seven Hundred and Thirty-nine* (London: T. Cooper, 1738), pp. 6–7.

21. Julia Kristeva, *Revolution in Poetic Language*, trans. Margaret Waller (New York: Columbia University Press, 1984).

22. Leitch, *Deconstructive Criticism*, pp. 175–76; Terry Eagleton, *Literary Theory: An Introduction* (Minneapolis: University of Minnesota Press, 1983), pp. 118–19.

23. *Correspondence of Alexander Pope*, 3:354.

24. Italics added.

25. Nuttall, *Pope's "Essay on Man,"* pp. 54, 59, 58, 48, 73, 84.

26. *Common Sense*, p. 16.

27. Nuttall, *Pope's "Essay on Man,"* p. 54.

28. Maynard Mack, *Collected in Himself*, p. 411.

29. John Dryden, *The Dramatic Works*, ed. Montague Summers, 6 vols. (London: Nonesuch, 1932), 4:388, 356.

30. *Dialogues of Plato*, 1:404, 405, 421.

31. *Complete Essays of Montaigne*, pp. 370–71, 407, 417.

32. Kallich, *Heav'n's First Law*, p. 73.

33. Morris, *Alexander Pope*, p. 167.

34. Spanos, "Breaking the Circle: Hermeneutics as Dis-closure," *Boundary 2* 5 (Winter 1977): 444.

35. Johnson's *Crousaz*, p. 23; Nuttall, *Pope's "Essay on Man,"* p. 54; Johnson, *Diaries*, pp. 383–84.

36. Julia Annas and Jonathan Barnes, *The Modes of Scepticism: Ancient Texts and Modern Interpretation* (Cambridge: Cambridge University Press, 1985), pp. 20–21, 119.

37. Cicero, *The Nature of the Gods*, trans. Horace C. P. McGregor (New York: Penguin, 1972), p. 234.

38. *Pascal's Pensées*, pp. 104, 111.

39. Cicero, *Tully's Two Essay* [*sic*] *of Old Age*, pp. 171, 179, 180, 186.

40. Annas and Barnes, *Modes of Scepticism*, p. 198.

41. Stanley, *History of Philosophy*, p. 737.

42. Terence Irwin, *Classical Thought* (Oxford: Oxford University Press, 1989), p. 48.

43. Stanley, *History of Philosophy,* pp. 789, 791.

44. Leo Spitzer, "Classical and Christian Ideas of World Harmony," *Traditio* 2 (1944): 409–64 and *Traditio* 3 (1945): 307–64.

45. Edward Hursey, *The Presocratics* (New York: Scribners, 1972), pp. 33–34.

46. Ibid., pp. 42, 48, 43.

47. Stanley, *History of Philosophy,* pp. 742, 741, 743.

48. Hursey, *The Presocratics,* pp. 43, 36.

49. Stanley, *History of Philosophy,* pp. 738–42.

50. Hursey, *The Presocratics,* p. 49.

51. *An Essay on Man,* ed. Mack, p. 92.

52. Cicero, *The Nature of the Gods,* pp. 73, 319.

53. Stanley, *History of Philosophy,* pp. 738, 743, 742.

54. Nuttall, *Pope's "Essay on Man,"* p. 86.

55. The literature on metaphor is vast. Many of the most salient questions regarding the relation of figurality to rational discourse are raised in a collection of essays from a conference on that subject: Andrew Ortony, ed. *Metaphor and Thought* (Cambridge: Cambridge University Press, 1979). Also interesting for its discussion of the cognitive force of metaphor is Eva Feder Kittay's *Metaphor: Its Cognitive Force and Linguistic Structure* (Oxford: Clarendon Press, 1987). An earlier formulation of my argument for metaphor as regulative hypothesis appears in "Reading Philosophical Poetry," in *The Philosopher as Writer: The Eighteenth Century,* ed. Robert Ginsberg (London: Associated University Presses, 1987), pp. 122–39.

56. Douglas Berggren, "The Use and Abuse of Metaphor," *The Review of Metaphysics* 16:1 (1962): 236.

57. Richetti, *Philosophical Writing,* p. 17.

58. Paul de Man, "The Epistemology of Metaphor," pp. 29, 13.

59. Culler, *On Deconstruction,* p. 147.

60. Max Black, *Models and Metaphors: Studies in Language and Philosophy* (Ithaca: Cornell University Press, 1962), pp. 47, 25.

61. Rorty, "Philosophy as a Kind of Writing," p. 156.

62. Philip Wheelwright, *The Burning Fountain* (Bloomington: Indiana University Press, 1954), p. 52.

63. Graff, *Poetic Statement and Critical Dogma,* p. xi.

64. I. A. Richards, *Creation and Discovery* (Chicago: Henry Regnery, 1955), p. 3.

65. *Correspondence of Alexander Pope,* 3:354.

66. For relevant analogues to this approach to metaphor as problem solving: Karl Popper, *Conjectures and Refutations* (London: Routledge & Kegan Paul, 1962), p. 199; and Friedel Weinert, "Tradition and Argument," *The Monist* 65:1 (January 1982): 88–105.

67. Warburton, *Critical and Philosophical Commentary,* p. 137.

68. Jerry Fodor, "Too hard for our kind of mind?" *London Review of Books* 13 (27 June 1991): 12, reviewing Colin McGinn, *The Problem of Consciousness* (Oxford: Blackwell, 1990).

69. Dorothy Emmet, *The Nature of Metaphysical Thinking* (London: Macmillan, 1957), p. 205.

70. Sherlock, *Discourse,* p. 348.

71. James Noxon, *Hume's Philosophical Development* (Oxford: Clarendon Press, 1975), p. 91.

72. Samuel Taylor Coleridge, *Biographia Literaria* (London: Dent, 1965), p. 174.

73. *Works of Joseph Butler,* 2:35.

74. Walker Percy, *The Message in the Bottle* (New York: Farrar, Strauss, and Giroux, 1975), p. 156.

75. Johnson's *Crousaz,* p. 207.

76. Spence, *Observations,* p. 114.

77. Lovejoy, *The Great Chain of Being,* p. 206; Kenneth MacLean, *John Locke and English Literature of the Eighteenth Century* (New Haven: Yale University Press, 1936), pp. 145–46; cf. White, *Pope and the Context of Controversy,* p. 153.

78. Johnson's *Crousaz,* p. 123.

79. Daniel J. Wilson, "Arthur O. Lovejoy and the Moral of *The Great Chain of Being,*" *Journal of the History of Ideas* 41:2 (April–June 1980): 249–65.

80. Lovejoy, *The Great Chain of Being,* pp. 183–84.

81. MacLean, *John Locke and English Literature of the Eighteenth Century,* pp. 145–46.

82. Guiseppa Saccaro-Battisti, "Changing Metaphors of Political Structures," *Journal of the History of Ideas* 44:1 (January–March 1983): 31.

83. Yasmine Gooneratne, *Alexander Pope* (Cambridge: Cambridge University Press, 1976), p. 107.

84. F. E. L. Priestly, "Pope and the Great Chain of Being," in *Essays in English Literature from the Renaissance to the Victorian Age,* ed. Millar MacLure and F. W. Watt (Toronto: University of Toronto Press, 1964), p. 213.

85. *Common Sense,* p. 10.

86. Robert Boyle, "A Free Inquiry into the Vulgarly Received Notion of Nature," *The Works of the Honourable Robert Boyle,* ed. Thomas Birch, 6 vols. (London: J. and F. Rivington, 1772), 5:183.

87. Keener, *An Essay on Pope,* p. 59.

88. John Macquarrie, *Thinking About God* (New York: Harper, 1975), p. 137.

89. So pervasive is the metaphor that it is insignificant that Pope's editors have cited neither Ralegh nor Dryden as analogues.

90. Richard S. Westfall, "The Career of Isaac Newton," *American Scholar* 50:3 (1981): 351–52.

91. Thomas F. Merrill, *Christian Criticism: A Study of Literary God Talk* (Amsterdam: Rodopi, 1976), pp. 15, 10. Literature on the theological use of language is extensive. Cf. Langdon Gilkey, *Naming the Whirlwind: The Renewal of God Language* (Indianapolis: Bobbs-Merrill, 1969); Raeburne S. Heimbeck, *Theology and Meaning: A Critique of Metatheological Skepticism* (Stanford: Stanford University Press, 1969); Kenneth Hamilton, *Words and the WORD* (Grand Rapids, MI: William B. Eerdmans, 1971); Anders Jeffner, *The Study of Religious Language* (London: SCM Press, 1972); Paul M. Van Buren, *The Edges of Language: An Essay in the Logic of a Religion* (New York: Macmillan, 1972); Earl R. MacCormac, *Metaphor and Myth in Science and Religion* (Durham: Duke University Press, 1976); Terrence W. Tilley, *Talking of God: An Introduction to Philosophical Analysis of Religious Language* (New York: Paulist Press, 1978). Three useful collections of essays are: Robert H. Ayers and William T. Blackstone, eds., *Religious Language and Knowledge* (Athens: University of Georgia Press, 1972); Ronald E. Santoni, ed., *Religious Language and the Problem of Religious Knowledge* (Bloomington: Indiana University Press, 1968); and Robert P. Scharlemann and Gilbert E. M. Ogutu, eds., *God in Language* (New York: Paragon House, 1987).

92. White, *Pope and the Context of Controversy*, p. 41.

93. Warton, *Essay*, 2:77.

94. John P. Sisk, "The Tyranny of Harmony," *American Scholar* 46 (1977): 204.

95. Stanley, *History of Philosophy*, pp. 739, 741.

96. Charron, *Of Wisdom*, 1:246. Italics added to Pope and Charron.

97. Northrop Frye, *Fables of Identity* (New York: Harcourt, 1963), p. 141.

98. William James, *The Varieties of Religious Experience*, ed. Bruce Kuklick (New York: Vintage, 1990), pp. 440–42.

99. Rorty, *Contingency, Irony, and Solidarity*, p. 112.

100. Quoted in Mack, *Alexander Pope*, p. 743.

101. Bayle, *Dictionary*, 4:90–97, 4:484–92.

102. Elizabeth Tebeaux, "Scepticism in Pope's *Essay on Man*," *College Literature* 10:2 (1983): 166, 168.

103. Ferguson, *The Unbalanced Mind*, p. 71.

104. Joseph Glanvill, *Scepsis Scientifica*, ed. John Owen (London: K. Paul, Trench, 1885), p. 182. Originally published in 1665, this is a revision of *The Vanity of Dogmatizing*.

105. Austin Farrer, *Reflective Faith: Essays in Philosophical Theology*, ed. Charles C. Conti (London: SPCK, 1972), p. 32.

106. William King, *Divine Predestination and Fore-Knowledge, Consistent with the Freedom of Man's Will* (London: J. Baker, 1709), pp. 5, 14.

107. Emmet, *Nature of Metaphysical Thinking,* p. 202. The criteria of importance and matter-of-factness as well as comprehensiveness and openness are discussed on pp. 195–202.

108. Berggren, "The Use and Abuse of Metaphor," p. 472.

Conclusion

1. Todorov, *Introduction à la littérature fantastique,* p. 29.

2. Culler, *Structuralist Poetics,* p. 137.

3. Nuttall, *Pope's "Essay on Man,"* p. 188: "This book is Crousazian."

4. G. S. Rousseau, *The Eighteenth Century,* pp. 258–59.

5. Nuttall, *Pope's "Essay on Man,"* pp. 51, 57–58.

6. *Essay on Man,* ed. Pattison, p. 77.

7. Kallich, *Heav'n's First Law,* p. 136. Kallich argues that the ideology of *An Essay on Man* is a "not unusual religious orthodoxy" (p. 97).

8. *Works,* ed. Elwin, 2:377; Bloom, *Alexander Pope,* p. 3.

9. Leitch, *Deconstructive Criticism,* pp. 77–78.

10. Jacques Derrida, "Structure, Sign, and Play in the Discourse of the Human Sciences," in *Contemporary Literary Criticism: Modernism through Poststructuralism,* ed. Robert Con Davis (New York: Longman, 1986), p. 492.

11. Morris, *Alexander Pope,* pp. 153, 156, 176.

12. Livingston, *Hume's Philosophy of Common Life,* pp. 35–36; Hume, *Treatise,* p. 215.

13. Nagel, *Mortal Thoughts,* p. 213.

14. Spence, *Observations,* p. 135.

15. Richard P. McBrien in *The New York Times Book Review* (11 January 1981) contends that this theme "permeates" Kung's *Does God Exist?*

16. Graff, *Poetic Statement and Critical Dogma,* p. 77.

17. David M. Vieth, "Divided Consciousness: Variations on a Theme in Literary Interpretation," *Tennessee Studies in Literature* 22 (1977): 50; J. Paul Hunter, *Occasional Form: Henry Fielding and the Chains of Circumstance* (Baltimore: Johns Hopkins University Press, 1975), p. 45.

18. Murray Krieger, *The Tragic Vision: Variations on a Theme in Literary Interpretation* (New York: Holt, 1960), pp. 233, 243.

19. Fish, "Rhetoric," p. 221.

20. Arthur C. Danto, "Philosophy as/and/of Literature," in *Literature and the Question of Philosophy,* ed. Anthony J. Cascardi (Baltimore: Johns Hopkins University Press, 1987), p. 3; Arthur C. Danto, *The Philosophical Disenfranchisement of Art* (New York: Columbia University Press, 1986), p. 21.

21. de Man, "The Epistemology of Metaphor," p. 28.

22. Stanley Cavell, *The Claim of Reason* (New York: Oxford University Press, 1979), p. 496.

23. Robert Nozick, *The Examined Life* (New York: Simon & Schuster, 1989), p. 18.

24. Martha C. Nussbaum, *The Fragility of Goodness: Luck and Ethics in Greek Tragedy and Philosophy* (Cambridge: Cambridge University Press, 1986).

25. Roger Scruton, "Modern Philosophy and the Neglect of Aesthetics," *Times Literary Supplement* 4392 (5 June 1987): 604, 616–17.

26. Johnson's *Crousaz*, p. 28.

BIBLIOGRAPHY

An Abstract Of the most Curious and Excellent Thoughts in Seigneur de Montaigne's Essays: Very Useful for Improving the Mind, and Forming the Manners of Men. London: R. Smith, 1701.

Adams, Robert M. "Putting Pope in His Place." *The New York Review of Books* (13 March 1986): 29–32.

Addison, Joseph, et al. *The Spectator.* Edited by Gregory Smith. 4 vols. London: Dent, 1945.

———. *The Spectator.* Edited by Donald F. Bond. 5 vols. Oxford: Clarendon Press, 1965.

Alderman, William E. "Pope's *Essay on Man* and Shaftesbury's *The Moralists.*" *Publications of the Bibliographical Society of America* 67 (1973): 131–40.

Annas, Julia, and Jonathan Barnes. *The Modes of Scepticism: Ancient Texts and Modern Interpretation.* Cambridge: Cambridge University Press, 1985.

Aristotle. *The Ethics of Aristotle: The Nicomachean Ethics.* Translated by J. A. K. Thompson. New York: Penguin, 1976.

Atkins, G. Douglas. "Pope and Deism: A New Analysis." In *Pope: Recent Essays by Several Hands,* edited by Maynard Mack, pp. 392–415. Hamden, CT: Archon, 1980.

———. *Quests of Difference: Reading Pope's Poems.* Lexington: University Press of Kentucky, 1986.

———. *Reading Deconstruction: Deconstructive Reading.* Lexington: University Press of Kentucky, 1983.

Austin, J. L. *How to do Things with Words.* Cambridge: Harvard University Press, 1975.

Ayer, A. J. *Voltaire.* New York: Random House, 1986.

Ayers, Michael. *Locke*. London: Routledge, 1992.

Ayers, Robert H., and William T. Blackstone, eds. *Religious Language and Knowledge*. Athens: University of Georgia Press, 1972.

Ayre, William. *Memoirs of the Life and Writings of Alexander Pope*. 2 vols. London: For the Author, 1745.

———. *Truth. A Counterpart to Mr. Pope's Esay* [*sic*] *on Man, Epistle the First*. London: R. Minors, 1739.

Bacon, Frances. *Essays, Advancement of Learning, New Atlantis, and Other Pieces*. Edited by Richard Foster Jones. New York: Odyssey, 1937.

Balfour, James. *Philosophical Essays*. Edinburgh: For John Balfour, 1768.

Balguy, John. *The Law of Truth: Or, the Obligations of Reason Essential to All Religion*. London: John Pemberton, 1733.

Barker, John. *Strange Contrarieties: Pascal in England during the Age of Reason*. Montreal: McGill-Queens University Press, 1975.

Barnouw, Jeffrey. "The Separation of Reason and Faith in Bacon and Hobbes, and Leibniz's *Theodicy*." *Journal of the History of Ideas* 42:4 (October–December 1981): 607–28.

Barthes, Roland. *Image, Music, Text*. Translated by Stephen Heath. New York: Hill and Wang, 1977.

Bayle, Pierre. *The Dictionary, Historical and Critical of Mr. Peter Bayle*. 2nd ed. 5 vols. London: J. J. and P. Knapton et al., 1734–38.

Bentley, Thomas. *A Letter to Mr. Pope, Occasion'd by Sober Advice From Horace*. London: T. Cooper, 1735.

Berggren, Douglas. "The Use and Abuse of Metaphor." *The Review of Metaphysics* 16 (1962–63): 237–58, 450–72.

Black, Max. *Models and Metaphors: Studies in Language and Philosophy*. Ithaca: Cornell University Press, 1962.

Blackmore, Sir Richard. *Creation: A Philosophical Poem. In Seven Books*. Reprinted in *Works of the English Poets*. Edited by Alexander Chalmers, 10:325–81. 21 vols. London: C. Whittingham, 1810.

Bloom, Harold. *Alexander Pope: Modern Critical Views*. New York: Chelsea House, 1986.

———. *The Anxiety of Influence*. New York: Oxford University Press, 1973.

Bogel, Fredric V. *Acts of Knowledge: Pope's Later Poems*. Lewisburg, PA: Bucknell University Press, 1981.

Bolingbroke, Henry St. John, Lord. *The Works of . . . Henry St. John, Lord Viscount Bolingbroke*. Edited by David Mallet. 5 vols. London: D. Mallet, 1754.

Boswell, James. *Life of Johnson*. Edited by G. B. Hill, revised by L. F. Powell. 6 vols. Oxford: Clarendon Press, 1934–50.

———. *Life of Johnson*. Edited by R. W. Chapman. London: Oxford University Press, 1953.

Boyle, Robert. *The Works of the Honourable Robert Boyle*. Edited by Thomas Birch. 6 vols. London: J. and F. Rivington, 1772.

Brett, R. L. *Reason and Imagination*. London: Published for the University of Hull by Oxford University Press, 1960.

Bridges, Mr. *Divine Wisdom and Providence: An Essay Occasion'd by The Essay on Man*. London: J. Roberts, 1736.

Broackes, Justin. "Hume and Scepticism." *London Review of Books* 8:4 (6 March 1986): 20–22.

Brower, Reuben. *Alexander Pope: The Poetry of Allusion*. Oxford: Oxford University Press, 1959.

Browne, Peter. *The Procedure, Extent and Limits of Human Understanding*. London: William Innys, 1728.

———. *Things Divine and Supernatural Conceived by Analogy with Things Natural and Human*. London: William Innys, 1733.

Butler, Joseph. *The Works of Joseph Butler*. Edited by W. E. Gladstone. 2 vols. Oxford: Clarendon Press, 1897.

Canfield, J. Douglas. "A. D. Nuttall. *Pope's 'Essay on Man.'*" *Eighteenth-Century Studies* 19:2 (1985–86): 290–92.

———. "The Fate of the Fall in Pope's *Essay on Man*." *The Eighteenth Century: Theory and Interpretation* 23 (1982): 134–50.

Cavell, Stanley. *The Claims of Reason*. New York: Oxford University Press, 1979.

Charron, Pierre. *Of Wisdom. In Three Books. Written Originally in French, By the Sieur de CHARRON*. Translated by George Stanhope. 2nd ed. 2 vols. London: J. Tonson et al., 1707. 1st ed. 1694; 3rd ed. 1729.

Chesterfield, Philip Dormer Stanhope, Fourth Earl of. *Characters by Lord Chesterfield Contrasted with Characters of the Same Great Personages by other respectable Writers*. London: Edward and Charles Dilly, 1778.

Ciceronis, M. Tullii. *Academica*. Londinenses: Jacobum Knapton, 1725. 2nd ed. 1736.

Cicero, Marcus Tullius. *Brutus, On the Nature of the Gods, On Divination, On Duties*. Translated by Hubert M. Poteat with introduction by Richard McKeon. Chicago: University of Chicago Press, 1950.

———. *The Nature of the Gods*. Translated by Horace C. P. McGregor. New York: Penguin, 1972.

———. *De Officiis*. Translated by Harry G. Edinger. New York: Bobbs-Merrill, 1974.

———. *Tully's Laelius: Or, Discourses upon Friendship. Translated from the Latin*. London: Richard Wilkin, 1713.

———. *Tully's Three Books of Offices, In English. with Notes explaining the METHOD and MEANING of the AUTHOR*. Translated by Thomas Cockman. 5th ed. London: A. Bettesworth et al., 1732.

———. *Tully's Two Essay* [*sic*] *of Old Age, and of Friendship with His Stoical Paradoxes, and Scipio's Dream*. Translated by Mr. [S.] Parker. 3rd ed. London: H. P. for J. Wilford, 1727.

———. *Tusculan Disputations*. Translated by J. E. King. London: William Heinemann, 1927.

Clarke, John. *An Enquiry into the Causes and the Origin of Moral Evil*. London: J. Knapton, 1721.

Coleridge, Samuel Taylor. *Biographia Literaria*. London: Dent, 1965.

Collier, Jeremy. *Essays upon Several Moral Subjects*. 6th ed. 2 vols. London: D. Brown, 1722.

Common Sense a Common Delusion . . . Mr. Pope's Essay on Man, Proved Ridiculous, Impious . . . By Almonides, a believing Heathen. London: T. Reynolds, 1751.

Courthope, William John. *The Life of Alexander Pope*. London: John Murray, 1889.

Crousaz, J. P. de. *A Commentary On Mr. Pope's Principles of Morality, Or Essay on Man*. Translated by Samuel Johnson. London: A. Dodd, 1739 (1738, cf. *Daily Advertiser*, 23 November 1738).

———. *A Commentary Upon Mr. Pope's Four Ethic Epistles, Intituled, An Essay on Man. Wherein His System is fully Examin'd*. Translated by Charles Forman. London: E. Curll, 1738.

———. *An Examination of Mr. Pope's Essay on Man*. Translated by Elizabeth Carter. London: A. Dodd, 1739 (1738, cf. *Daily Advertiser* and *General Evening Post*, 23 November 1738).

Cuddon, J. A. *A Dictionary of Literary Terms and Literary Theory*. 3rd ed. Oxford: Blackwell, 1991.

Culler, Jonathan. *On Deconstruction*. Ithaca: Cornell University Press, 1982.

———. *Structuralist Poetics*. Ithaca: Cornell University Press, 1975.

Damrosch, Leopold, Jr. *The Imaginative World of Alexander Pope*. Berkeley: University of California Press, 1987.

Danto, Arthur C. *The Philosophical Disenfranchisement of Art*. New York: Columbia University Press, 1986.

———. "Philosophy as/and/of Literature." In *Literature and the Question of Philosophy*, edited by Anthony J. Cascardi, pp. 3–23. Baltimore: Johns Hopkins University Press, 1987.

De Man, Paul. *Blindness and Insight: Essays in the Rhetoric of Contemporary Criticism*. 2nd ed. Minneapolis: University of Minnesota Press, 1983.

———. "The Epistemology of Metaphor." *Critical Inquiry* 5 (1978): 13–30.

Dennis, John. *The Age of Pope*. London: G. Bell, 1894.

Dennis, John. *The Critical Works of John Dennis*. Edited by Edward Niles Hooker. 2 vols. Baltimore: Johns Hopkins University Press, 1939.

De Quincey, Thomas. *The Collected Writings of Thomas De Quincey*. Edited by David Masson. 14 vols. London: A. and C. Black, 1896–97.

Derrida, Jacques. "Living On: Border Lines." In *Deconstruction and Criticism*, edited by Harold Bloom et al., pp. 75–175. New York: Seabury Press, 1979.

———. *Of Grammatology*. Translated by G. C. Spivak. Baltimore: Johns Hopkins University Press, 1976.

———. "Structure, Sign, and Play in the Discourse of the Human Sciences." In *Contemporary Literary Criticism: Modernism through Poststructuralism*, edited by Robert Con Davis, pp. 480–98. New York: Longman, 1986.

A Dialogue on One Thousand Seven Hundred and Thirty-eight: Together with a Prophetic Postscript as to One Thousand Seven Hundred and Thirty-nine. London: T. Cooper, 1738.

Dodsley, Robert. *An Epistle to Mr. Pope, Occasion'd by his Essay on Man*. London: L. Gilliver, 1734.

Donaldson, Ian. "Author of Himself." *Times Literary Supplement* (13 September 1985): 997–98.

Donini, Pierluigi. "The History of the Concept of Eclecticism." In *The Question of "Eclecticism": Studies in Later Greek Philosophy*, edited by John M. Dillon and A. A. Long, pp. 15–33. Berkeley: University of California Press, 1988.

Dryden, John. *The Dramatic Works*. Edited by Montague Summers. 6 vols. London: Nonesuch, 1932.

———. *Poems of John Dryden*. Edited by James Kinsley. 4 vols. Oxford: Clarendon Press, 1958.

———. *The Poems and Fables of John Dryden*. Edited by James Kinsley. London: Oxford University Press, 1962.

———. *Works of John Dryden: Poems 1685–1692*. Edited by H. T. Swedenberg, Jr. Berkeley: University of California Press, 1969.

Dudgeon, William. *The Philosophical Works of Mr. William Dudgeon*. Edinburgh: privately printed, 1765.

———. *A View of the Necessitarian or Best Scheme: Freed From The Objections of M. Crousaz, in his Examination of Mr. Pope's "Essay on Man."* London: T. Cooper, 1739.

Eagleton, Terry. *Literary Theory: An Introduction*. Minneapolis: University of Minnesota Press, 1983.

Edwards, Thomas R., Jr. *This Dark Estate: A Reading of Pope*. Berkeley: University of California Press, 1963.

———. "Visible Poetry: Pope and Modern Criticism." In *Twentieth-Century Literature in Retrospect*, edited by Reuben A. Brower, pp. 299–321. Harvard English Studies 2. Cambridge: Harvard University Press, 1971.

Emmet, Dorothy. *The Nature of Metaphysical Thinking*. London: Macmillan, 1957.

Encyclopedia. Translated by Nelly S. Hoyt and Thomas Cassirer. Indianapolis: Bobbs-Merrill, 1965.

Erasmus, Desiderius. *All the Familiar Colloquies of Desiderius Erasmus, Of Roterdam, Concerning Men, Manners, and Things*. Translated by N. Bailey. London: J. Darby et al., 1727. Second edition 1733.

———. *The Praise of Folly and Other Writings*. Translated by Robert M. Adams. New York: Norton, 1989.

———. *Twenty Two Select Colloquies out of Erasmus Roterdamus, Pleasantly representing several Superstitious Levities That were Crept into the Church of Rome In His Days. By Sir Roger L'Estrange, Kt. To which are added, Seven More Dialogues, with the Life of the Author. By Mr. Tho. Brown*. London: B. Motte et al., 1725.

———. *Wit against Wisdom: Or The Praise of Folly. Made English from the Latin of Erasmus. By an Eminent Hand*. 3rd ed. London: John Wilford, 1722.

Fabian, Bernhard. "On the Literary Background of the *Essay on Man*: A Note on Pope and Lucretius." In *Pope: Recent Essays by Several Hands*, edited by Maynard Mack and James A. Winn, pp. 416–27. Hamden, CT: Archon, 1980.

The False Patriot. An Epistle to Mr. Pope. London: James Roberts, 1734.

Farrer, Austin. *Reflective Faith: Essays in Philosophical Theology*. Edited by Charles C. Conti. London: SPCK, 1972.

Felman, Shoshana. *Jacques Lacan and the Adventure of Insight: Psychoanalysis in Contemporary Culture*. Cambridge: Harvard University Press, 1987.

Ferguson, Rebecca. *The Unbalanced Mind: Pope and the Rule of Passion*. Philadelphia: University of Pennsylvania Press, 1986.

Fish, Stanley. "Rhetoric." In *Critical Terms for Literary Study*, edited by Frank Lentricchia and Thomas McLaughlin, pp. 203–22. Chicago: University of Chicago Press, 1990.

Fodor, Jerry. "Too hard for our kind of mind?" *London Review of Books* 13 (27 June 1991).

Fogelin, Robert J. "The Tendency of Hume's Skepticism." In *The Skeptical Tradition*, edited by Myles Burnyeat, pp. 397–412. Berkeley: University of California Press, 1983.

Force, James E. "Hume and the Relation of Science to Religion among Certain Members of the Royal Society." *Journal of the History of Ideas* 45:4 (October–December 1984): 517–36.

Foxon, David. *Pope and the Early Eighteenth-Century Book Trade*. Revised and edited by James McLaverty. Oxford: Clarendon Press, 1991.

Fraser, George S. *Alexander Pope*. London: Routledge, 1978.

Frye, Northrop. *Fables of Identity*. New York: Harcourt, 1963.

Gay, Peter. *The Enlightenment: An Interpretation*. 2 vols. New York: Norton, 1977.

Geertz, Clifford. "Thick Description: Toward an Interpretive Theory of Culture." In *The Interpretation of Cultures*, pp. 3–30. New York: Basic Books, 1973.

Gilkey, Langdon. *Naming the Whirlwind: The Renewal of God Language*. Indianapolis: Bobbs-Merrill, 1969.

Giroud, Vincent. "An Early French Commentary on Pope's *Essay on Man*." *Yale University Library Gazette* 57:1 (October 1982): 10–17.

Glanvill, Joseph. *Essays on Several Important Subjects in Philosophy and Religion*. London: J. D. for John Baker and Henry Mortlock, 1676.

———. *Scepsis Scientifica, or, Confest Ignorance*. London: Henry Eversden, 1665.

———. *Scepsis Scientifica*. Edited by John Owen. London: K. Paul, Trench, 1885.

———. *The Vanity of Dogmatizing: or Confidence in Opinions. Manifested in a Discourse of the Shortness and Uncertainty of our Knowledge . . .* London: Henry Eversden, 1661.

Goldberg, S. L. "Integrity and Life in Pope's Poetry." In *Studies in the Eighteenth Century: III*, edited by R. F. Brissenden and J. C. Eade, pp. 185–207. Toronto: University of Toronto Press, 1976.

Goldgar, Bertrand A. "Pope's Theory of the Passions: the Background of Epistle II of the *Essay on Man*." *Philological Quarterly* 41 (1962): 730–43.

Gooneratne, Yasmine. *Alexander Pope*. Cambridge: Cambridge University Press, 1976.

Gordon, I. R. F. *A Preface to Pope*. London: Longman, 1976.

Graff, Gerald. *Poetic Statement and Critical Dogma*. Chicago: University of Chicago Press, 1970.

Greene, Donald J. "'Logical Structure' in Eighteenth-Century Poetry." *Philological Quarterly* 31 (1952): 315–36.

———. *The Politics of Samuel Johnson*. 2nd ed. Athens: University of Georgia Press, 1990.

Gretton, Phillips. *A Review of the Argument A Priori, In Relation to the Being and Attributes of God*. London, 1726.

Griffin, Dustin. *Alexander Pope: The Poet in the Poems*. Princeton: Princeton University Press, 1978.

Hamilton, Kenneth. *Words and the WORD*. Grand Rapids, MI: William B. Eerdmans, 1971.

Hammond, Brean S. *Pope and Bolingbroke: A Study of Friendship and Influence*. Columbia: University of Missouri Press, 1984.

Hampson, Norman. *The Enlightenment*. Baltimore: Penguin, 1968.

Harth, Phillip. "The New Criticism and Eighteenth-Century Poetry." *Critical Inquiry* 7 (1981): 521–37.

Heidegger, Martin. *Martin Heidegger: Basic Writings*. Edited by David Farrell Knell. New York: Harper, 1977.

Heimbeck, Raeburne S. *Theology and Meaning: A Critique of Metatheological Skepticism*. Stanford: Stanford University Press, 1969.

Helm, Paul. "Locke on Faith and Knowledge." *Philosophical Quarterly* 23 (1973): 52–66.

Hervey, John, Lord. *A Letter To Mr. C——b-r, On his Letter to Mr. P——*. London: J. Roberts, 1742.

Hobbes, Thomas. *Leviathan*. Edited by C. B. Macpherson. New York: Penguin, 1968.

———. *Thomas White's De Mundo Examined*. Translated by Harold Whitmore Jones. London: Bradford University Press, 1976.

Hudson, Nicholas. *Samuel Johnson and Eighteenth-Century Thought*. Oxford: Clarendon Press, 1988.

Hume, David. *Dialogues Concerning Natural Religion*. Edited by Norman Kemp Smith. New York: Macmillan, 1947.

———. *Enquiries Concerning the Human Understanding and Concerning the Principles of Morals*. Edited by L. A. Selby-Bigge. 2nd ed. Oxford: Clarendon Press, 1902.

———. *New Letters of David Hume*. Edited by Raymond Klibansky and Ernest L. Mossner. Oxford: Clarendon Press, 1954.

———. *A Treatise of Human Nature*. Edited by L. A. Selby-Bigge with text revised and notes by P. H. Nidditch. 2nd ed. Oxford: Clarendon Press, 1978.

Hunter, J. Paul. *Occasional Form: Henry Fielding and the Chains of Circumstance*. Baltimore: Johns Hopkins University Press, 1975.

Hursey, Edward. *The Presocratics*. New York: Scribners, 1972.

Irwin, Terence. *Classical Thought*. Oxford: Oxford University Press, 1989.

Jackson, Wallace. *Vision and Re-vision in Alexander Pope*. Detroit: Wayne State University Press, 1983.

Jaki, Stanley L. *The Road of Science and the Ways to God*. Chicago: University of Chicago Press, 1978.

James, William. *The Varieties of Religious Experience*. Edited by Bruce Kuklick. New York: Vintage, 1990.

Jardine, Lisa. "Lorenzo Valla: Academic Skepticism and the New Humanist Dialectic." In *The Skeptical Tradition*, edited by Myles Burnyeat, pp. 253–86. Berkeley: University of California Press, 1983.

Jeffner, Anders. *The Study of Religious Language*. London: SCM Press, 1972.

Jenkins, Robert. *The Reasonableness and Certainty of the Christian Religion*. London: Richard Sare, 1715.

Johnson, Samuel. *Diaries, Prayers, and Annals*. Edited by E. L. McAdam, Jr., with Donald and Mary Hyde. New Haven: Yale University Press, 1958.

———. *Lives of the Poets*. Edited by G. B. Hill. 3 vols. Oxford: Clarendon Press, 1905.

———. *Lives of the English Poets*. Introduction by L. Archer-Hind. 2 vols. London: Dent, 1925.

Kallich, Martin. *Heav'n's First Law: Rhetoric and Order in Pope's Essay on Man*. De Kalb: Northern Illinois University Press, 1967.

Kant, Immanuel. *Kant's Gesammelte Schriften*. 29 vols. Berlin: G. Reimer, Walter de Grunter et al., 1902–.

———. *Lectures on Philosophical Theology*. Translated by Allen W. Wood and Gertrude M. Clark. Ithaca: Cornell University Press, 1978.

———. *The Philosophy of Kant: Immanuel Kant's Moral and Political Writings*. Edited by Carl J. Friedrich. New York: Random House, 1949.

Keener, Frederick M. *An Essay on Pope*. New York: Columbia University Press, 1974.

Kidd, I. G. "Greek Academy." In *The Encyclopedia of Philosophy*, edited by Paul Edwards, 3:382–85. 8 vols. New York: Macmillan, 1967.

King, Albion Roy. *The Problem of Evil: Christian Concepts and the Book of Job*. New York: Ronald Press, 1952.

King, William. *Divine Predestination and Fore-Knowledge, Consistent with the Freedom of Man's Will*. London: J. Baker, 1709.

———. *Essay on the Origin of Evil . . . Translated from the Latin, with large Notes; tending to explain and vindicate some of the Author's Principles . . .* London: J. and J. Knapton et al., 1731.

Kittay, Eva Feder. *Metaphor: Its Cognitive Force and Linguistic Structure*. Oxford: Clarendon Press, 1987.

Knapp, Richard Gilbert. *The Fortunes of Pope's "Essay on man" in 18th century France*. Vol. 82 of *Studies on Voltaire and the Eighteenth Century*, edited by Theodore Besterman. Geneva: Institut et Musée Voltaire, 1971.

Krieger, Murray. *The Tragic Vision: Variations on a Theme in Literary Interpretation*. New York: Holt, 1960.

Kristeva, Julia. *Revolution in Poetic Language*. Translated by Margaret Waller. New York: Columbia University Press, 1984.

Kung, Hans. *Does God Exist?: An Answer for Today*. Garden City, NY: Doubleday, 1980.

Lee, Henry. *Anti-Scepticism: or, Notes upon . . . Mr. Lock's "Essay. . ."* London: R. Clavel and C. Harper, 1702.

Leibniz, Gottfried Wilhelm. *Theodicy*. Introduction by Austin Farrer. New Haven: Yale University Press, 1952.

Leitch, Vincent B. *Deconstructive Criticism*. New York: Columbia University Press, 1983.

Leranbaum, Miriam. *Alexander Pope's "Opus Magnum," 1729–1744*. Oxford: Clarendon Press, 1977.

Lipking, Lawrence. "Wise Guy." *American Scholar* 56:3 (Summer 1987): 435–39.

Livingston, Donald W. *Hume's Philosophy of Common Life*. Chicago: University of Chicago Press, 1984.

Locke, John. *An Essay Concerning Human Understanding*. Edited by Alexander Campbell Fraser. 2 vols. Reprint. New York: Dover, 1959.

———. *An Essay Concerning Human Understanding*. Edited by Peter H. Nidditch. Oxford: Clarendon Press, 1975.

Lovejoy, A. O. *The Great Chain of Being*. Cambridge: Harvard University Press, 1936.

McBrien, Richard P. *New York Times Book Review,* 11 January 1981.

MacCormac, Earl R. *Metaphor and Myth in Science and Religion*. Durham: Duke University Press, 1976.

Macintyre, Alasdair. *After Virtue: A Study in Moral Theory*. 2nd ed. Notre Dame: University of Notre Dame Press, 1984.

McGinn, Colin. *The Problem of Consciousness*. Oxford: Blackwell, 1990.

Mack, Maynard. *Alexander Pope: A Life*. New York: Norton, 1985.

———. *Collected in Himself: Essays Critical, Biographical, and Bibliographical on Pope and Some of His Contemporaries*. Newark: University of Delaware Press, 1982. Pp. 394–460 are "A Finding List of Books Surviving from Pope's Library."

———, ed. *Essential Articles for the Study of Alexander Pope*. Hamden, CT: Archon, 1964.

———, ed. *"The Last and Greatest Art": Some Unpublished Poetical Manuscripts of Alexander Pope*. Newark: Delaware University Press, 1984. Pp. 190–418 are facsimiles with a printed transcription of the Pierpont Morgan and the Houghton Library manuscripts of *An Essay On Man*.

———, ed. *Pope: Recent Essays by Several Hands*. Hamden, CT: Archon, 1980.

———. "Pope's Books: A Biographical Survey with a Finding List." In *English Literature in the Age of Disguise*, edited by Maximillian Novak, pp. 209–305. Berkeley: University of California Press, 1977.

MacLean, Kenneth. *John Locke and English Literature of the Eighteenth Century*. New Haven: Yale University Press, 1936.

Macquarrie, John. *Thinking About God*. New York: Harper, 1975.

Maner, Martin. *The Philosophical Biographer: Doubt and Dialectic in Johnson's "Lives of the Poets."* Athens: University of Georgia Press, 1988.

Mandelbaum, Maurice. "On Lovejoy's Historiography." In *The History of Ideas*, edited by Preston King, pp. 198–210. Totowa, NJ: Barnes & Noble, 1983.

Mansfield, Bruce. *The Phoenix of His Age: Interpretations of Erasmus c 1550–1750*. Toronto: University of Toronto Press, 1979.

Merrill, Thomas F. *Christian Criticism: A Study of Literary God Talk*. Amsterdam: Rodopi, 1976.

Middleton, Conyers. *The History of the Life of Marcus Tullius Cicero*. 2 vols. Dublin: John Smith, 1741.

Miller, J. Hillis. "Ariachne's Broken Woof." *Georgia Review* 31 (1977): 44–60.

———. "Stevens' Rock and Criticism as Cure." *Georgia Review* 30 (1976): 5–33, 330–48.

Milton, John. *Complete Poems and Major Prose*. Edited by Merritt Y. Hughes. New York: Odyssey, 1957.

Moltmann, Jurgen. *Theology of Hope*. New York: Harper and Row, 1967.

Montagu, Lady Mary Pierrepont Wortley. *Essays and Poems and Simplicity: A Comedy*. Edited by Robert Halsband. Oxford: Clarendon Press, 1977.

Montaigne, Michel de. *Essays of Michael Seigneur de Montaigne. In Three Books*. Translated by Charles Cotton. 3 vols. London: T. Basset, M. Gilliflower, and W. Hensman, 1685–93. Pope owned Cotton's translation and a 1652 French folio edition. The third edition of Cotton's translation (1700) adds "a full defense of the Author."

———. *The Complete Essays of Montaigne*. Translated by Donald M. Frame. Stanford: Stanford University Press, 1958.

Moore, Cecil A. "Did Leibniz Influence Pope's *Essay*?" *Journal of English and German Philology* 16 (1917): 84–102.

Morrice, Bezaleel. *To the Falsely Celebrated British Homer. An Epistle*. London: Printed for the Author, 1742.

Morris, David B. *Alexander Pope: The Genius of Sense*. Cambridge: Harvard University Press, 1984.

Motto, Anna Lydia. *Seneca Sourcebook: Guide to the Thought of Lucius Annaeus Seneca*. Amsterdam: Adolf M. Hakkert, 1970.

Nagel, Thomas. *Mortal Questions*. Cambridge: Cambridge University Press, 1979.

———. *The View from Nowhere*. New York: Oxford University Press, 1986.

Natanson, Maurice. "Rhetoric and Philosophical Argumentation." In *Philosophical Style*, edited by Berel Lang, pp. 221–33. Chicago: Nelson-Hall, 1980.

Newton, Isaac. *Newton's Philosophy of Nature: Selections from His Writings*. Edited by H. S. Thayer. New York: Hafner, 1953.

Nicolson, Marjorie Hope. *Newton Demands the Muse: Newton's Opticks and the Eighteenth-Century Poets*. Princeton: Princeton University Press, 1946.

Niebuhr, Reinhold. *The Nature and Destiny of Man, A Christian Interpretation*. 2 vols. New York: Scribner, 1941–43.

Nokes, David. "A Bout of Commentary." *Times Literary Supplement* 4246 (17 August 1984): 925.

Noxon, James. *Hume's Philosophical Development*. Oxford: Clarendon Press, 1975.

Nozick, Robert. *The Examined Life*. New York: Simon & Schuster, 1989.

Nussbaum, Martha C. *The Fragility of Goodness: Luck and Ethics in Greek Tragedy and Philosophy*. Cambridge: Cambridge University Press, 1986.

Nuttall, A. D. *Pope's "Essay on Man."* London: George Allen & Unwin, 1984.

Odell, Daniel W. "Young's *Night Thoughts* as an Answer to Pope's *Essay on Man*." *Studies in English Literature* 12 (1972): 481–501.

Ortony, Andrew, ed. *Metaphor and Thought*. Cambridge: Cambridge University Press, 1979.

The Oxford Companion to English Literature. Edited by Margaret Drabble. 5th Edition. Oxford: Oxford University Press, 1985.

The Oxford Dictionary of the Christian Church. Edited by F. L. Cross and E. A. Livingstone. 2nd ed. Oxford: Oxford University Press, 1978.

Pascal, Blaise. *Pascal's Pensées*. Translated by W. F. Trotter with introduction by T. S. Eliot. New York: Dutton, 1958.

———. *Pensées*. Translated by A. J. Krailsheimer. New York: Penguin, 1966.

———. *Thoughts on Religion, and other Curious Subjects . . . By Monsieur Pascal*. Translated by Basil Kennet. 3rd ed. London: John Pemberton, 1731.

Passmore, John. *Hume's Intentions*. Cambridge: Cambridge University Press, 1952.

Patey, Douglas Lane. *Probability and literary form: Philosophical theory and literary practice in the Augustan age*. Cambridge: Cambridge University Press, 1984.

Pattison, Mark. *Essays by the Late Mark Pattison*. Edited by Henry Nettleship. 2 vols. Oxford: Clarendon Press, 1889.

Pelikan, Jaroslav. *The Melody of Theology: A Philosophical Dictionary*. Cambridge: Harvard University Press, 1988.

Pemberton, Henry. *A View of Sir Isaac Newton's Philosophy*. Edited by I. B. Cohen. New York: Johnson Reprint, 1972.

Percy, Walker. *The Message in the Bottle*. New York: Farrar, Strauss, and Giroux, 1975.

Pierce, Charles E. *The Religious Life of Samuel Johnson*. Hamden, CT: Archon, 1983.

Piper, William Bowman. "Leopold Damrosch, Jr. *The Imaginative World of Alexander Pope*," *The Scriblerian* 24:1 (Autumn 1991): 47–48.

———. "Pope's Vindication." *Philological Quarterly* 67:3 (Summer 1988): 303–21.

Plato. *The Dialogues of Plato*. Translated by Benjamin Jowett. 2 vols. New York: Random House, 1937.

Plutarch. *Plutarch's Morals: Translated from the Greek by Several Hands*. 3rd ed. London: Tho. Braddy II, 1694.

Pope, Alexander. *The Correspondence of Alexander Pope*. Edited by George Sherburn. 5 vols. Oxford: Clarendon Press, 1956.

———. *Epistles To Several Persons*. Edited by F. W. Bateson. 2nd ed. New Haven: Yale University Press, 1961 (vol. III–ii of *Twickenham Edition*).

———. *An Essay on Man*. Edited by Maynard Mack. New Haven: Yale University Press, 1950 (vol. III-i of *Twickenham Edition*).

———. *Essay on Man*. Edited by Mark Pattison. Oxford: Clarendon Press, 1904.

———. *An Essay on Man: Reproductions of the Manuscripts in the Pierpont Morgan Library and the Houghton Library with Printed Text of the Original Edition*. Introduction by Maynard Mack. Oxford: Roxburghe Club, 1962.

———. *Imitations of Horace*. Edited by John Butt. 2nd edition revised. New Haven: Yale University Press, 1961 (vol. IV of *Twickenham Edition*).

———. *Poems in Facsimile*. Introduction by Geoffrey Day. Aldershot: Scolar Press, 1988. Contains a facsimile of *An Essay on Man* (London: Printed by John Wright, for Lawton Gilliver, 1734).

———. *The Twickenham Edition of the Poems of Alexander Pope*. Edited by John Butt et al. 11 vols. New Haven: Yale University Press, 1738–68.

——. *The Works of Alexander Pope*. Edited by William Warburton. 9 vols. London, 1751.

———. *The Works of Alexander Pope*. Edited by Joseph Warton et al. 9 vols. London: B. Law, 1797.

———. *The Works of Alexander Pope*. Edited by William Roscoe. 10 vols. London: Longman, 1824.

———. *The Works of Alexander Pope*. Edited by Rev. Whitwell Elwin and W. J. Courthope. 10 vols. London: John Murray, 1871–89.

Popkin, Richard H. *The History of Scepticism from Erasmus to Descartes*. Rev. ed. New York: Harper, 1964.

Popper, Karl. *Conjectures and Refutations*. London: Routledge & Kegan Paul, 1962.

Price, Martin. *To the Palace of Wisdom: Studies in Order and Energy from Dryden to Blake*. Garden City, NY: Anchor, 1964.

Priestly, F. E. L. "Pope and the Great Chain of Being." In *Essays in English Literature from the Renaissance to the Victorian Age*, edited by Millar MacLure and F. W. Watt, pp. 213–28. Toronto: University of Toronto Press, 1964.

Prince, Michael B. "Hume and the End of Religious Dialogue." *Eighteenth-Century Studies* 25:3 (Spring 1992): 283–308.

Princeton Encyclopedia of Poetry and Poetics. Edited by Alex Preminger. Enlarged Edition. Princeton: Princeton University Press, 1974.

Prior, Matthew. *The Literary Works of Matthew Prior*. Edited by H. Bunker Wright and Monroe K. Spears. 2nd ed. 2 vols. Oxford: Clarendon Press, 1971.

———. *Poems on Several Occasions*. Edited by A. R. Waller. Cambridge: Cambridge University Press, 1905.

Puckle, James. *The Club: Or, A Grey-Cap for a Green Head. Containing Maxims, Advice, and Cautions*. 7th ed. Dublin: Peter Wilson, 1743.

Quintilian, Marcus Fabius. *The Instituto Oratoria of Quintilian*. Translated by

H. E. Butler. 4 vols. Cambridge: Loeb Classical Library by Harvard University Press, 1922.

Randall, John Herman, Jr. *The Career of Philosophy*. 2 vols. New York: Columbia University Press, 1976.

Rawson, Claude. "Pope's '*Opus Magnum*' and An Essay on Man." In *Order from Confusion Sprung: Studies in Eighteenth-Century Literature from Swift to Cowper*, 222–34. London: Allen & Unwin, 1985.

Reeves, James. *The Reputation and Writings of Alexander Pope*. London: Heinemann, 1976.

Richards, I. A. *Creation and Discovery*. Chicago: Henry Regnery, 1955.

Richetti, John J. *Philosophical Writing: Locke, Berkeley, Hume*. Cambridge: Harvard University Press, 1983.

Rogers, Robert W. "Critiques of the *Essay on Man* in France and Germany 1736–1755." *ELH* 15:3 (1948): 176–90.

Rorty, Richard. *Contingency, Irony, and Solidarity*. Cambridge: Cambridge University Press, 1989.

———. "Philosophy as a Kind of Writing: An Essay on Derrida." *New Literary History* 10 (1978): 141–60.

——. *Philosophy and the Mirror of Nature*. Princeton: Princeton University Press, 1979.

Rosslyn, Felicity. *Alexander Pope: A Literary Life*. New York: St. Martin's, 1990.

Rousseau, G. S. *The Eighteenth Century: A Current Bibliography*. n.s. 3 (1981): 258–59.

Rousseau, Jean-Jacques. *The Indispensable Rousseau*. Edited by John Hope Mason. London: Quartet Books, 1979.

Saccaro-Battisti, Guiseppa. "Changing Metaphors of Political Structures." *Journal of the History of Ideas* 44:1 (January–March 1983): 31–54.

Santoni, Ronald E., ed. *Religious Language and the Problem of Religious Knowledge*. Bloomington: Indiana University Press, 1968.

Scharlemann, Robert P., and Gilbert E. M. Ogutu, eds. *God in Language*. New York: Paragon House, 1987.

Schiffman, Zachary S. "Montaigne and the Rise of Skepticism in Early Modern Europe: A Reappraisal." *Journal of the History of Ideas* 45:4 (October–December 1984): 499–516.

———. *On the Threshold of Modernity: Relativism in the French Renaissance*. Baltimore: Johns Hopkins University Press, 1991.

Scruton, Roger. "Modern Philosophy and the Neglect of Aesthetics." *Times Literary Supplement* 4392 (5 June 1987): 604, 616–17.

Seneca, Lucius Annaeus. *Seneca's Morals by Way of Abstract*. Translated by Sir Roger L'Estrange. 12th ed. London: W. Meadows, 1722.

Shackleton, Robert. "Pope's *Essay on Man* and the French Enlightenment." In *Studies in the Eighteenth Century II: Papers Presented at the Second David Nichol*

Smith Memorial Seminar, Canberra 1979, edited by R. F. Brissenden, pp. 1–15. Toronto: University of Toronto Press, 1973.

Shaftesbury, Anthony Ashley Cooper, Third Earl of. *Characteristics of Men, Manners, Opinions, Times*. Edited by John M. Robertson. Indianapolis: Bobbs-Merrill, 1964.

Sherlock, William. *A Discourse Concerning the Divine Providence*. London: William Rogers, 1694.

Sisk, John P. "The Tyranny of Harmony." *American Scholar* 46 (1977): 193–205.

Sitter, John. *Literary Loneliness in Mid-Eighteenth-Century England*. Ithaca: Cornell University Press, 1982.

———. "Theodicy at Mid-century: Young, Akenside, and Hume." *Eighteenth-Century Studies* 12:1 (Fall 1978): 90–106.

Sloane, Thomas O. *Donne, Milton, and the End of Humanist Rhetoric*. Berkeley: University of California Press, 1985.

Snyder, David C. "Faith and Reason in Locke's *Essay*." *Journal of the History of Ideas* 47:2 (April–June 1986): 197–213.

Solomon, Harry M. "Reading Philosophical Poetry." In *The Philosopher as Writer: The Eighteenth Century*, edited by Robert Ginsberg, 122–39. London: Associated University Presses, 1987.

———. *Sir Richard Blackmore*. Boston: Twayne, 1980.

Spacks, Patricia Meyer. *An Argument of Images: The Poetry of Alexander Pope*. Cambridge: Harvard University Press, 1971.

Spanos, William V. "Breaking the Circle: Hermeneutics as Dis-closure." *Boundary 2* 5 (Winter 1977): 421–57.

———. "Heidegger, Kierkegaard, and the Hermeneutic Circle: Toward a Postmodern Theory of Interpretation as Dis-closure." In *Martin Heidegger and the Question of Literature: Toward a Postmodern Literary Hermeneutics*. Edited by William V. Spanos, pp. 115–48. Bloomington: Indiana University Press, 1976.

Sparrow, John. *Independent Essays*. London: Faber and Faber, 1963.

Spence, Joseph. *Observations, Anecdotes, and Characters of Books and Men*. Edited by James Osborn. 2 vols. Oxford: Clarendon Press, 1966.

Spitzer, Leo. "Classical and Christian Ideas of World Harmony." *Traditio* 2 (1944): 409–64 and 3 (1945): 307–64.

Stanley, Thomas. *The History of Philosophy: Containing the Lives, Opinions, Actions and Discourses of the Philosophers of Every Sect. Illustrated with the Effigies of divers of Them*. 2nd ed. London: Thomas Bassett, Dorman Newman, and Thomas Cockerill, 1687.

Stephen, Leslie. *Alexander Pope*. London: Macmillan, 1880.

Stock, R. D. *The Holy and the Demonic from Sir Thomas Browne to William Blake*. Princeton: Princeton University Press, 1982.

Striner, Richard. "Felicity Rosslyn. *Alexander Pope: A Literary Life.*" *The Scriblerian* 24:1 (Autumn 1991): 49–51.

Stroud, Barry. *Hume*. London: Routledge & Kegan Paul, 1977.

Sykes, Arthur Ashley. *The True Foundations of Natural and Reveal'd Religion Asserted*. London: James and John Knapton, 1730.

Taine, H. A. *History of English Literature*. Translated by H. Van Laun. 4 vols. Edinburgh: Edmonston and Douglas, 1873.

Tebeaux, Elizabeth. "Scepticism in Pope's *Essay on Man*." *College Literature* 10:2 (1983): 158–71.

Thilly, Frank, and Ledger Wood. *A History of Philosophy*. 3rd ed. New York: Holt, Rinehart, 1963.

Tilley, Terrence W. *Talking of God: An Introduction to Philosophical Analysis of Religious Language*. New York: Paulist Press, 1978.

Tillotson, Geoffrey. *Pope and Human Nature*. Oxford: Clarendon Press, 1958.

Tillotson, Geoffrey, Paul Fussell, Jr., and Marshall Waingrow. *Eighteenth-Century English Literature*. New York: Harcourt, 1969.

Todorov, Tzvetan. *Introduction à la littérature fantastique*. Paris: Seuil, 1970.

Troy, Frederick S. "Pope's Images of Man." *Massachusetts Review* 1 (1960): 359–84.

Tuveson, Ernest. "*An Essay on Man* and 'The Way of Ideas.'" *ELH* 26 (1959): 368–86.

Uphaus, Robert. *The Impossible Observer: Reason and the Reader in 18th-Century Prose*. Lexington: University Press of Kentucky, 1979.

Van Buren, Paul M. *The Edges of Language: An Essay in the Logic of a Religion*. New York: Macmillan, 1972.

Varey, Simon. "Rhetoric and *An Essay on Man*." In *The Art of Alexander Pope*, edited by Howard Erskine-Hill and Anne Smith, pp. 132–43. New York: Barnes and Noble, 1979.

Vieth, David M. "Divided Consciousness: Variations on a Theme in Literary Interpretation." *Tennessee Studies in Literature* 22 (1977): 46–62.

Vlastos, Gregory. *Socrates, Ironist and Moral Philosopher*. Ithaca, NY: Cornell University Press, 1991.

Voltaire, François Marie de. *Philosophical Letters*. Translated by Ernest Dilworth. Indianapolis: Bobbs-Merrill, 1961.

Wain, John. "A Proper Study of the Man." *New York Times Book Review* (2 March 1986): 11.

Walker, R. C. S. *Times Literary Supplement* 4023 (2 May 1980): 506.

Walker, William. "Locke Minding Women: Literary History, Gender, and the *Essay*." *Eighteenth-Century Studies* 23:3 (Spring 1990): 245–68.

Warburton, William. *A Critical and Philosophical Commentary on Mr. Pope's Essay on Man*. London: John and Paul Knapton, 1742.

———. *A View of Lord Bolingbroke's Philosophy*. 3 vols. in 1. London: J. and P. Knapton, 1754–55.

———. *A Vindication of Mr. Pope's Essay on Man, from the Misrepresentations of Mr. de Crousaz*. London: J. Robinson, 1740.

———. *The Works of the Right Reverend William Warburton*. 12 vols. London: Printed by L. Hansard for T. Cadell and W. Davies, 1811.

Warton, Joseph. *An Essay on the Genius and Writings of Pope*. 2 vols. London: J. Dodsley, 1782.

Watts, Isaac. *The Works of the Rev. Isaac Watts*. Edited by Edward Parsons. 7 vols. Leeds: Printed by Edward Baines for the editor et al. (preface dated 25 August 1800).

———. *The Works of the Reverend and Learned Isaac Watts*. London: J. Barfield, 1810.

Weinbrot, Howard D. *Alexander Pope and the Tradition of Formal Verse Satire*. Princeton: Princeton University Press, 1982.

Weinert, Friedel. "Tradition and Argument." *The Monist* 65:1 (January 1982): 88–105.

Westfall, Richard S. "The Career of Isaac Newton." *American Scholar* 50:3 (1981): 341–53.

Wheelwright, Philip. *The Burning Fountain*. Bloomington: Indiana University Press, 1954.

———. *Metaphor and Reality*. Bloomington: Indiana University Press, 1962.

White, Douglas H. *Pope and the Context of Controversy: The Manipulation of Ideas in An Essay on Man*. Chicago: University of Chicago Press, 1970.

White, Douglas H., and Thomas P. Tierney. "*An Essay on Man* and the Tradition of *Satires on Mankind*." *Modern Philology* 85:1 (1987): 27–41.

White, Hayden. *Metahistory: The Historical Imagination in Nineteenth-Century Europe*. Baltimore: Johns Hopkins University Press, 1973.

Whiteley, Paul. "'Enchained Philosophy': Pope's *An Essay on Man*." *Critical Quarterly* 22:4 (1980): 65–74.

Wilkins, John. *The Principles and Duties of Natural Religion*. London: T. Basset, 1678.

Willey, Basil. *The Eighteenth-Century Background*. London: Chatto and Windus, 1940.

Williams, Aubrey L. *An Approach to Congreve*. New Haven: Yale University Press, 1979.

Williams, Charles. *Reason and Beauty in the Poetic Mind*. Oxford: Clarendon Press, 1933.

Willis, Richard. *The Occasional Paper: Number III. Being Reflections on Mr. Toland's Book, call'd Christianity Not Mysterious: With Some Considerations about the Use of Reason in Matters of Religion*. London: M. Wotton, 1697.

Wilson, Daniel J. "Arthur O. Lovejoy and the Moral of *The Great Chain of Being*." *Journal of the History of Ideas* 41:2 (April–June 1980): 249–65.

Wollaston, William. *The Religion of Nature Delineated*. 7th ed. London: J. and P. Knapton, 1750. First edition privately printed in 1722, then "Re-printed in the Year 1724" (London: Sam. Palmer).

Wood, Allen. *Kant's Rational Theology*. Ithaca: Cornell University Press, 1978.

Wood, James. "Derrida in Oxford." *Times Literary Supplement* 4644 (3 April 1992): 13.

Young, Edward. *The Complaint: or, Night-Thoughts on Life, Death, & Immortality*. London: R. Dodsley, 1742.

———. *The Complete Works, Poetry and Prose*. Edited by James Nichols. 2 vols. London: William Tegg, 1854.

———. *The Correspondence of Edward Young, 1683–1765*. Edited by Henry Pettit. Oxford: Clarendon Press, 1971.

———. *Night Thoughts*. Edited by Stephen Cornford. Cambridge: Cambridge University Press, 1989.

———. *A Paraphrase on Part of the Book of Job*. London, 1719.

———. *A Vindication of Providence: or, A True Estimate of Human Life*. London: T. Worrall, 1728.

INDEX

Abstract of the most Curious and Excellent Thoughts in Seigneur de Montaigne's Essays, 141
Academica (Cicero), 124, 130, 133
Academic discourse, 122, 134–36, 148, 162, 164–65, 184–86
Academic doubt, 155
Academic skepticism, 119–23, 165, 178–81
Academics and Pyrrhonians contrasted, 124–25, 126, 133
Adams, Robert M., 1, 33
Addison, Joseph, 17, 27–28, 44, 52, 66, 84, 115–16, 170, 177, 179–80
Advancement of Learning (Bacon), 81
Aeneid (Virgil), 173
Aesthetic: definition of, 3
Against Confidence in Philosophy (Glanvill), 88
Against the Dogmatists (Sextus Empiricus), 121
The Age of Pope (Dennis), 23
Akenside, Mark, 167, 170
Alderman, William E., 34
Alexander Pope (Stephen), 16
Allen, Ralph, 124, 131
Analogical versus empirical reasoning, 73–76
Analogy of Nature (Butler), 41
Anthropocentrism, 79–81, 84, 107, 122, 151–52, 175–76, 178
Antiochus of Ascalon, 122
Apology (Plato), 72, 155
Apology for Raymond Sebond (Montaigne), 83, 85
Aporia, 64–66, 76, 112
A posteriori and a priori reasoning, 69, 77, 79, 93, 106
Aquinas, Saint Thomas, 26
Aristotelian empiricism versus Platonic rationalism, 86
Aristotle, 27–28, 54, 62, 86, 115–16, 159, 168
Art of Poetry (Boileau), 105
Atkins, G. Douglas, 2
Austin, J. L., 97
Autobiography (Mill), 187
Ayers, Michael, 4
Ayre, William, 18–19, 21–22, 60

Bacon, Frances, 81, 89, 101–102, 120, 163, 165, 170, 173, 179

Balfour, James, 133
Balguy, John, 74
Barnouw, Jeffrey, 107
Barthes, Roland, 56
Bateson, F. W., 127
Bayle, Pierre, 68, 101, 121, 123–26, 129, 137, 139, 141–42, 178, 180, 188
Bellarmine, Robert, 173
Bentley, Richard, 69, 88
Bentley, Thomas, 9, 20, 86–88
Berggren, Douglas, 163, 169, 180
Berkeley, George, 3, 45, 66–67, 145
Biographia Literaria (Coleridge), 167
Black, Max, 163
Blackmore, Sir Richard, 26–27, 29, 43–49, 52–54, 56, 69, 78–79, 82, 87, 101, 116
Blair, Hugh, 142
Blake, William, 116
Bloom, Harold, 1, 19, 28, 43, 186
Bogel, Fredric V., 105
Bohr, Niels, 156, 169
Boileau-Despreaux, Nicolas, 105, 115
Bolingbroke, Henry St. John, Lord, 7–8, 10, 13–14, 16–17, 20, 25, 34–35, 49, 55, 59, 67, 71–72, 74, 77, 81, 107–108, 115, 119, 120, 124, 127–32, 138–39, 142, 147–49, 162, 166, 170, 176, 180, 185
Boswell, James, 20, 25
Boyle, Robert, 69, 77, 172–73
Brett, R. L., 16
Bridges, Mr., 10
British Quarterly Review, 15
Broackes, Justin, 144
Brower, Reuben, 55, 59, 65
Browne, Peter, 73, 82, 101, 165
Brucker, Jakob, 137
Butler, Joseph, 41, 54, 66–73, 82, 87, 90, 97–101, 135, 168, 180
Byron, George Gordon, Lord, 30

Caligula, 140
Candide (Voltaire), 71, 80, 116
Canfield, J. Douglas, 31
Carneades of Cyrene, 121–22, 124, 129–30
Carter, Elizabeth, 11
Cartesian clarity, 185
Caryll, John, 8, 75–76, 91–93, 102, 150, 164, 173–76
Cato (Addison), 52, 116
Cavell, Stanley, 189
Charron, Pierre, 54, 68, 123, 125–27, 129–30, 139, 177, 180
Chaucer, Geoffrey, 161
Chesterfield, Philip Dormer Stanhope, Fourth Earl of, 58, 149
Cheyne, George, 73
Christianity Not Mysterious (Toland), 77
Chrysostom, Saint John, 26
Cicero, Marcus Tullius, 17, 54, 63, 72, 119–25, 128–31, 133–34, 137–42, 148, 155–57, 159, 161, 180, 185
Ciceronian *controversia,* 147–48, 153
Clarke, John, 17
Clarke, Samuel, 41, 67, 69, 77–79, 101, 120, 135
Clito (Toland), 173
The Club: Or, A Grey-Cap for a Green Head (Puckle), 137
Cockman, Thomas, 138
Coleridge, Samuel Taylor, 167
Collier, Jeremy, 83
Commentaire sur la traduction en vers . . . de l'Essai . . . sur l'Homme (Crousaz), 11–12, 18
Common Sense a Common Delusion, 22, 61, 63, 80, 94, 152, 154, 172
Common Sense: Or, The Englishman's Journal, 20
Complementarity, 156–57, 168–69
Conjectures on Original Composition (Young), 180
"A Consideration upon Cicero" (Montaigne), 138
Constative and Performative Speech Acts, 97, 180–81
The Context of Controversy (White), 49
Corinthians, 111
Cotton, Charles, 83, 141

Courthope, W. J., 2, 23
Creation (Blackmore), 26–27, 43–49, 52–54, 69, 78, 116
Critique of Judgment (Kant), 106; all *Critiques,* 116
Crousaz, J. P. de., 11–13, 15–19, 21, 23–25, 28–30, 34, 36, 39, 42, 59–60, 71, 73, 95, 98, 100, 112, 115, 117, 140–41, 146, 148, 150–51, 156, 158, 163–64, 170, 184–87, 189
Crousazian criticism, 57–58, 60, 97, 105, 151–52
Crousazian versus Warburtonian criticism, 12, 25, 33–34, 73, 147, 149
Cudworth, Ralph, 173
Culler, Jonathan, 33, 65, 184
Curll, Edmund, 11–12, 19

Damrosch, Leopold, Jr., 6, 28, 35, 92
Dante, 30
Danto, Arthur C., 189
The Dean's Provocation for Writing the Lady's Dressing-Room (Montagu), 8
Deconstruction, 65, 148, 180
De Man, Paul, 3–4, 163, 189
De Natura Deorum (Cicero), 17, 120, 133, 156
Dennis, John, 23
Dennis, John (Pope's contemporary), 26, 44
De Officiis (Cicero), 139
De Origine Mali (King), 34, 38, 116
De Quincey, Thomas, 6–7, 14–15, 19, 24, 28, 117, 186
De Rerum Natura (Lucretius), 32, 34, 47, 51, 56, 100, 116, 162
Derham, William, 69
Derrida, Jacques, 2, 5, 33, 55, 71, 148, 150, 153
Descartes, René, 27, 122, 189
A Dialogue on One Thousand Seven Hundred and Thirty-eight, 152
Dialogues Concerning Natural Religion (Hume), 63, 68, 133
Dictionary, Historical and Critical (Bayle), 121, 124–26
Diderot, Denis, 137, 170
Diogenes Laertius, 156
Discordia concors, 158–59, 167, 169, 176, 184–85, 187
Discourse Concerning the Divine Providence (Sherlock), 40, 44, 62
Discourses on the Deceitfulness of Humane Virtues (Espirit), 150
Dissemination, 32, 37, 40–41, 43, 49, 54–56, 81, 147
Divine Wisdom and Providence (Bridges), 10
Dodd, Anne, 11
Dodsley, Robert, 8, 13, 36, 102, 115, 131
Dryden, John, 50–52, 54, 62, 74, 89, 96, 100, 154, 160–62, 174
Dudgeon, William, 42–43
The Dunciad (Pope), 7, 46, 77, 79

Eagleton, Terry, 148
Ecclesiastes, 142
Eclecticism, 137, 141
Edwards, Thomas R., Jr., 3, 104–105
Eighteenth-Century Studies, 31
Elwin, Whitwell, 14–16, 19, 21–22, 24–25, 28–29, 152, 184, 186
Emerson, Ralph Waldo, 167
Emmet, Dorothy, 165, 173, 180
Empiricism versus rationalism, 71, 73, 102, 135
Encyclopedie (Diderot), 137
Enquiries Concerning the Human Understanding and Concerning the Principles of Morals (Hume), 143
Enquiry Concerning Human Understanding (Hume), 134, 144, 147
Epicurus, 27, 44
Epistle to Cobham (Pope), 127
An Epistle to Dr. Arbuthnot (Pope), 9, 15
Erasmus, Desiderus, 120, 123–24, 139
Espirit, Jacques, 150
An Essay Concerning Human Understanding (Locke), 17, 67, 72, 74, 115–16, 142, 163
An Essay on Criticism (Pope), 44, 92, 123, 164, 172, 189

An Essay on the Genius and Writings of Pope (Warton), 14, 19, 39
Essay on the Universe (Morrice), 20
Essays of Michael Seigneur De Montaigne, 141
Ethics (Spinoza), 68
Euripides, 161
Examen de l'Essai de M. Pope sur l'Homme (Crousaz), 11
The Examined Life (Nozick), 189
The Excursion (Wordsworth), 30

Fabian, Bernhard, 34, 49
The False Patriot, 9
Farrer, Austin, 179
Felman, Shoshana, 36
Ferguson, Rebecca, 105, 179
Fichte, Johann Gottlieb, 116
First Satire of the Second Book of Horace (Pope), 7, 123
Fish, Stanley, 97, 188
Fodor, Jerry, 165
Fogelin, Robert J., 145
Forman, Charles, 11
Foucault, Michel, 183
Four Quartets (Eliot), 32
The Fragility of Goodness (Nussbaum), 189
Fragments or Minutes of Essays (Bolingbroke), 129
Frame, Donald, 136
Fraser, George S., 21
A Free Inquiry into The Nature and Origin of Evil (Jenyns), 25
Frye, Northrop, 177, 188

Gay, Peter, 119, 122
Genesis, 116
Gentleman's Magazine, 8, 114
Glanvill, Joseph, 75, 88–89, 121, 162, 179
Goethe, Johann Wolfgang von, 116
Goldberg, S. L., 60
Gooneratne, Yasmine, 29, 171
Graff, Gerald, 164, 188
Great chain metaphor, 84–85
Greene, Donald J., 16
Gretton, Phillips, 78
Griffin, Dustin, 3, 59, 103
Guardian, 53
Gulliver's Travels (Swift), 87

Hammond, Brean S., 20, 32, 49, 131
Hampson, Norman, 76
Hartley, David, 66
Hegel, Georg Wilhelm Friedrich, 178
Heidegger, Martin, 4, 30, 71, 178, 186
Helm, Paul, 142
Heraclitus, 157–62, 167, 169, 172, 176–78, 180, 185
Hervey, John, Lord, 8–9, 15–16, 36, 54, 136, 141, 143, 148, 150, 162
Hesiod, 119
His Stoical Paradoxes (Cicero), 157
Historia critica philosophiae (Brucker), 137
History of Philosophy (Stanley), 72, 120–21, 157, 160, 172, 176
History of the Works of the Learned, 12
Hobbes, Thomas, 17, 27, 66–67, 71, 145
Homer, 17, 28, 115, 188–90
Horace, 54, 59, 102, 105
Hosea, 73
Hudson, Nicholas, 25, 147
Humanitas, 122
Hume, David, 3, 5, 17, 57, 63, 66–67, 81, 89, 106, 131–35, 139, 142–47, 150–51, 156, 165–68, 178–80, 185, 187
Hunter, J. Paul, 188
Hursey, Edward, 159–60
Hutcheson, Francis, 150
Hypothetical dialect, 109, 149–50

The Imaginative World of Alexander Pope (Damrosch), 28
Incarnative language, 169
Inquiry into the Original of Our Ideas of Beauty and Virtue (Hutcheson), 150
Interpretive openness, 87
Intertextuality, 37, 41, 50, 53, 55, 185
Irony, 65–66
Irwin, Terence, 157

Jackson, Wallace, 1, 104
Jaki, Stanley L., 62, 143
James, William, 178
Jardine, Lisa, 130
Jenkins, Robert, 68, 70
Jenyns, Soame, 25, 35, 171
Job, 40–41, 54, 100–102
Johnson, Samuel, 6, 11–12, 16–20, 22, 25–30, 50, 59, 89, 95, 140–41, 156, 162, 167, 170, 187

Kallich, Martin, 24, 155, 186
Kant, Immanuel, 1, 5, 23, 66, 81, 97, 106–107, 109, 116, 122, 132, 134, 142–43, 147, 165–67, 169–70, 177–80, 184, 189
Keats, John, 30, 183
Keener, Frederick M., 172
Kennet, Basil, 75
Kierkegaard, Søren, 189
King, William, 34, 38, 54, 116, 170, 179–80, 188
King Lear (Shakespeare), 32
Knightes Tale (Chaucer), 161
Knowledge versus opinion, 89, 92
Kristeva, Julia, 153
Kung, Hans, 188

La Rochefoucauld, François, Duc de, 99, 111–12, 150
Leavis, F. R., 1
Lectures on Philosophical Theology (Kant), 81, 109
Leibniz, Gottfried Wilhelm, 1, 4, 13, 23, 34–35, 38–39, 55, 66, 71–72, 77, 93, 101, 107–108, 116, 120, 130–32, 142, 180, 185
Leibnizian versus Lockean, 73
Leitch, Vincent B., 4, 35, 40, 117, 148, 186
Leranbaum, Miriam, 1
Lessing, Gotthold, 23
L'Estrange, Roger, 140
A Letter to Mr. Pope (Bentley), 9
Leviathan (Hobbes), 163
Life of Alexander Pope (Courthope), 23
Life of Marcus Tullius Cicero (Middleton), 119, 147
Life of Pope (Johnson), 12, 16, 18
Lipking, Lawrence, 3
The Lisbon Earthquake (Voltaire), 71, 80
Livingston, Donald W., 143, 146
Locke, John, 3–4, 17, 35, 58, 66–67, 71–74, 89, 115–16, 120, 122, 139, 142, 145–46, 185
Logocentric: definition of, 3
Logocentric versus Aesthetic, 23, 30–31, 117–18, 163–64, 169, 183, 186, 188
Logocentricism, 65, 72, 136–37, 139, 144, 155, 162, 172, 184–86
Logospeak, 117
London Evening Post, 7, 117
Lovejoy, A. O., 35, 170–71
Lucretius, 9, 32, 34–35, 44–45, 47, 49, 51, 54–56, 79, 100–102, 106, 116, 162

McGill, Colin, 165
Macintyre, Alasdair, 145
Mack, Maynard, 2–3, 11–12, 24–25, 28, 31, 33–34, 50, 83, 119, 129, 131–32, 145, 161, 184
MacLean, Kenneth, 170
Macquarrie, John, 173
Mandeville, Bernard, 113
Maner, Martin, 25
Matthew, 151, 153, 175
Mémoires de Trévoux, 11, 115
Memoirs of the Life and Writings of Alexander Pope (Ayre), 18, 22
Mendelssohn, Moses, 23
Merrill, Thomas F., 174
Metaphysics (Aristotle), 116
Middleton, Conyers, 63, 119, 120, 138–39, 147
Mill, John Stuart, 187
Miller, J. Hillis, 65
Milton (Blake), 116
Milton, John, 30, 39–40, 43, 45, 50–51, 54, 56, 116, 180
Mitigated skepticism, 134–35, 144, 146–47, 177

Moltmann, Jurgen, 83
Montagu, Lady Mary Pierrepont Wortley, 8
Montaigne, Michel de, 54, 68 , 83, 85, 87, 96, 106, 110–11, 120–21, 123–27, 129, 134, 136–38, 141, 155, 165–66, 170, 180
Monumentalization, 56
Moore, Cecil A., 16
Moralists (Shaftesbury), 38, 116
Morrice, Bezaleel, 7, 20
Morris, David B., 3, 16, 34, 145, 155, 187
Mortal Questions (Nagel), 64
Motto, Anna Lydia, 141

"Nadir of Augustan poetry," 112
Nadir of modern criticism, 113
Nagel, Thomas, 64–65, 70, 76, 84, 103, 106, 112, 165, 177, 187
Natanson, Maurice, 146
Naturalization, 184
Natural theology, 173, 178
Natural Theology (Sebond), 83
The Nature and Destiny of Man (Niebuhr), 64
"Nature, Extent and Reality of Human Knowledge" (Bolingbroke), 120
The Nature of Metaphysical Thinking (Emmet), 165
Nero, 140
Newton, Isaac, 41, 62, 85–88, 101–102, 116, 164, 167, 174, 176
Newton Demands the Muse (Nicolson), 88
Nicolson, Marjorie Hope, 88
Nicomachean Ethics (Aristotle), 62
Niebuhr, Reinhold, 64
Nietzsche, Friedrich Wilhelm, 189
Night Thoughts (Young), 9, 19, 43, 146, 180
Nokes, David, 2, 36
Noxon, James, 167
Nozick, Robert, 189
Nussbaum, Martha, 198
Nuttall, A. D., 2, 6, 12, 25, 28, 31, 34–35, 38–39, 49, 56, 59, 87–88, 91, 93, 95, 100, 102, 112–13, 131, 146, 151–54, 156, 185

Objective versus subjective perspectives, 64–66, 83, 85–86, 99, 101, 103, 177
"Ode on a Grecian Urn" (Keats), 32
Odes on Various Subjects (Warton), 19
Oedipus (Dryden), 154
Of Wisdom (Charron), 125–27
"On the Folly and Presumption of Philosophers" (Bolingbroke), 129
Optimism versus pessimism, 104–106, 108
Outlines of Pyrrhonism (Sextus), 121
Oxford Companion to English Literature, 39, 71

Paine, Thomas, 74
Paradise Lost (Milton), 38–40, 45, 50, 53, 55–56, 81, 116
Paradox, 156–57
A Paraphrase on Part of the Book of Job (Young), 68
Pascal, Blaise, 54, 67, 70, 75–76, 83, 93, 101, 106, 126, 145, 151, 153, 162, 178, 180, 189
Passmore, John, 142
Patey, Douglas Lane, 92
Pattison, Mark, 3, 14–16, 21–22, 24–25, 28–29, 34, 87, 186
Paul, Saint, 101
Pelikan, Jaroslav, 123
Pemberton, Henry, 62
Pensées (Pascal), 75
Percy, Walker, 169
Peri Bathos (Pope), 26, 54
Philips, Ambrose, 53
Philosophers and phenomenologists, 58
Philosophical Essays (Balfour), 133
Philosophical poetry, 12–16, 57, 114–18, 145, 168
Physico-theology, 78–81, 107
Piper, William Bowman, 59
Plato, 17, 86, 130, 134, 136, 150, 155, 189

Pleasures of the Imagination (Akenside), 167
Pliny the Younger, 138
Plotinus, 189
Plutarch, 63, 120, 132, 134, 136, 138–41, 155, 160
Plutarch's Morals, 139
Pope ein Metaphysiker! (Lessing and Mendelssohn), 23
"Pope to Bolingbroke" (Montagu), 9
Popkin, Richard H., 133
The Present State of the Republic of Letters, 9, 58, 140
Presumption, 81–90, 126, 129, 175, 187
"Presumption" (Montaigne), 83
Price, Martin, 60
Priestly, F. E. L., 171
Princeton Encyclopedia of Poetry and Poetics, 32
Principia Mathematica (Newton), 85, 116, 174
The Principles and Duties of Natural Religion (Wilkins), 63
Prior, Matthew, 41, 82–83, 86
The Procedure, Extent and Limits of Human Understanding (Browne), 74, 101
The Prompter, 9
Puckle, James, 137
Pyrrho, 121–22
Pyrrhonians and Dogmatists, 75–76
Pyrrhonism, 127, 130, 144, 156

Quintilian, Marcus Fabius, 49, 139, 141

Ralegh, Sir Walter, 173
Randall, John Herman, Jr., 34–35, 99, 102, 142
Rasselas (Johnson), 30
Ray, John, 69
The Reasonableness and Certainty of the Christian Religion (Jenkins), 68
Reeves, James, 16
"Reflections upon the Excellencies of *Socrates* and *Cicero*" (Erasmus), 124
Reflective judgment, 106–10, 136, 167, 179
Regulative metaphor, 167–77, 179
Religio Laici (Dryden), 50, 62, 74, 89
The Religion of Nature Delineated (Wollaston), 63, 132
The Republic (Plato), 17, 189
Resnel, Jean-François Du, 11, 17, 45, 115
Richards, I. A., 164
Richardson, Samuel, 19
Richetti, John J., 3–4, 142, 146, 163
Rochester, John Wilmot, Second Earl of, 80
Rorty, Richard, 29, 60, 65, 163, 178
Roscoe, William, 14–15
Rosslyn, Felicity, 60
Rousseau, G. S., 1, 3, 185
Rousseau, Jean-Jacques, 1, 3–5, 33, 84, 108–109, 137, 147–50, 156, 184
Ruffhead, Owen, 58

Saccaro-Battisti, Guiseppa, 171
A Satyr Against Mankind (Rochester), 80
Savage, Richard, 43
Scruton, Roger, 189
Sebond, Raymond, 83, 85
Selby-Bigge, L. A., 143
Senault, J. F., 173
Seneca, Lucius Annaeus, 120, 136, 138–41, 159
Sextus Empiricus, 121, 130, 156–57
Shaftesbury, Anthony Ashley Cooper, Third Earl of, 9, 20, 34, 38, 54–55, 59, 63, 115–16, 142
Shakespeare, William, 30, 39
Sherlock, William, 40–41, 43–44, 47, 52, 54, 62, 82, 98, 166, 180
Silhouette, Etienne de, 10, 115
Sisk, John P., 176
Situational heresy, 55
Skepticism, 66, 68
Sloane, Thomas O., 147–48
Snyder, David C., 142
Socrates, 72–73, 97, 120, 124, 126–27, 130–31, 133–34, 137, 148, 155, 157, 160–61, 180, 185, 189
Solomon, Harry M., 82, 97

Solomon, King, 69, 101
Solomon (Prior), 41, 82, 86–87
Sophocles, 161
The Soul's Ascension to God (Bellarmine), 173
Sous rature [Under erasure], 95, 99–100, 107, 149, 151, 153
Spacks, Patricia Meyer, 74, 104
Spanos, William V., 2, 30, 155, 186
Sparrow, John, 21
The Spectator, 84, 86–87, 115, 177, 179
Spence, Joseph, 20, 21, 77, 84, 91–92, 96, 98, 127, 150, 170, 187
Spenser, Edmund, 39
Spinoza, Benedict de (Baruch), 11, 13, 27, 34, 68
Spitzer, Leo, 158
Sprat, Thomas, 18
Stanhope, George, 125–26
Stanley, Thomas, 72, 120–21, 157, 160–61, 172, 176
The State of the Moral World Considered (Dudgeon), 42
Stephen, Leslie, 14–16, 20–22, 24–25
Sterne, Laurence, 116
Stock, R. D., 94–95
Stoic apathy and Pyrrhonic indisturbance, 121, 158
Stoics versus Skeptics, 90, 118–21, 130, 157, 179
"The Strength and Weakness of Human Reason" (Watts), 63
Striner, Richard, 60
Stroud, Barry, 145
Supplementarity, 148–49, 157
Swift, Jonathan, 9, 51, 72, 87
Sykes, Arthur Ashley, 41–43, 54
Sylvae (Dryden), 100

Taine, H. A., 23
Tebeaux, Elizabeth, 179
Tennyson, Alfred Lord, 165, 178
Theodicee (Leibniz), 34, 38–39, 71–72, 116
Theodicy, 25, 30, 32, 35, 38–39, 56, 107, 162
Theogony (Hesiod), 116
Theophrastus, 159
Thick description, 37, 49–56, 188
Things Divine and Supernatural Conceived by Analogy with Things Natural and Human (Browne), 74, 165
Tillotson, Geoffrey, 6, 28
Tillotson, John, 63, 96
Todorov, Tzvetan, 33, 183
Toland, John, 77, 173
A Treatise of Human Nature (Hume), 66–67, 132–33, 135, 143, 145, 147, 168
Tristram Shandy (Sterne), 116
Troy, Frederick S., 16
The True Foundations of Natural and Reveal'd Religion Asserted (Sykes), 41–42, 54
The True Intellectual System of the Universe (Cudworth), 173
Truth (Ayre), 18
Tully's Laelius: Or, Discourse upon Friendship (Cicero), 128
Tully's Three Books of Offices (Cicero), 138
Tusculan Disputations (Cicero), 130
Twenty Two Select Colloquies out of Erasmus Roterdamus, 123

Univocation, 55, 87
Uphaus, Robert, 103
"Upon the Ignorance of Man" (Butler), 68–73
The Uses of Passion (Senault), 173

The Vanity of Dogmatizing (Glanvill), 75, 88–89, 121
Varey, Simon, 59
Via media methodology, 62–63
Vieth, David M., 188
View of Lord Bolingbroke's Philosophy (Warburton), 13, 129
A View of the Necessitarian or Best Scheme (Dudgeon), 42
A Vindication of Mr. Pope's Essay on Man (Warburton), 12–13, 21

A Vindication of Providence (Young), 42–43, 180
Virgil, 30, 189
The Vocation of Man (Fichte), 116
Voltaire, François Marie de, 1, 5, 11, 23, 39, 71, 80, 86, 99, 108–10, 116–17, 131, 137–39, 142–43, 147, 149, 156, 180, 184, 190

Wain, John, 144
Walker, R. C. S., 143
Walker, William, 142
Walpole, Sir Robert, 9
Warburton, William, 13, 15, 21, 23, 28, 34, 38, 70, 73–74, 84, 86, 93, 112, 115, 117, 129, 131–32, 146, 165, 178
Warton, Joseph, 12–15, 20, 24, 28, 30, 32, 38–39, 56, 59, 65, 70, 93, 175, 186
Waterland, Daniel, 42
Watts, Isaac, 96
Weekly Miscellany, 8–9
Weinbrot, Howard D., 106
Welsted, Leonard, 7
Westfall, Richard S., 174
Wheelwright, Philip, 32, 164, 168–70
White, Douglas H., 24, 34–35, 42, 49, 73, 92–93, 131, 145, 170, 175
White, Hayden, 65, 112
White, Thomas, 71
Wilhelm Meister (Goethe), 116
Wilkins, John, 63
Willey, Basil, 35
Williams, Aubrey L., 151
Williams, Charles, 59, 94–95
Willis, Richard, 77
The Wisdom of God Manifested in the Works of Creation (Ray), 69
Wit and Wisdom: Or, The Praise of Folly (Erasmus), 124
Wollaston, William, 63, 132
Wordsworth, William, 30

Xenophon, 130, 134

Young, Edward, 10, 19, 42–43, 47, 68, 93, 101, 146, 180